From Summit to Sea

The second location of Rogers Pass station and yards, 1901.
Although not as dangerous as the first site, this location was
subject to inundation from several streams.

CITY OF VANCOUVER ARCHIVES/2–113

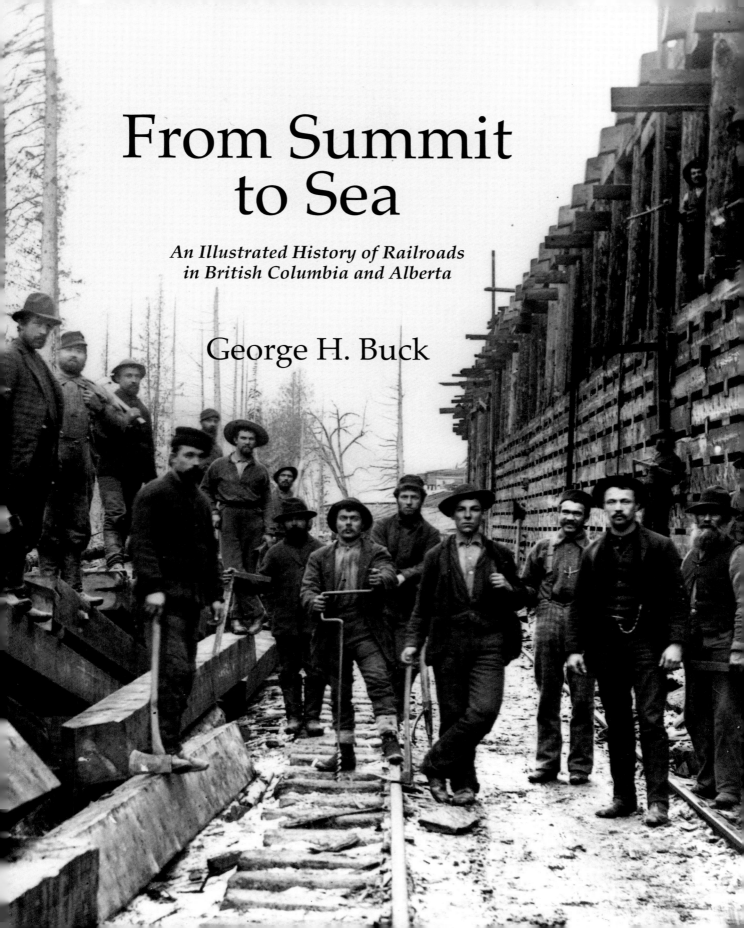

From Summit to Sea

An Illustrated History of Railroads in British Columbia and Alberta

George H. Buck

Front cover photograph: Royal train at Glacier House, September 29, 1901. A popular activity of celebrities of the time was riding on the pilot of a locomotive, a fad aided by Lady Macdonald, wife of Prime Minister Sir John A. Macdonald. Arriving from Rogers Pass, the Duke of York (later George V), third from left, his wife, and members of his household, are comfortably ensconced on the pilot of a heavy Consolidation locomotive just before the train proceeds east through the Loops. The two rods sloping from the front of the pilot to the top of the smokebox underneath the headlight are braces to hold the pilot in position when the locomotive is used in pusher service. *Vancouver Public Library/38753*

To maintain the atmosphere of the period and to minimize confusion by including two sets of numbers, Imperial measurements are used within the text. Imperial values were, and remain, the system of measurement used by railroads in Canada.

Back cover photograph: A publicity shot of the new Stoney Creek bridge, 1894. The single locomotive in the centre was to convey a sense of size to the viewer. *Vancouver Public Library/835*

Layout and design by John Luckhurst/GDL

THE CANADA COUNCIL FOR THE ARTS SINCE 1957 | LE CONSEIL DES ARTS DU CANADA DEPUIS 1957

The publisher gratefully acknowledges the support of the Department of Canadian Heritage and the Canada Council for the Arts for our publishing program.

Printed and bound in Canada by Friesens, Altona, MB

97 98 99 00 01 / 5 4 3 2 1

CANADIAN CATALOGUING IN PUBLICATION DATA

Buck, George H. (George Henry), 1957–

From summit to sea

Includes bibliographical references.
ISBN 1–895618–94–0 (bound)
ISBN 1–895618–93–2 (paperback)

1. Railroads – British Columbia – History. 2. Railroads – Alberta – History. 3. Railroads – British Columbia – Pictorial works. 4. Railroads – Alberta – Pictorial works. I. Title.
HE2809.B7B83 1997   385'.09711   C97–920077–6

FIFTH HOUSE LTD.
#9–6125 11th Street S.E.
Calgary AB Canada T2H 2L6

1-800-360-8826

Contents

To my parents, with thanks

Preface and Acknowledgements

Railroads and Canada. The two words seem almost inseparable. As Donald Cardwell says, "The establishment of railroad networks had enormous, irreversible consequences for society ... The railroad made possible great continent-wide nations such as Australia, Canada, the USA and Russia."[1] Railroads also made possible the settlement and economic development of western Canada. While the fur trade and the North West and Hudson's Bay Companies established the white man's presence in the West, it was the railroads that brought the masses of people who settled the land, exploited its resources, and transformed the environment.

Railroads themselves comprised communities. Many individuals were required to construct, operate, and service the railroads and related infrastructure, and they usually resided along its route. A railroad thus became a linear town—a thin line of civilization—to which became tethered larger communities and expanses of settled land.

Although the coastal areas of British Columbia were accessible by water long before the coming of railways, the area was isolated physically from the remainder of North America that had remained loyal to the British Crown. When Canada invited British Columbia to join Confederation, many residents believed that unity with the rest of the country was not possible without some tangible and permanent link with points east. Besides sheer distance, several formidable and imposing mountain ranges reinforced the impression that British Columbia was cut off from the halls of power in Ontario and Quebec.

Augmented by written accounts from the period and archival photographs, this book chronicles the development of larger railroads and related enterprises in what are now the provinces of British Columbia and Alberta, from the beginnings through 1939, when the advent of the Second World War created changes that would irrevocably alter the appearance, operation, and future of railroads in western Canada. The two provinces are particularly significant because the railways played so decisive a role in their development, and also because the terrain posed such a challenge to construction. Alberta and British Columbia represent a geographical and economic transition unique in Canada, from prairie to alpine to coastal, all within the space of approximately eight hundred miles. Both provinces have areas rich in natural resources and others well suited to farming and ranching. In no small way, therefore, chronicling the establishment of railroads across the region also reflects the simultaneous development and growth of settlement and various economies.

Railroads might be viewed in a number of different ways, depending upon one's perspective—as businesses, modes of transportation, means to political ends, examples of the entrepreneurial and pioneering spirit, or as essential elements in the fabric of the country. But however one regards them, it is clear that *people* imagined them, constructed them, operated and changed them. To consider railroads simply as corporate entities, as assemblages of equipment and infrastructure, or as economic instruments, is to ignore the very heart and soul of railroads—the people. This book, therefore, deals not only with the corporate and physical aspects of railroads, but also with the individuals who made them a reality.

In keeping with the general theme of development and expansion, the focus is on larger railroads—the major players—although smaller concerns are represented both in the text and photographs. And rather than a comprehensive history of each railroad, this work provides instead a convenient starting point, where one may gain some insight into construction, operation, development, and other ventures related to railroads in Alberta and British Columbia.

I wish to acknowledge and thank the following individuals, who, with kindness and enthusiasm, assisted and encouraged me in the preparation of *From Summit to Sea*. Brock Silversides recommended me for the project. His experienced hand guided me along the path he knows well. My parents, Helen Buck and Dr. Robert J. Buck, selflessly acted as my eyes and agents in distant archives and also prepared the index. Dr. Edward G. Wilson assisted with archival research, and Les S. Kozma, a living encyclopaedia of railroad information, willingly shared his knowledge. Laurel Wolanski's excellent photographic and artistic skills are evident on the cover. Sabrina Fox and Doug Blackley directed me to useful material not readily available in archives. Dr. Stephen M. Hunka, in the manner of former days as my doctoral supervisor, critiqued the manuscript and offered valuable information about railroads from his perspective as the son of a section foreman. Melvin P. Marshall shared reminiscences from his fifty-year railroading career, beginning with the Grand Truck Pacific. Ron Blond and James Higham's valuable input ensured the readability and accuracy of the manuscript. Dr. Genevieve M. Johnson's keen eye helped in the selection of many of the images. I am grateful to the staff of the City of Edmonton Archives, especially June Honey, for being so helpful over the years. I also wish to thank the Winnipeg *Free Press*, the Revelstoke and District Historical Society, and the Canadian Pacific Railway Company.

Special thanks to Nora Russell, who did an excellent job of editing the manuscript, and to the staff at Fifth House Publishers, who have been most helpful.

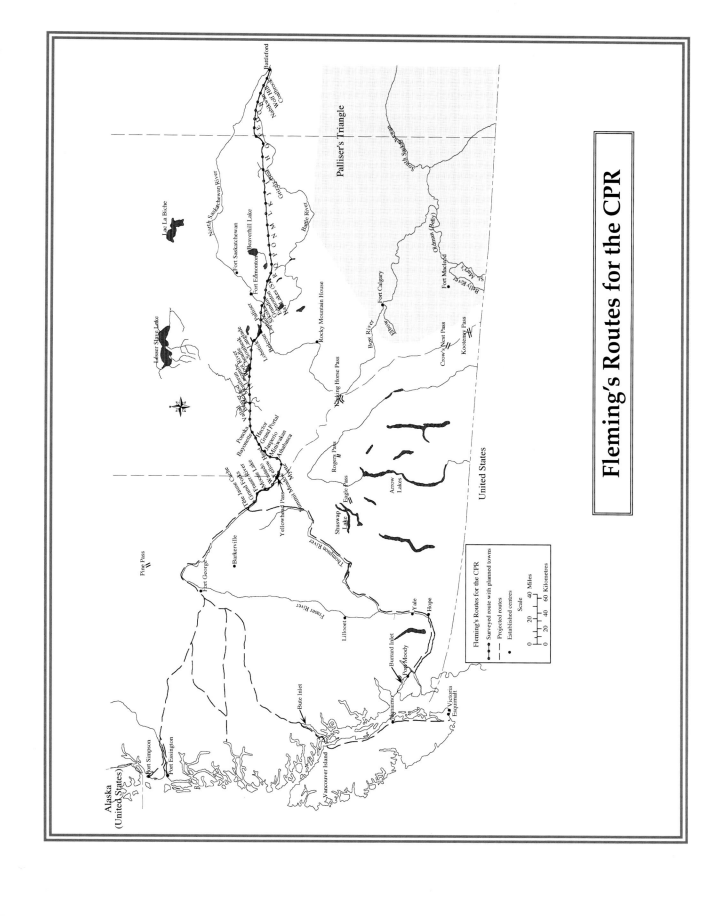

Fleming's Routes for the CPR

Alaska
(United States)

Fort Simpson

Fort Essington

Pine Pass

Fort George

• Barkerville

Fraser River

Lillooet

Bute Inlet

Nanaimo

Vancouver Island

Victoria
Esquimalt

Burrard Inlet

Port Moody

Hope

Yale

Thompson River

Shuswap Lake

Eagle Pass

Arrow Lakes

Rogers Pass

United States

Kicking Horse Pass

Crow's Nest Pass

Kootenay Pass

Bow River

Fort Calgary

Fort Macleod

Oldman (Belly)

St. Mary's

Belly River

Elbow

Palliser's Triangle

South Saskatchewan

Rocky Mountain House

Battle River

North Saskatchewan River

Fort Saskatchewan

Beaverhill Lake

Fort Edmonton

Lac La Biche

Lesser Slave Lake

Battleford

Wolf Hills

Tête Jaune Cache

Grand Forks

Moose Lake

Yellowhead Pass

Pine River

Tête Jaune Pass

Athabasca

Ponoka

Bayonette

Hector

Grand Portal

Minnewakan

Tête Jaune Cache

Fleming's Routes for the CPR

—•— Surveyed route with planned towns

----- Projected routes

• Established centres

Scale

0   20   40   Miles

0   20   40   60 Kilometres

Prelude

While it might at first appear that a railway to link British Columbia with eastern Canada was a capricious and greedy demand by an aspiring province, consideration of earlier events reveals that it was in the best interests of Canada if it wanted to retain British Columbia as well as the territory comprising Alberta. There had been interest in the area from the earliest days of European contact. Juan de Fuca is reputed to have explored the southern part of the B.C. coast as early as 1592, and explorations of the Interior were made in earnest two hundred years later, largely through the impetus of the fur trade. The efforts of Alexander Mackenzie in the late 1700s, and Simon Fraser and David Thompson in the early 1800s, including information gathered from native Indians, established a rudimentary record of some of the major geographical features of the area. Further exploration was carried out by individuals connected with the Hudson's Bay Company, especially after it took over the North West Company in 1821.[1]

The fur trade brought the first permanent European settlement to British Columbia in the early nineteenth century. Some of these people farmed along the southern coast of the mainland and on sections of Vancouver Island, especially after 1830. Then gold was discovered, first in 1857 along parts of the Fraser River and its tributaries, and beginning in 1860, at several locations in the area now referred to as the Cariboo. Word spread rapidly, and British Columbia was soon inundated by prospectors hoping to strike it rich. Many of these were Americans who had come up from San Francisco, where, by this time, the California gold rush of 1849 had lost some of its lustre.[2] The sudden increase in population and business was a great boost to the economy, and many British Columbians became wealthy meeting the needs of the gold-seekers. But existing means of transportation could not adequately accommodate the large movement of people and goods. Several rivers were navigable, at least for some distance, but many of the gold centres were near unnavigable waterways, or not near waterways at all. And the numerous trails and simple roads already in existence were quite inadequate. The governor of the British Columbia colony at that time, James Douglas, sometimes called the "King of Roads," managed to convince the imperial government in London to fund and supply some Royal Engineers to help construct several ambitious wagon roads in the early 1860s.[3] One of the most remarkable of these was the Cariboo Wagon Road, which wound its way from Yale along the steep palisades of the Fraser and Thompson Rivers, crossing them several times before heading off towards Barkerville. While a vast improvement over the old trails, and providing routes where none had existed, these roads were treacherous and circuitous.

In spite of such limitations, Governor Douglas was convinced that further construction would open up the interior to increased settlement. But officials in both the colony and in England expressed concern that additional development would bring in more Americans, whose numbers would eventually swell to the extent that allegiance would shift to the United States, with the result that the colony and its revenues would be lost to the Empire.[4]

It was not only the gold rushes, however, that brought Americans into British Columbia. Beginning in 1865, the Collins Overland Telegraph Company embarked on the construction of a line to connect American systems to those in Europe via the Bering Strait and the Russian telegraphs. Although surveys were done and construction began, the whole effort was abandoned in 1867, after the completion of the trans-Atlantic cable.[5]

To preserve a connection with Britain and its colonies to the east, Douglas wanted to build a road that would traverse British Columbia from west to east. Entering the new territory now known as Alberta from one of the known passes through the Rocky Mountains, the road would proceed to Edmonton House, where it would connect with a road constructed from points east. The final proposal—a wagon road and accompanying telegraph line entirely through British territory—attracted interest in both eastern Canada and England. One of the foremost promoters of the project was Edward Watkin, president of the Grand Trunk Railway of Canada. Watkin and others had formed the Atlantic and Pacific Telegraph Company to construct the telegraph line and a wagon road, and it seems that Watkin had designs for the Grand Trunk Railway eventually to supplant the road.[6] Insurmountable financial difficulties, however, ensured that the Atlantic and Pacific Telegraph Company remained solely a paper entity.

As far as the B.C. government was concerned, a wagon road was the only way to go, but before it could be started, surveyors had to find the shortest and gentlest routes through the mountain ranges in the Interior. Among those hired for this purpose was Walter Moberly, a civil engineer from Ontario, who had come to British Columbia in 1858. In 1865, hoping to discover a pass for the road, Moberly explored the seemingly impenetrable Gold Range (now known as the Monashees),[7] but he believed that a railroad would be more efficient for moving goods and people quickly. In a report to Joseph Trutch, surveyor general of the colony of British

Columbia,[8] Moberly wrote that he "had succeeded in accomplishing one of the chief objects of the expedition of which I had charge, namely, the connection of the valleys of the Fraser, Thompson and Shuswap waters with those of the Columbia river by a low pass, suitable either for a wagon road or a railway ..."[9] Having discovered the pass by following some eagles he had disturbed while exploring the area, Moberly named it Eagle Pass.

The territory that became Alberta was sparsely populated at this time, most of it the realm of the Hudson's Bay Company, which was not interested in having outsiders come onto its land and disrupt the fur trade. While the plains and the eastern approaches to the Rocky Mountains had been traversed for centuries by native Indians and later by fur traders, little of their knowledge had been gathered and written down in a systematic way. Filling in such gaps in knowledge piqued the interest of Captain John Palliser, an Irishman who had visited North America in 1847-48 and explored the wilds of Missouri with fur traders. Curious to explore the British possessions in western North America, Palliser approached the Royal Geographic Society in England in 1856 to underwrite an excursion. While amenable, the society recommended that several scientists accompany him, so that a more accurate account of the terrain could be made. Besides some official financial support from the Colonial Office, Palliser's expedition was promised the assistance of the Hudson's Bay Company. As well as investigating the terrain, its resources, and potential for settlement, Palliser was also charged with ascertaining whether or not a railroad could be constructed along the plains and through the Rocky Mountains, so as to create a transcontinental railroad in British North America.[10] Palliser noted that the government of the United States had undertaken surveys as early as 1853, hoping to find a suitable route for an American transcontinental railroad.

> None of these surveys, however, offers a favourable prospect for the ultimate construction of a line of railway connecting the Atlantic to the Pacific, principally from the fact that in the central part of the continent there is a region, desert, or semi-desert in character, which can never be expected to become occupied by settlers.
>
> It was, therefore, with considerable interest and anxiety that public attention was turned to our own territories ...[11]

Arriving in Canada in 1857, Palliser and his team began the slow and arduous trek west, investigating the terrain as they went and relying heavily on the accounts of Hudson's Bay Company officials, Indians, and Métis. The explorations were concluded in the fall of 1859. Among the significant features of the southern prairies bordering on the United States was a vast, arid, wedge-shaped region devoid of trees and substantial vegetation that subsequently became known as Palliser's Triangle.

Palliser was of the opinion that settlement within this area was not a wise idea, given the evidence of low precipitation and poor growing conditions.[12] Later events during the Great Depression would support this contention.

The Palliser Expedition also explored known passages through the Rocky Mountains and searched for new ones. In August 1858, Dr. James Hector, a geologist with the Palliser group, discovered a narrow, steep pass through the Rockies west of present-day Lake Louise. Through a mishap, Hector's horse fell into the torrent running through the pass. During his rescue of the beast, Hector received a nasty kick to the chest, and this episode led to the area being named the Kicking Horse Pass.[13] Farther south, Thomas Blakiston, another member of the expedition, explored the North Kootenay Pass, which he believed to be the most southerly pass in British territory. He was equally convinced that a transcontinental railroad should take the North Kootenay Pass as the easiest and most direct route. In his final report, Blakiston remarked that a railroad would be a comparatively easy undertaking because most of it would be constructed "over level prairies, and but 40 miles through the mountains."[14] Palliser did not share his colleague's conclusions. He felt strongly, in fact, that the Kicking Horse Pass had much smoother and more gradual gradients, so much so that "the construction of a wagon road, and even the project of a railway by this route across the Rocky mountains might be reasonably entertained."[15] But Palliser was far less optimistic about the prospect of a transcontinental railroad, stating, "The knowledge of the country on the whole would never lead me to advocate a line of communication from Canada across the continent to the Pacific, exclusively through British territory."[16]

Kootenay Plains, from a sketch by The Marquis of Lorne.

PUBLISHED IN *PICTURESQUE CANADA*, VOLUME 1, 1882.

Given the road-building activity in British Columbia, the exploration by Moberly and others, and the Palliser Expedition's acknowledgement that a railroad was possible, although not feasible economically, a railroad traversing British North America became an option. But Palliser's disparaging remarks, coupled with the fact that individuals such as Edward Lytton, former British colonial secretary, who favoured the construction of a railroad, were no longer in government, meant that funding and support for such a project would not come from the imperial government in England. It was up to interests in Canada.

The Canadian Pacific Railway: The Making of a Prima Donna

ritish Columbians had decided to join Confederation by 1871, and having dropped the idea of a cross-country road, proposed instead that the dominion government construct a railway across the continent to the west coast. The enterprise was to be completed within ten years. In return, British Columbia agreed to provide a land grant within the province of twenty miles on either side of the railway.[1] The terms of Confederation were ratified on July 20, 1871, and surveys for the Canadian Pacific Railway began in British Columbia that day. The survey was under the direction of Sandford Fleming, an experienced railway engineer who had worked on various projects in eastern Canada. Fleming hired surveyors who were familiar with particular regions. Walter Moberly, for example, took charge of the survey between Shuswap Lake and the eastern foothills of the Rockies.[2] While the government undertook the survey, it was hoped that private enterprise would construct the railroad, since many in Parliament thought it politically unwise to raise taxes to pay for a railroad that would benefit so few, so far removed from the centres of population and commerce.

To the surprise of some, Canada's largest and arguably best established railway, the Grand Trunk, took no direct involvement with the new railway. The president, Edward Watkin, the same man who had represented the ill-fated Atlantic and Pacific Telegraph Company, saw the Grand Trunk's future growth to the Pacific coast taking place largely through Canada, apart from sections that would make use of the Grand Trunk lines in the United States to avoid heavy construction north of the Great Lakes. Most of the shareholders and board members, however, were British and knew very little about western Canada, and while a few of them agreed with Watkin, the majority were afraid of the risks. There was also concern that previous political scandals involving the Grand Trunk would prejudice the railway's chances of being treated fairly by politicians of any stripe. This spirit was personified in Sir Henry Tyler, who not only defeated Watkin's initiatives, but eventually became president of the Grand

Trunk, and steadfastly maintained a conservative policy regarding expansion into virgin territory. Moreover, the Canadian government felt that a transcontinental railroad should be built entirely within Canadian territory.[3] The Grand Trunk's failure to seize the opportunity to expand westward led eventually to calamity for the company.

Sir John A. Macdonald's administration favoured the entrepreneurial initiative of individuals for the construction of the railway. This approach would not only minimize government expenditure, and thus taxes on the electorate, but it would also enable the party faithful to get something in return for their support. But this policy proved disastrous for Macdonald in the first instance. In 1872, a private syndicate was granted a charter with a $30-million cash subsidy, a land grant of 50 million acres, and perpetual exemption from property taxes.[4] But the syndicate did not begin construction, and by 1873, allegations of graft and corruption began to circulate, and soon even Macdonald was implicated. As a result of the Pacific Scandal, Macdonald resigned and his Conservative government was defeated in the 1874 election by Alexander Mackenzie's Liberals.[5] Mackenzie was intent on continuing with the Canadian Pacific Railway, but as a public venture that would be proceeded with as finances permitted. The latter proviso was popular, at least in eastern Canada, as the country wallowed in the grips of a severe economic depression.

The survey for the location of the Canadian Pacific Railway proceeded slowly during the course of the political tumult and change in Ottawa. Many routes were explored and considered, the main criteria being cost, ease of gradient, ease of construction, and directness. By 1872, Fleming decided that the Yellowhead Pass was the easiest route through the Rocky Mountains, although its selection would add many miles to the line.[6] The approach from the east was not a simple matter of laying tracks in a straight line across flat prairie, since much of Alberta consisted of rolling parkland prairie bisected by deep, wide watercourses created through glacial till.

The Canadian Pacific was to be a trunk railroad, its primary purpose to link the East with the west coast by the easiest and least expensive route. As it was intended to pass through areas most suitable for future habitation, it avoided Palliser's Triangle. And dodging geographical obstacles that would be expensive to pass through usually took precedence over locating the line through pre-existing settlements. So, for example, to avoid both the steep banks and broad valley of the North Saskatchewan River at Fort Edmonton, and the Beaver Hills to the east, the projected line passed by Hay Lakes, about thirty miles to the southeast, where a new station named Edmonton would be established. Not all obstacles, however, could be avoided. Fleming noted that the railroad would have to cross the Grizzly Bear Coulee, a broad ravine south of present-day Vermilion that would require a large bridge or viaduct for the crossing.[7]

Fleming planned to locate stations at intervals of approximately six to ten miles

The station at Hope on the CPR. The building is an example of the standard design stations erected on portions of the CPR constructed under the auspices of the dominion government. Besides examples in British Columbia, this type of station was also erected in parts of Ontario, 1897.

CITY OF VANCOUVER ARCHIVES/ CANP. 235 N.182

along the flatter sections of the projected railway. This was necessary for several reasons. First, the line was to be single track, and frequent passing tracks would be required to accommodate traffic in both directions. Stations were positioned at critical points along sidings to control train movement. Before the era of radio communication, orders had to be delivered to the crews directly, although information was often transmitted by telegraph between stations. Since delays on the line often meant modifying schedules, train crews received written instructions from station personnel as their trains passed by. The orders would inform them whether they should stop immediately, stop at the next siding, or proceed until further orders were received. Second, maintenance and operations personnel had to be located along the line, rather than at terminal points, and it would be necessary to provide some means of supplying them and enabling them to live reasonably normal lives. Third, when the areas adjoining the railway were settled and farmed, stations had to be convenient for loaded, horse-drawn wagons. These had a limit of about twenty miles a day, so the one-way trip should not exceed ten miles. Much of the line east of Edmonton passed through uninhabited territory, and it is for this reason that several stations on the first route maps are indicated simply by letters of the alphabet, proceeding east to west.

Distance was not the only criterion for the location of station sites. Fleming had other concerns as well:

> Care should be taken to have them [stations] on the level, and as far as practicable, on straight sections of the Railway … they should not be near the foot of long steep grades, nor any grade exceeding fifteen feet to a mile. The points selected should not be where the Railway is on embankment or in cutting, but where the grading necessary for station purposes, could be done at least cost.[8]

Fleming also devised a standard plan for towns or villages near a station. The general layout was in the shape of an X, with the station being the focal point. By arranging settlements in this way, only two roads would have to cross the tracks. Apart from reducing the costs of constructing and maintaining grade crossings, the arrangement would minimize crossing mishaps. Station buildings as well were to have a common design—a two-storey, combination station- and freight-house, with the upper storey to serve as a dwelling for the agent and his family. Inexpensive board-and-batten siding helped keep the cost down.

Big problems faced the survey in British Columbia. Eleven different routes through the mountains to the coast had been deemed possible by 1873. All of them entered British Columbia via the Yellowhead Pass and then fanned out in various directions to the coast.[9] But none of them had been surveyed completely, nor was any one considered entirely satisfactory. Reasons included excessive length, snow accumulation problems, severe engineering difficulties, expensive construction, and in the case of more southerly routes, the possibility of attack by Americans from Washington Territory.[10] The dithering in selecting a final route was tolerated for a time, but the delay over deciding upon the western terminus, however, enraged many British Columbians to the point of taking drastic action.

The first conceptions of the transcontinental railway envisioned Esquimalt, on the southern end of Vancouver Island, as the western terminus. Fleming investigated the idea during the surveys of 1872. The easiest route involved crossing the islands between Bute Inlet and Vancouver Island via Seymour Narrows, from whence the line would proceed south to Esquimalt, mainly along the eastern shore of Vancouver Island. By 1873, however, it was clear that such construction was impractical; extensive tunnelling would be required to reach Bute Inlet in the first place; and about a mile and a half of bridges would be necessary for the line to reach Vancouver Island. Fleming remarked that the bridging was not only a daunting task of engineering and construction, "but without precedent."[11] His disparaging comments, combined with the reluctance of Prime Minister Mackenzie to spend much on the railway project, caused many British Columbians to conclude that they would never see the railway reach Esquimalt, much less Vancouver Island. Moreover, after nearly four years of survey, not one rail had been laid in British Columbia. This state of affairs resulted in many protests being lodged with both the dominion and imperial governments, the culmination of which was an appeal to Lord Carnarvon, the colonial secretary, accusing Canada of a breach of contract by not honouring the terms of Confederation. In a difficult position, Carnarvon did his best to mediate the dispute. He recommended that construction of the line from Esquimalt up-island be commenced immediately; that the survey on the mainland be accelerated; that a telegraph and wagon road along the railway line be constructed as a stop-gap measure; and that the entire transcontinental line be finished by January 1, 1891. In keeping with the spirit of the Carnarvon terms, British Columbia passed legislation in 1875 giving the dominion government a land grant for the construction of a railroad between Esquimalt and Nanaimo. But while Ottawa introduced legislation in 1875 agreeing to the Carnarvon terms, the Senate defeated the bill, thus prolonging the disagreement and postponing, once again, the construction of the island railroad.[12]

Prime Minister Mackenzie, who was also minister of public works, took action before the Carnarvon terms were dealt with in Parliament. To show that he meant to have the Canadian Pacific Railway constructed, he ordered Fleming to build a telegraph line to British Columbia. Wherever possible, it was to follow the surveyed route of the railway. To further justify his action, Mackenzie resurrected the old view that a transcontinental telegraph was an important means of communication between east and west, and according to Fleming, "it was held that the telegraph running continuously along the line of railway, would not only facilitate its construction, but favourably affect its cost, and at the same time largely assist in the settlement of the country."[13] Fleming called for tenders, and by the end of 1874, contracts had been let for construction from Fort William, Ontario, to the existing telegraph system in British Columbia, with a completion date of December 31, 1876.[14] These contracts represented the first construction of the Canadian Pacific Railway.

The contracts called for the erection of poles, insulators, and wires; the construction of log or frame station-houses about every fifty miles; the clearing of a path 132 feet wide along the line, which meant removing brush and trees through most of Alberta; and maintaining the line for a period of five years. The telegraph was in operation to Hay Lakes by July 1876, although service was sporadic because of improper site preparation, poor construction, and because some poles were pushed over by buffalo.[15] Unfortunately, the contractor for the section between Hay Lakes and the B.C. border did not honour his contract, and the telegraph line never made it into the province. The failure of the telegraph line, the continued indecision regarding a route, and the apparent abandonment of Esquimalt as the terminus rekindled the urge in many British Columbians to secede from Confederation. And a visit in 1876 by Lord Dufferin, the Governor-General, did little to relieve the situation.

By 1878, at the end of their tether, officials in B.C. sent a petition to the Queen requesting permission to leave Confederation. It was an election year in Canada, and Prime Minister Mackenzie realized that railway construction had to begin in British Columbia to avoid catastrophe. This meant that he would have to decide on a route. Asked his opinion, Sandford Fleming indicated that he preferred a delay in order to undertake further exploration of possible routes through the Pine Pass. Mackenzie found this response unacceptable and pressed further. In return, Fleming wrote:

> If a decision cannot be postponed until further examination be made, if the construction of the railway must at once be proceeded with, the line to Vancouver Island should, for the present, be rejected, and the Government should select the route by the Rivers Thompson and Fraser to Burrard Inlet.[16]

He chose this route because the line would pass through more settled areas of the mainland; it was the shortest route; and it was thought to be easier to construct and operate than any of the others.[17] The prime minister accepted these recommendations and ordered Fleming to proceed with construction.

Before it could begin, however, the election of 1878 intervened, and Mackenzie and the Liberals were defeated at the hands of Sir John A. Macdonald's Conservatives. Macdonald lost his seat in Kingston, however, and turned this setback into a golden opportunity to appease those British Columbians outraged that Esquimalt had been forsaken as the western terminus for the railway. He arranged to run in a by-election in Victoria, where he won. Although Macdonald did not state that he would shift the terminus back to Esquimalt, he hinted that it was crucial for some sort of railroad building to occur on Vancouver Island.[18]

Macdonald retained the southerly route to Burrard Inlet, and through an Order in Council of October 4, 1878, directed Fleming to commence construction of the most difficult section of the railway in western Canada, a 127-mile stretch along the canyon of the Fraser River, between Yale and Savona. Calling for tenders, Fleming had awarded by the end of 1879 all but twenty-nine miles of construction to an American contractor, Andrew Onderdonk. Work was to begin in the West and proceed eastwards, with the last contract scheduled for completion by June 30, 1885.[19] While economic conditions were better by the time these contracts were awarded, the Conservative government maintained the Liberal's policy of constructing the line as

The dapper American Andrew Onderdonk, who had the difficult task of constructing the CPR through most of the mountainous territory of the line.

PROVINCIAL ARCHIVES OF BRITISH COLUMBIA/HP2917

inexpensively as possible. In a letter to Fleming on April 12, 1880, the minister of railways and canals, Charles Tupper, wrote:

> The policy of the Government is to construct a cheap railway, following, or rather, in advance of settlement, with any workable gradients that can be had, incurring no expenditure beyond that absolutely necessary to effect the rapid colonization of the country.[20]

Fleming suggested methods that would minimize construction cost, specifically, "the production of timber trestle-work in the place of solid earth or rock embankments, and by the use of temporary structures in place of permanent and more costly ones."[21]

Construction of the Canadian Pacific Railway in British Columbia began with a bang at eleven o'clock, May 14, 1880, when the first rock was blasted away at Emory's Bar, about four miles west of Yale. Onderdonk and his crews had the daunting task of carving out a roadbed along the side of the Fraser and Thompson Rivers without disrupting the Cariboo Wagon Road. Moreover, many tunnels were required, most of which had to be blasted through solid rock. Although the Cariboo Road was near

A typical example of a rock-cut tunnel with wood lining. Difficult to blast out of the surrounding rock, lining was required to prevent small sections of rock working loose and either blocking the line or falling on a passing train.

PROVINCIAL ARCHIVES OF BRITISH COLUMBIA/61402

much of the construction, it proved inadequate for moving heavy objects and large quantities of supplies, so Onderdonk had a small steamboat—the *Skuzzy*—built at Yale.[22] Although the *Skuzzy* fulfilled its purpose—moving supplies up the Fraser to the construction site—it did so with great difficulty, since the river is both swift-flowing and rough in that area. The railroad itself was later used to move supplies as sections were completed. Great rejoicing ensued when the first locomotive for the Onderdonk section arrived at Yale a year later, May 15, 1881.[23] Transportation difficulties eased somewhat after 1881, when Onderdonk won the contract for construction from Port Moody, on Burrard Inlet, to Emory's Bar, a distance of almost eighty-six miles.[24]

Finding sufficient labour at cheap prices was also a problem, solved by importing large numbers of labourers from China, in much the same manner as was done earlier in the construction of America's Central Pacific.[25] The Chinese were not only inexpensive to hire, but it was considered largely unnecessary to be overly concerned about safe working and sanitary conditions, with the result that many of them lost their lives or were injured. The appalling treatment and working conditions fueled the long-standing myth that each tie of the CPR main line in British Columbia represents one dead Chinese worker.

The government's policy of frugality—even stinginess—resulted in changes to the construction of bridges on the government-built sections. Bridges were to be built of the indigenous Douglas fir, which was plentiful, easy to harvest, and easy to prepare, so trestles could be constructed cheaply. Where trestles could not be used, such as over large chasms, bridges of the Howe truss pattern could be substituted. Basically, these bridges consisted of surfaced timbers keyed together in a criss-cross pattern, with the whole structure kept under tension by iron rods bolted through the timbers. There was no local supply of iron or steel, so these materials had to be imported, usually from England or Europe, which made the cost prohibitive. In consequence, the government reduced the number of iron rods in some bridges, and also substituted double-intersection Howe truss spans, which used twice the amount of wood, but only half the number of rods as a regular truss. While reducing costs, these measures inevitably created weaker bridges. Inferior design coupled with the heavy use of completed sections by Onderdonk's crews resulted in many bridges being worn out before the line entered regular service.[26]

In spite of his government's concern for fiscal responsibility, Macdonald remained keenly aware that if the government constructed the entire line, taxes would have to rise, and the electorate would likely seek retribution. He therefore felt he had no choice but to revert to his earlier policy of soliciting private enterprise to construct the line with the aid of government subsidies. Dismayed at this prospect, Sandford Fleming advised the government against it, contending that in the long

Chinese labourers, formerly employed by the CPR, working on the construction of Hill's Great Northern.

PROVINCIAL ARCHIVES OF
BRITISH COLUMBIA/72553

Newly finished Salmon River bridge, an example of a double-truss, 1884.

PROVINCIAL ARCHIVES OF BRITISH COLUMBIA/74897

term, more public money would be spent supporting private companies than if the Canadian Pacific were to be constructed solely with public funds.[27] His views were contrary to those of the government, however, and some of the surveyors involved in the project began to intrigue against him. Moreover, a royal commission investigating alleged impropriety in the survey and construction of the railway concluded that there was much waste and inefficiency, and Fleming was eventually invited to resign amicably as engineer-in-chief.[28] He was replaced by Collingwood Schreiber, a man who kept his opinions largely to himself and consequently enjoyed a long tenure in the government's employ.

The new syndicate formed in 1880 included George Stephen (later Lord Mount Stephen), president of the Bank of Montréal; Donald Smith (later Lord Strathcona), member of Parliament, who had attacked Macdonald during the Pacific Scandal; and James Jerome Hill, originally a Canadian and the only experienced railroad builder of the lot, whose recent work centred on the American concern, the St. Paul, Minneapolis and Manitoba Railroad, a forerunner to the Great Northern. The agreement between the syndicate and the government was ratified by Parliament on February 15, 1881. For undertaking to build the remainder of the Canadian Pacific Railway, to be completed by May 1, 1891, the syndicate would receive a cash subsidy of $25 million; a land grant of 25 million acres, not including the B.C. land grant; right of way through public lands; free importation of all construction materials; a free gift of all government-constructed sections upon their completion, minus locomotives and rolling stock; a full exemption from property tax; and a guarantee that no other railroad would be allowed to construct a line south of the Canadian Pacific in an easterly direction for twenty years.[29]

Jim Hill took charge of the project and almost immediately decided to abandon the Yellowhead Pass in favour of a more direct route. His decision was influenced in part by the findings of John Macoun, a professor of botany at Albert College, Belleville, Ontario. While exploring the southern half of Alberta for Sandford Fleming, Macoun found that the territory seemed to be lush and well-watered, in sharp contrast to Palliser's findings. Moreover, Macoun was convinced that this was the normal state of the area, and felt that it was most suitable for settlement.[30] In March 1881, Hill hired an eccentric but competent American locating engineer, Major A.B. Rogers, and put him in charge of finding the most direct route between Savona, B.C., and Moose Jaw, in the territory later to become Saskatchewan.[31] There were several known passes through more southerly sections of the Rocky Mountains, but little saving in distance would result if the line had to follow the Columbia River, which made a great loop to the north called the Big Bend. A pass had to be found through the Selkirk Mountains.

By the end of April, Rogers was in Kamloops, and having studied Walter Moberly's surveys of 1865, concluded that there was a pass through the Selkirks near the head of the Illecillewaet River.[32] Rogers and his party reached this point in late May, after an arduous trek involving an excursion up the wrong fork, which ended in a box canyon (later named Albert Canyon in honour of Rogers's nephew), and numerous altercations with a particularly nasty, long-thorned plant called Devil's Club.[33] Unfortunately, the snow was too heavy to enable the party to proceed farther east, although there did appear to be an opening into the valley of the Beaver River. Rogers spent the rest of the season scouting other passes.

Major A.B. Rogers, a locating engineer who possessed the dogged persistence that led to the discovery of the high, narrow pass through the Selkirk Mountains. Ironically, Rogers died before he had the opportunity to travel by train through the pass named in his honour.

COLLECTION OF THE AUTHOR

The bill that permitted the Canadian Pacific to abandon the Yellowhead Pass also stipulated that any new pass had to be at least a hundred miles from the U.S. border, largely to protect the line in the event of American attack. In view of this restriction and his own findings, Rogers concluded that the best route through the Rockies was the Kicking Horse Pass, an ironic echo of John Palliser's recommendation of 1858, which was subsequently abandoned in favour of the Yellowhead.[34]

In July 1882, Rogers approached the headwaters of the Illecillewaet River from the east, eventually reaching the point where he had stopped the year before. Rogers Pass had been discovered, offering the possibility of a more southerly, direct route for the railway.[35] Extremely pleased with Rogers's success, the CPR presented him with a five-thousand-dollar cheque. Living up to his reputation as an eccentric, however, Rogers did not cash the cheque, but framed it instead and placed it in his brother's house in Minnesota. The large outstanding cheque concerned CPR accountants, who were worried that it might be cashed unexpectedly, at a time when money was scarce. A year later, after much pleading on the part of the CPR, and the presentation of an engraved gold watch, Rogers was finally convinced to cash the cheque.[36]

Although news of a more direct route was welcome, both the Kicking Horse and Rogers Passes were at high elevations, and even with careful planning, the grades required would be to the maximum stipulated by the government—2.2 percent, or a rise of about 116 feet per mile.[37] Realizing that he required a strong, experienced individual to oversee construction of the Canadian Pacific, Hill hired William Cornelius Van Horne, an American railway official with excellent managerial skills.[38] Van Horne took charge of planning and construction in 1882, and quickly proved his abilities, accelerating progress and hiring the best people as required. Jim Hill, like Edward Watkin of the Grand Trunk years before, wanted the main line of the Canadian Pacific to pass south of the Great Lakes, using some of his lines. But having any part of the main line pass through American territory was untenable for Macdonald, and so in mid-1883, Hill left the Canadian Pacific to return to expanding his American lines.[39]

With the location of the main line finally settled, Van Horne spurred construction on from the east. The Minnesota contracting firm of Langdon, Shepard and Company was responsible for constructing the roadbed and track through most of western Canada to Calgary, and more than sixty subcontractors were involved in the operation.[40] To speed progress, bridge gangs preceded most other crews. While most bridges were either trestles or Howe trusses, substantial crossings such as that over the South Saskatchewan near Medicine Hat received steel structures, although a temporary trestle was constructed first to allow track laying to continue uninterrupted.[41]

After bridge gangs, grading crews appeared, followed by a track gang. Although the southern Alberta prairie is flatter than the parkland farther north, considerable earth moving was required to provide a smooth, relatively level grade. Earth removed from high spots usually filled in low spots, and most of this work was done with horse-drawn scoops and shovels known as Fresnos. Track gangs consisted of about 182 men, most of them immigrants from Europe, who did everything from unloading ties and rails from flatcars, to cutting, laying, and spiking. The rail used was commonly referred to as T-rail; most laid on the prairie sections weighed fifty-six pounds per yard, while the standard in the mountains was seventy-two.[42] On the prairies, with little or no gravel available, ballast under the rails consisted mainly of native soil piled on top of the ties and sloped from the centre out to the edges, which facilitated drainage. Other crews built stations, section houses for track maintenance forces, and water tanks for locomotives. Since coal was scarce, many tanks were filled by wind-powered pumps, usually constructed beside the tank.

As with Fleming's original plan, sidings were located at regular intervals, but at

Sir William Cornelius Van Horne, dynamic general manager, then president, Canadian Pacific Railway. Unlike Andrew Onderdonk, who returned to the United States once his work was finished, Van Horne fell in love with the CPR and Canada, and remained, becoming a citizen and earning high honours from his adopted country.

COLLECTION OF THE AUTHOR

distances of approximately seven to ten miles. Where no settlement existed, sidings were numbered from east to west, rather than given letters of the alphabet, as on the first route maps. No interest was shown, however, in Fleming's townsite plan. To prevent problems with drifting snow caused by parked rolling stock, most sidings were located thirty or forty feet away from the main line.[43] Divisional points were set at intervals of 100 to 150 miles, except in the mountains, where terrain and operational difficulties influenced their location. A divisional point, located, where possible, in an established settlement, is a terminal where crews change, with substantial facilities for fuelling and servicing locomotives, as well as for making minor repairs to rolling stock.

Another crew erected poles, crossarms, insulators, and wires for a telegraph line alongside the railroad. Besides being a requirement in the 1881 charter, the telegraph facilitated operation by transmitting train orders quickly between stations. It also provided an all-Canadian route for commercial communication between British Columbia and eastern Canada.[44]

Construction crews did not arrive in Alberta until June 1883, but progress to Calgary was rapid. On more than one occasion, crews laid more than six miles of track in a day, owing largely to the fairly flat terrain and hot, dry weather.[45] Such rapid progress presented problems for the crews. Camps adjacent to the line were impractical, since they would be left many miles behind the next day. Boarding cars, which resembled long boxcars, solved the problem to some degree. Two storeys tall, with windows along the sides, each car could accommodate up to eighty men in the upper storey; the lower level contained a kitchen and eating area.[46]

The dry conditions east of Calgary, and the scarcity of water, prompted several individuals to remark that Palliser had been correct in stating that the area was unsuitable for colonization, and that Fleming's choice of route had been right all along. Such comments enraged Van Horne, and after touring the entire western route of the line, he stated publicly:

> I feel justified in expressing my opinion in the strongest terms, that no mistake was made by the company in adopting the more direct and southerly route, instead of that by way of the Yellow Head Pass … Reports about alkali districts and sandy stretches have been circulated by parties ignorant of the country.[47]

The line reached the little settlement of Calgary in mid-August, and an old converted boxcar body was placed along the siding as the first station building. By the end of 1883, rails reached almost to the border of British Columbia, and at this point the company dispensed with contractors and undertook construction itself under the direction of James Ross. To speed things up, as revenues and funds were low, Van Horne compromised directness and gentle curves to eliminate as many tunnels as possible, as they were both expensive and time-consuming to build.[48] This policy resulted in the omission of a tunnel through a mountain near Banff, though the mountain still continues to be referred to as Tunnel Mountain.[49]

Meanwhile, construction in British Columbia was proceeding well. By the end of 1883, Onderdonk's crews had completed most grading to Savona, and track was laid from Port Moody to Spences Bridge, about a hundred miles inland. The Fraser River at Cisco presented a particularly difficult obstacle. Neither a trestle nor a Howe truss bridge would do at this point, known as bridge 417, as the crossing was more than five hundred feet long and the turbulence of the river precluded building any piers in the water. These facts, combined with the government's strictures about expense, required the construction of a unique and relatively inexpensive bridge. Rising to the task, consulting engineer Charles Schneider designed an iron and steel cantilever structure that would rest on stone piers built into each bank of the river.[50] The cantilever requires less material than other bridge designs, does not need supports in the river during either erection or use, and can be erected quickly.[51] Fabricated in England, the bridge was shipped in pieces to Port Moody, arriving in December 1883. The pieces were moved to the site by rail, and the San Francisco Bridge Company undertook the installation. Although there were questions concerning the standard of

The unique iron and steel cantilever bridge at Cisco, 1884, with one of Onderdonk's locomotives crossing. This bridge was state-of-the art engineering for the day, as it was only the second of its type constructed in North America.

PROVINCIAL ARCHIVES OF BRITISH COLUMBIA/51761

construction on Onderdonk's section, his work seemed satisfactory to the Canadian Pacific, and he received a final contract to carry on from Savona to Eagle Pass, where his forces would meet those approaching from the east.[52]

On the other side of the mountains, moving westwards, Ross's crews faced some of the most difficult terrain—the Kicking Horse and Rogers Passes. It was estimated that adhering to the surveyed line, which would honour the 2.2 percent maximum grade, would add several years to the construction, time that the company did not have. Following negotiations, the government granted permission for a temporary maximum grade of 4.5 percent along the west side of the Kicking Horse Pass, and the steep section of the line was built in 1884.[53]

The area became widely known as the Big Hill, and to prevent trains from careening down if they lost control, three safety switches were installed at points along the descent. Switch tenders monitored approaching trains, and if one appeared to be out of control, the tender would not throw his switch, and the train would travel up the safety spur, lose momentum, and stop. By 1888, a telephone and electric gong system informed switch tenders and the operator at Field of the progress and problems of trains descending the Big Hill.[54] Trains ascending the grade either had to be pulled up in two or more short sections (a procedure sometimes referred to as doubling), or have extra engines added to the head end, and sometimes as midtrain helpers and/or pushers on the tail end. In view of operational difficulties, heavier locomotives were especially ordered for service on the Big Hill between Field and Stephen, and east to Laggan (Lake Louise).

The most common type of locomotive on the Canadian Pacific in the early years possessed four small pony trucks (nonpowered wheels) in front to guide the locomotive around curves, and four large driving wheels (drivers). Locomotives with this wheel

A typical example of a 4–4–0 (American), outfitted for burning wood, in front of the wooden twelve-stall roundhouse at Canmore, Alberta, 1887. The locomotive is half on the turntable, which, at that time, was moved by men pushing on angled wooden poles attached to the ends of the table. Such a pole is visible underneath the locomotive's cab.

COLLECTION OF THE AUTHOR

arrangement—referred to as 4–4–0, or Americans—were equipped to consume either coal or wood, depending upon their operating territory. In the first years of operation, most locomotives in British Columbia burned wood. Locomotives with the wheel arrangement 2–8–0, or Consolidations, were ordered in 1884 from the Baldwin Locomotive Works in Philadelphia, Pennsylvania, for service on the Big Hill. These locomotives, which were fitted with small-diameter drivers (51 inches), were joined in 1886 and 1887 by six similar units constructed by the Canadian Pacific in its own shops. As the Consolidations were longer than the 4–4–0s, yet still had to negotiate the same sharp curves, the two middle driving wheels were blind, that is, fitted with tires that had no flange to grip the edge of the rail. Encountering a sharp curve, the blind drivers would extend over the far edge of the rails, but the locomotive would be able to negotiate the curve without derailing.[55]

Number 321, one of the heavy Consolidations 2–8–0 from Baldwin Locomotive Works for helper service on the Big Hill, photographed next to the fuel shed at Field, B.C., 1889. Note the blind second and third drivers. The shed contained split wood in bins on either side of the central portion, which was equipped with platforms to help crews load tenders.

PROVINCIAL ARCHIVES OF ALBERTA/B5975

The Atlantic Express emerging from the Kicking Horse Canyon (Big Hill), 1890. The eastbound transcontinental is about to pass the first safety switch, with the assistance of a midtrain helper and a pusher.

COLLECTION OF THE AUTHOR

Although the Big Hill saved time in constructing the line, the grade slowed the passage of trains severely, even on the descent. Depending upon the length of the train, it would take from forty-five minutes to an hour to get to the bottom of the Big Hill and reach the divisional point at Field.[56]

The next major obstacle facing Ross and his crews was the ascent to Rogers Pass from the east, and the descent to the west. To reach the summit, the line followed the western side of the Beaver River valley, where many creeks and raging torrents entered the river, and there were enormous gorges and chasms that had to be bridged either by trestles or Howe trusses. As before, bridge crews preceded the track-laying crews. One of the firms contracted to construct bridges along this section was headed by William Mackenzie, who later became president of the Canadian Northern Railway. It was during his work for the CPR that Mackenzie met his future partner, Donald Mann, who also worked for the company.[57] The largest bridge in British Columbia (438A, with a length of 1,086 feet and a height of 154 feet) was built across Mountain Creek.[58] But perhaps the most spectacular bridge was the original structure across Stoney Creek (bridge 433A), a few miles east of Rogers Pass, designed by Charles Schneider. Supported by three elaborate wooden towers, Stoney Creek bridge was a set of three linked Howe trusses that stood 192 feet above a picturesque and extremely rugged gorge.

The route west from Rogers Pass was intended initially to descend gradually along the north side of the Illecillewaet River. Ross noted, however, that there were

Mountain Creek Bridge, 1886, the largest bridge on the CPR, consuming over 2 million board feet of lumber. The Howe truss across the watercourse wore out within ten years and had to be braced with an elaborate wooden tower until it could be replaced in 1898.

GLENBOW ARCHIVES/NA–4498–1

Heading west, the
Atlantic Express is
gradually making its way
east towards Rogers Pass.
Although not pulling a
dining-car, the passenger
train was sufficiently
heavy to require a pusher
locomotive to make the
grade, 1888.

PROVINCIAL ARCHIVES OF
ALBERTA/67.143/203

severe avalanches along this section, requiring additional expense to make the line safe. Guided by the practices of some Swiss railways, Ross suggested a descent from the south side of the Illecillewaet, forming the line into two broad loops in the form of a reversed S, which would snake across the valley. Although this added nearly four miles to the length of the line, Ross believed the extra distance would be offset by the savings in construction time and cost.[59] This portion of the line became known as the Loops, and it was comprised mostly of large, curving wooden trestles. Apart from the second crossing of the Columbia River near Revelstoke (originally Farwell), construction farther west was comparatively easy.

At 9:00 a.m., November 7, 1885, the last rail was laid in Eagle Pass, at a place named Craigellachie. At approximately 9:21 a.m., in the presence of a large entourage including Sandford Fleming, Van Horne, and Onderdonk, Donald Smith prepared to drive the last spike. His first attempt bent the spike, but he successfully tapped home a second. After the conclusion of the ceremony, the party boarded the westbound train for Burrard Inlet.

While the driving of the last spike might signify a conclusion to the construction, the work, in fact, was only beginning. The rapid line of communication, and the operational brain of the railroad—the telegraph—considered so important by earlier politicians and interested parties, was not completed until 1886. Nevertheless, the railroad formed a permanent link between British Columbia and the rest of the country, establishing an efficient means of moving settlers into that province, as well as into Alberta.

One of the first trains across the Stoney Creek bridge, which spanned a gorge almost 200 feet deep. Although not worn out, the bridge was replaced after seven years with a steel structure thought to be more resistant to fire, 1885.
GLENBOW ARCHIVES/ NA–4140–40

Early Supporting Players and Growth

The Esquimalt and Nanaimo Railway Company

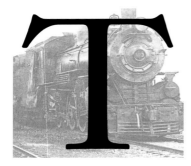

T he construction of the Canadian Pacific Railway encouraged the establishment of other railways. When it became clear that the terminus for the Canadian Pacific was to be on the mainland and not at Esquimalt, the British Columbia government tried several strategies to have a railroad built on Vancouver Island. In 1881, when the Canadian Pacific became a private company, the former premier of British Columbia, Amor de Cosmos, asked it to construct a railroad on the island, even if it was not connected directly to the mainland. Canadian Pacific was not interested, however, so the government turned to others.

One early impetus had been the discovery of considerable coal deposits along the east coast near Nanaimo and at points farther north. By the mid-1860s, production at the mines near Nanaimo warranted the construction of a railroad to transport the coal to the docks. In the early 1870s, Robert Dunsmuir, a mining engineer, started his own mine near Wellington, and he had soon built an extensive system of mine railways.[1]

One offer to construct a railroad up-island came from the Vancouver Land and Railway Company, a syndicate comprised mainly of American interests. Although some trepidation was expressed over the predominance of Americans, British Columbia passed legislation in 1882 incorporating the Esquimalt and Nanaimo Railway Company (the E&N), which was "to build railway of the same gauge as *Canadian Pacific Ry.* from Esquimalt Harbour to Nanaimo; with power to extend the line to Comox and to Victoria."[2] A telegraph line was also to be constructed along the right of way. When a lack of funding prevented the syndicate from starting work, Robert Dunsmuir entered the scene. Although railroads were not his main interest, he realized that a railroad from Nanaimo to Victoria would provide his company with additional profits by expanding his market for coal, and also by providing transportation for people and goods. In 1884, the Esquimalt and Nanaimo Railway was re-incorporated, this time under a syndicate headed by Dunsmuir. An additional boost for the E&N came with the passage of the Settlement Act, under which, among other things, the federal government pledged a subsidy of $750,000 for the construction of the island railway. In turn, the province was to provide a liberal land grant of more than 2 million acres, encompassing most of the eastern half of Vancouver Island from Saanich Inlet to just south of present-day Campbell River. The E&N also gained mineral and logging rights, and did not have to pay taxes until the land was used.[3]

Surveying began immediately under the direction of Joseph Hunter, formerly a locating engineer on the CPR, and the route selection was largely complete by the end of September 1884. The line would travel from Thetis Cove northwesterly towards Langford Lake and Saanich Inlet, then northeasterly to the coast, where it would proceed to Nanaimo. The construction was divided into two sections, a twenty-four-mile stretch beginning at Esquimalt, and another of approximately fifty miles extending south from Nanaimo. Several contractors were involved, some responsible for clearing the heavily forested route, others for preparing the grade, building bridges, and laying track. Since some had recently worked on the Onderdonk sections of the CPR, they had plenty of experience with the harsh British Columbia conditions.

Construction began January 12, 1885, with simultaneous ground breaking at Esquimalt and Nanaimo.[4] While construction of the E&N was not as difficult as certain sections of the CPR, some formidable obstacles confronted crews, requiring massive wooden trestles in some cases and truss-type bridges in others. Although the line had to negotiate rocky terrain, grades were kept to a maximum of 1.5 percent. In some locations, rock had to be blasted to clear the roadbed, and one outcropping, about fifteen miles from Esquimalt, required a tunnel. It was the only one on the line, however, and it was short—approximately 145 feet long. Like the CPR, the E&N tried to minimize expensive construction and permanent bridges. The railway also copied Onderdonk's practice of hiring cheap Chinese labour, many of whom came directly from working on the CPR.

By July 1885, grading was progressing and shipments of rail, telegraph wire, and locomotives began to arrive on Vancouver Island. Most of the rail was lighter than that on the CPR, ranging from fifty to fifty-four pounds per yard. The E&N's first locomotives were small but powerful 4–4–0s, much like the first ones ordered for the CPR. Four of these came from the Schenectady Locomotive Works in New York. They could burn either coal or wood, and were equipped with diamond smokestacks to reduce the number of sparks. The first locomotive, Number 1, arrived by ship at Oyster Harbour at present-day Ladysmith in July 1885, and was soon put to work moving supplies and personnel along the northern section of line. Number 2 arrived in Esquimalt in August, accompanied by several flatcars to assist in the construction of the southern portion of the line.[5] Other rolling stock was acquired either new or used from diverse sources, including Andrew Onderdonk, who sold the E&N his private car.

The E&N used light motive power in its early years. Number 1998, shown here, was a small 2–4–2 Tank engine, which carried both coal and water in tanks attached to the locomotive, eliminating the need for a tender. Tank locomotives could negotiate extremely sharp curves, an attribute beneficial for logging lines.

Construction continued generally at a fast pace, and it was predicted that the E&N would be completed about mid-1886. By fortuitous coincidence, Sir John A. Macdonald travelled westward via the newly completed CPR in the summer of 1886 and was available to drive the last spike on the E&N. Construction crews met at the end of their respective sections in early August at a place called Cliffside on the east side of Shawnigan Lake. Early on the morning of August 13, the prime minister travelled from Esquimalt by train, and in the presence of a large gathering, including Premier Smithe, Robert Dunsmuir, and Joseph Hunter, he drove the last spike. Macdonald's train then made its way to Nanaimo at the end of the line. Although Macdonald alluded to the E&N as an extension of the CPR, a claim made credible by the stipulation in its charter that it be built to the same gauge, no unbroken connection was ever made between the two. Like the CPR, however, the telegraph was not completed at the same time as the railway, although it was only a few weeks late—September 24.[6]

Although it was evident that the E&N would help colonize and develop Vancouver Island, towns were not laid out at specific intervals as on the CPR. Instead, small combination freight and passenger stations were placed at frequent, if not equally spaced points, and larger stations were erected at centres of greater popula-

Sir John A. Macdonald pauses at the Stave River in B.C. on his transcontinental journey to Victoria. In less than two days, Macdonald would be wielding a hammer at Cliffside, driving the last spike on the E&N. In uncustomary manner, Lady Macdonald is seen at the rear of the train. Her preferred location was on a seat placed on the pilot of the locomotive, 1886.

GLENBOW ARCHIVES/NA–4967–132

tion, or where settlers agitated for them. In its early years, the E&N was the sole means of access to many locations, and the railroad tried to accommodate the needs of travellers. In spite of the large number of stopping places, trains could be flagged down almost anywhere along the line, and would also stop to detrain passengers at will, practices that were discouraged by 1899.[7]

The E&N was extended soon after its completion, reaching north from Nanaimo in 1887 to Dunsmuir's mines at Wellington, about five miles away. The extension provided a useful link between the mines and coal markets down-island. Wellington was also the logical place to locate the facilities for heavy locomotive repair, since the installation could serve both the E&N and the mine railways. An extension to Victoria

Strathcona Lodge, c1890s, was one of the well-appointed resort hotels located at scenic vacation spots along the E&N.

PROVINCIAL ARCHIVES OF BRITISH COLUMBIA/HP49606

begun in 1887 was not completed until March 1888 because a large, moveable bridge had to be constructed across the narrows of Victoria Harbour. The bridge was designed to pivot on a central pier, thus allowing ships to pass by. After crossing the swing bridge, trains terminated at an attractive, single-storey brick and masonry station.[8]

With the addition of rolling stock and four heavier locomotives, the Esquimalt and Nanaimo Railway continued to function as a private company until 1905, when the line was sold to the CPR for $2.3 million, including the land grant. To preserve the tax-free status of the land grant, however, the CPR ran the E&N as a subsidiary company.[9] Although the name continued, the E&N had been devoured.

The Turkey Track

The imminent arrival of the CPR in southern Alberta prompted at least one entrepreneur to develop some of the known coal beds in the southeast, with the hope of supplying fuel to the railway. Sir Alexander Galt, former president of the St. Lawrence and Atlantic Railroad in Québec, backed by English investors including William Lethbridge and William Ashmead-Bartlett Burdett-Coutts, was very much interested in mining the coal in this area. Largely through Galt's initiative, the North Western Coal and Navigation Company (NWC&NC) was formed in 1882 to mine and transport coal by water, and by 1883, coal was being extracted from mines along the banks of the Belly River (now the Oldman) at Coal Banks, south of present-day Lethbridge.[10] Local craftsmen, with the aid of shipwrights brought in from Mississippi, built several barges and stern-wheeled steamboats to move passengers, coal, and other freight along the Belly River, into the South Saskatchewan, and east to Medicine Hat.[11]

The service proved unsatisfactory, however, because low water levels in the rivers caused the boats to ground, and when the levels were sufficiently high, the steamboats were under-powered against the current.[12] A better means of transportation was necessary: a railroad. After much wrangling and political manœuvring, the CPR and the federal government came to support Galt's railway. Besides providing an efficient means of moving coal, it would open the area for colonization. When pressed for a land grant and a subsidy, Prime Minister Macdonald complained that money was tight, so Galt proposed a relatively inexpensive, light, narrow-gauge line. He even managed to appoint Sir Casimir Gzowski, a well-respected railway engineer from eastern Canada, as a consultant.

In 1884, the North Western Coal and Navigation Company received a charter to construct a three-foot, narrow-gauge railroad from Dunmore, on the CPR line near Medicine Hat, to its mines about 110 miles to the southwest, and permission to extend the line farther west to Fort Macleod. It also got a land grant of about 422,400 acres, consisting of odd-numbered sections within twelve miles of the line.[13]

Final location of the line was approved in March 1885, and construction to the cliffs overlooking the Belly River, using light, twenty-eight-pound-per-yard rail, was finished by mid-October. The Baldwin Locomotive Company supplied six small loco-

One of the ubiquitous CPR D–10s (4–6–0) lettered for service on the E&N, September 2, 1939.

PROVINCIAL ARCHIVES OF ALBERTA/FS2

motives, with a 2–6–0 wheel arrangement, sometimes referred to as Moguls, as well as more than one hundred small hopper cars and some passenger rolling stock. The townsite that sprang up almost overnight at the end of the line was named Lethbridge in honour of William Lethbridge. A small incline railway carried coal from the mines up the steep bank to the new line at Lethbridge, where the contents of the mine cars were dumped into the NWC&NC's hoppers. At Dunmore, a trestle coal dock was built to enable the unloading of the narrow-gauge cars into the CPR's standard-gauge stock. The line was opened officially on October 19, 1885.[14] Called variously the Turkey trail, or the Turkey tracks, the line did facilitate colonization in the area and also provided the main means of importing goods to Lethbridge.

To minimize the loss of the lucrative land grant if the NWC&NC went bankrupt, Galt and others started another concern in 1884 known as the Alberta Railway and Coal Company (AR&CC), which would take over the assets and charter of the earlier com-

Number 1, a small Mogul at the NWC&N Co. station at Dunmore Junction, c1890, the line's connection with the standard-gauge CPR main line.

GLENBOW ARCHIVES/NA–17–4

pany if it could not construct its railroad. The provision proved unnecessary, but the fact that the CPR was the NWC&NC's biggest customer was unsettling to both management and the many people whose livelihood depended on the narrow-gauge line. Although the CPR was purchasing large quantities of coal, it was finding mines of its own along its main line, and also importing cheap coal from Pennsylvania. To offset the possibility that the CPR might curtail its demand, or stop buying coal altogether, the company wisely decided to look for other markets. The Northern Pacific Railway ran through Montana, and Galt thought it would be a good idea to construct a railroad to the south. But this initiative was stopped quickly by President Stephen of the CPR, as the line would run within thirty miles of the American border, thus contravening one of the dominion government's commitments to the CPR. Galt's protests, however, combined with separate pressure from interests in Manitoba, resulted in the government repealing the CPR's southern monopoly early in 1888.[15] With the CPR out of the way, a line to Montana was possible.

In 1889, the Alberta Railway and Coal Company was re-incorporated and given permission to construct a three-foot-gauge line from east of Lethbridge to the American border, where the line would connect with the Great Falls and Canada Railway. The latter was built at the same time, running north from the Great Northern line at Great Falls.[16] The terms of the charter also permitted the AR&CC to acquire the assets of the North Western Coal and Navigation Company, if necessary.

Construction on the Great Falls and Canada began in April 1890 with a crew of five hundred, while work on the AR&CC began near Lethbridge in May. Donald Grant, president of the Great Falls and Canada, was also the contractor both for grading and track laying, and by the end of May it was reported that up to two miles of track were being laid per day. The line was completed by October, with through traffic to the United States commencing in December. The company purchased additional locomotives from Baldwin Locomotive Works, and several pieces of passenger rolling stock lettered for the Great Falls and Canada from the Wells and French Car Company. The rolling stock was also used on the Galt lines in Canada.[17]

In 1891, the AR&CC purchased the assets of the NWC&NC and relettered its locomotives and much of the rolling stock to reflect the change. The Dunmore-to-Lethbridge line was losing money, since the CPR, had reduced its demand for Galt coal. To avoid losing CPR business completely, the AR&CC needed to devise suitable enticements to buy. By this time, Alexander Galt's son Elliott was in charge, and he came up with a gambit that worked. In 1892 he applied for and received approval to extend the Lethbridge line to Hope, British Columbia, via the Crowsnest Pass. The CPR wanted the Crowsnest for itself, since it had undertaken surveys in the area as early as 1890, and Vice-President Shaughnessy soon began negotiating with Galt.[18] The end result was that in 1893, the Dunmore-to-Lethbridge line was leased to the CPR, which rebuilt it to standard gauge. The CPR also agreed to buy more coal from the Galt mines. The lines were relaid quickly and the first CPR locomotive entered Lethbridge on November 28, 1893. The CPR had the option of purchasing the line outright at the end of the lease in 1897, which it did, and it then became part of the CPR's Crowsnest Pass branch. The lines south of Lethbridge remained in Galt's hands.

The large influx of settlers anticipated by Alexander Galt did not occur because the land south and west of Lethbridge was too dry. Charles Magrath, the AR&CC's land agent, spearheaded a movement to develop irrigation southeast of Lethbridge near the St. Mary's River, where many Mormons had settled under the leadership of Charles Ora Card. The dominion government eventually provided a small grant for the project in 1897, with most of the labour coming from the Mormons, and as a result of the improvements, more Mormon settlers did move up from Utah.[19] In 1900, to serve the area better, an extension of the narrow-gauge line was incorporated as a separate entity—the St. Mary's River Railway Company. The railroad was distinct in name only, however, since the station buildings were identical to those on the other Galt lines and the same rolling stock was used. The line travelled west from Stirling to Spring Coulee, the intake of the irrigation canal, and was opened November 28, 1900, although the dominion government's reluctance to provide further subsidies delayed the extensions to Cardston and Kimball until 1904. Also at this time, as a means of increasing profits, all the Galt railroads were amalgamated under a new corporation—the Alberta Railway and Irrigation Company.[20] And it was at this juncture that the Great Falls and Canada Railway was sold to James J. Hill and his Great Northern Railway.

Even before the amalgamation, Elliott Galt began to have his lines converted to standard gauge. The process was slow, and for several years three rails existed in many places to accommodate both standard and narrow-gauge equipment. Attracted by the amalgamation and conversion process, the CPR began to buy stock in the company until it became the largest shareholder. The end of the Alberta Railway and Irrigation Company and the Turkey tracks came on January 1, 1912, at which time the lines were leased to the CPR for 999 years[21].

The Calgary and Edmonton Railway

The citizens of Edmonton were not impressed or pleased with the CPR, since the railroad seemed determined to bypass the largest population centre in the area. Sandford Fleming's provisional route for the CPR avoided Edmonton by passing through Hay Lakes to the south, and the situation did not improve when construction was assumed by private concerns, which moved the line much farther south. To make matters worse, when a delegation approached the CPR in mid-1883 to petition for a branch line to Edmonton, they were more or less ignored, even though it was pointed out that Edmonton possessed many coal seams.[22] So Edmonton continued to remain isolated from established railways. In 1889, several businessmen, including Mackenzie and Mann, talked about building their own railway between Edmonton and Calgary, and even before a company was formed, the CPR showed great interest in the venture. The Calgary and Edmonton Railway Company (C&E) was incorporated in 1890, with provision in its charter to allow it to be leased to the CPR. The charter enabled the company to build between Calgary and Edmonton, with provisions to extend the line northwest to the Peace River, south to Fort Macleod, and on to the United States boundary. The company would receive both a cash subsidy and land

Lieutenant-governor of the North-West Territories, Edgar Dewdney, breaking the ground, at Calgary, for the Calgary and Edmonton Railway, April 15, 1890. The photographic evidence here differs from the account by P. Turner Bone, who claims that Dewdney "simply took his place between the handles of a wheelbarrow, in which a few sods had been placed; and on a given signal, he took hold of the handles, and dumped out the sods." (Bone, 1947, pp. 159–60)

CITY OF EDMONTON ARCHIVES/EA–10–1290

grant from the dominion government.[23] The subsidies, combined with the likelihood that the railroad would carry large amounts of coal, lumber, and agricultural produce, motivated the CPR to take control of the C&E as a prelude to taking ownership should it prove successful. So before any work was done, the CPR entered into an agreement with the C&E to construct a line from Calgary to Edmonton, another line from Calgary to Fort Macleod, and to operate the railroad for the company for at least six years.[24] Surveys for the line from Calgary to Edmonton began on April 15, 1890, and by July, the project was ready for an official ground-breaking ceremony, carried out by Edgar Dewdney, lieutenant-governor of the North-West Territories.[25]

Although the line had to cover more than 190 miles to Edmonton, construction proceeded quickly, and by December 1890, the railroad had reached Red Deer, a divisional point. The work went well partly because many of those involved were veterans from the main-line construction of the CPR, including James Ross, P. Turner Bone, and William Mackenzie. In addition, few large obstacles hindered progress, and only two large bridges were required—one across the Bow River near Calgary, and the other across the Red Deer River north of Red Deer. Both were spanned initially by

Two bunk cars in the first
work train to reach
Strathcona, July 1891.
The cars provided moving
room and board for up to
eighty-five men.

PROVINCIAL ARCHIVES OF
ALBERTA/B6220

Some towns on the C&E, such
as Leduc, shown here, c1920,
flourished and grew. The large
number of grain elevators
attests to Leduc's importance
as a grain collection point.
The station building replaced
the original combination
station/section house that
had been destroyed by fire
in 1914.

PROVINCIAL ARCHIVES
OF ALBERTA/BA32

Beginning in 1886, in areas of heavy snowfall, the CPR erected standard combination station/section houses with steeply pitched roofs. This example, at Shuswap, c1890 functioned as a train order station, passenger and freight depot, telegraph office, and dwelling. The CPR got its money's worth from the Shuswap station, as the building lasted until it was rendered unnecessary in the 1960s.

PROVINCIAL ARCHIVES OF BRITISH COLUMBIA/27227

The original placement of the Rogers Pass station and yards was aligned with a large avalanche path. Besides the station/section house, Rogers Pass also possessed a two-stall engine house (seen at left) and a standard forty-thousand-gallon water tank. The train, the Atlantic Limited, c1890, will likely stop to detrain baggage and express, and take on water. When an unexpected avalanche destroyed the station and engine shed in 1899, a new station was built to the west, near the summit of the pass.

VANCOUVER PUBLIC LIBRARY/31070

Howe trusses. The practice of using bunk cars rather than pitching camps also helped to keep up the pace. Besides roadbed and track construction, crews also erected combination station/section houses, water tanks, and a telegraph line. On July 25, the first train reached the south bank of the North Saskatchewan River, at a point variously called South Edmonton or Strathcona. The last spike was driven on July 27 by Donald Ross, a pioneer settler in the area.[26] Although there was great excitement and celebration, Edmonton, which was on the north side of the river, still did not have a railroad. The deep valley of the North Saskatchewan required either a high bridge across it, or a circuitous descent to the water's edge, where a shorter bridge could be constructed. Neither the C&E nor the CPR was interested in building a bridge at this time.

The CPR turned its attention instead to the line from Calgary to Fort Macleod, completing the extension by November 1892.[27] Although the CPR eventually undertook the construction of a high-level bridge to reach Edmonton, the first railroad to actually enter the town was a subsidiary of a company controlled by Mackenzie and Mann. As for the C&E, the CPR initially postponed purchasing it because of disagreements with the management, but by the turn of the century, the situation had changed. CPR directors were fearful of the C&E "passing into unfriendly hands," most likely those of Mackenzie and Mann of the Canadian Northern, who were determined to construct a transcontinental line of their own. In 1904, consequently, the CPR secured the lease and all outstanding capital stock of the C&E for ninety-nine years.[28]

CPR Improvements

Snowsheds

While feeder railroads were being established, the CPR itself undertook massive improvements. Shortly after the driving of the last spike, the line through the mountains was closed for the winter of 1885–86. Officials were familiar with the severity of the winter in the area, and engineers were stationed throughout the mountains to monitor snowfall. Heavy snowfalls and severe avalanches in January and February indicated the necessity for some sort of protection for the line. Snowsheds, wooden structures built over the track, were already used on the Central Pacific–Union Pacific, but these models were thought to be too flimsy for the amount and weight of snow found in Rogers Pass and its approaches.[29] Much heavier structures were designed for the CPR, and these were of several configurations, depending upon terrain and whether the snow came from one side or both. In 1886 and 1887, fifty-three snowsheds were built between Bear Creek and Griffin Lake stations, a distance of seventy miles. Numbered from east to west, the snowsheds were made primarily of

A typical crew engaged in
snowshed construction during 1886. While sawmills
dressed the timbers, manual
labour was required to fit and
build the sheds. Besides the
handtools, the lack of hard
hats and other safety equipment should be noted.

PROVINCIAL ARCHIVES
OF ALBERTA/B6014

The winter of 1886–87
soon proved that the initial
snowsheds were too short,
as shown by this photograph.
Although snow removal
was necessary in any event,
clogged snowsheds were
especially hated and were
considered an unnecessary
problem, so additions were
made to several of them
during 1887.

CITY OF VANCOUVER
ARCHIVES/CAN P 202 N164

The longest snowshed, Number 17, was built at the summit of Rogers Pass, shown here in 1886. Although the remnants of the construction settlement are still standing, the CPR felt the track was in danger from avalanches on both sides. And believing an avalanche might be capable of collapsing a free-standing structure, railroad officials had the shed buried after construction.

NOTMAN ARCHIVES, MCCORD MUSEUM/1686

A typical wedge plough used to remove large drifts, 1893. The damp snow did not co-operate with this type of plough, and frequently the plough succeeded only in compacting the drifts, which then required teams of workers with shovels to remove them.

GLENBOW ARCHIVES/NA–237–33

large cedar and Douglas fir timbers held together with long iron and steel bolts. To minimize cost and possible damage by locomotive-induced fires, snowsheds were separated by open spaces. A few of the longer ones were equipped with steel pipes,

hydrants, and hoses supplied with water under pressure, so that watchmen would have a reasonable chance of extinguishing fires. Snow was diverted away from the spaces between snowsheds by glance cribs, rows of wooden piles with boards attached to them, braced by a crib filled with rocks and rubble. The glance cribs proved inadequate in some instances, and many sheds had to be extended in 1887. Slightly more than six miles of snowsheds had been constructed by the end of 1887, at a cost of more than $2 million. The longest at that time was Number 17—3,098 feet—at the summit of Rogers Pass.[30] Wherever possible, a track was laid outside the longer snowsheds for use in summer. The so-called summer tracks were built primarily to minimize fire risk, and also to allow passengers a better view of the mountains.[31]

The snow removal team at Rogers Pass station, c1887, which accompanied the wedge ploughs. Most of these men were recent immigrants from Finland.

PROVINCIAL ARCHIVES OF BRITISH COLUMBIA/34454

Snow clearing was attempted at first by fitting steel ploughs to the front of loco-motives. While this arrangement was satisfactory for light snowfall, it failed miser-ably with large drifts and the aftermath of avalanches. The railroad then tried larger, winged, wedge ploughs, which packed the snow so tightly that it was extremely dif-ficult for crews equipped with shovels to remove. Success was finally achieved in 1888 with a Canadian invention, the rotary snowplough, consisting of a large-diam-eter steel wheel nine to eleven feet across, containing several radially arranged pivot-ing steel plates. Chambers behind the plates caught the snow and ejected it through centrifugal force. The entire assembly was held in a circular housing mounted on a frame, and a two-cylinder steam engine and a system of gears rotated the wheel in either direction at speeds up to four hundred r.p.m. These ploughs were not self-pro-pelled, and had to be pushed by one or more locomotives. Unless rocks or trees were anticipated, which could break the cutters or the drive shaft, the rotary ploughs were usually pushed through snow at speeds of eight to ten miles per hour.[32]

In spite of such extensive construction and elaborate snow-clearing equipment, snowfall and avalanches continued to be a problem in Rogers Pass. In 1899, a massive avalanche destroyed the station, section house, water tank, and roundhouse, killing eight people. The station and yard were relocated closer to the summit at a wider point in the area, but the ongoing problems and expenses associated with the wea-ther led to the decision in the early 1900s to abandon the pass.

One of the first tests of a rotary snowplough, Rogers Pass, 1888. Note the wooden covers on the tenders of the plough and locomotive to protect the fuel from snow.

GLENBOW ARCHIVES/NA–2216–5

A Consolidation fitted with a large plough, c1887. While sufficient for removing small accumulations of snow, these ploughs were woefully inadequate for contending with large drifts and avalanches.

CANADIAN PACIFIC CORPORATE ARCHIVES/NS 124

A westbound freight on the newly completed Surprise Creek steel bridge, c1899. Smaller deck spans at either end enabled the track to reach the main arch. By the mid 1920s, such bridges were scheduled for replacement because the weight of trains and locomotives started to exceed the designed loading limits. Sometimes, replacement did not occur soon enough. On January 28, 1929, while its replacement was being built a few feet away, the

lattice deck span at the left gave way as two heavy Decapod locomotives (5767 and 5779) crossed. Tragically, 5767 fell into the gorge, killing both the engineer and fireman. The remains of 5767 were retrieved, and the locomotive returned to service. The surprise demise of the bridge resulted in the line remaining closed for about a month, as workers rushed completion of the new bridge.

VANCOUVER PUBLIC LIBRARY/843

Bridges

As noted earlier, many of the bridges and much of the initial construction were considered temporary. Some of the bridges on the Onderdonk sections of the main line, in fact, were worn out before regular service even commenced. At first, the CPR braced the worn bridges, but it planned to replace most of them with more permanent structures during the 1890s.[33] Besides fatigue, wooden bridges were vulnerable to fire, and there were many conflagrations along the main line, the CPR itself being responsible for a good number of them. Small bridges were replaced either with rock and soil fill, or by arched masonry structures, and steel bridges of several varieties replaced larger ones. Wherever possible, as at Mountain Creek and the Loops, considerable filling took place before steel bridges were installed. Filling techniques included the use of air-operated, side-dump cars, designed by the CPR, which would dump their loads over the sides of bridges in a more efficient manner than the older method of pushing and shovelling fill off flatcars, and hydraulic filling. The latter entailed using a large hose or monitor, similar to that used in hydraulic mining. Water from the monitor would wash soil and gravel from higher elevations to the area beneath a bridge. Flumes directed the course of the soil and gravel slurry, and wooden crib-work held it in place. This method was used at Mountain Creek and Chapman's Creek, enabling the original bridges to be replaced by much shorter steel structures.[34]

No filling or line relocation was possible at Stoney Creek. Although the bridge was not worn out, it was replaced in 1893 because of the fear of fire, a legitimate concern given the fact that a forest fire reached the western end of the new bridge in 1894, soon after its completion. The new structure, designed by CPR engineer P. Alex Peterson, consisted of a graceful steel arch with a span of 336 feet, which supported a single-track, steel-lattice deck truss with a total length of 484.5 feet. Although the steel was imported from England, the bridge components were fabricated in Canada by the Hamilton Bridge Company and shipped to the site ready to assemble. With the aid of elaborate wooden false works, the new bridge was constructed around the old one, which was removed after the new bridge became operational in November 1893.[35] Although some mourned the passing of the old bridge, the new steel arch figured prominently in CPR promotional literature and was noted in guidebooks as something to see.[36] Steel arch bridges also replaced Howe trusses at Salmon River (now the Nahatlatch River) and Surprise Creek.

Erecting the new steel arch bridge across Stoney Creek, 1893. Although the false work supported the new structure in progress, it was designed to straddle the old bridge so that service would not be disrupted during construction.

PROVINCIAL ARCHIVES OF
BRITISH COLUMBIA/77633

The masonry arch constructed across Cascade Creek at the eastern edge of Rogers Pass, 1898. It was hoped that the new bridge would last longer than the earlier wooden trestles, which were often washed out each year. The arch has met expectations as it continues to span Cascade Creek, although the CPR is long-gone from Rogers Pass.

VANCOUVER PUBLIC LIBRARY/829

A train of air-operated dump cars contributes to the filling-in of the Loop bridges, 1900. Stress on the bridge was minimized by dumping half the cars one way and half the other. Filling in as much as possible reduced the length and cost of replacement steel bridges.

PROVINCIAL ARCHIVES
OF BRITISH COLUMBIA/41741

A view of the Loops after filling and replacement with steel bridges, c1913. Compare this photograph with the one above. The building to the right of the freight train is a section house at a siding known as Cambie.

WHYTE MUSEUM OF THE CANADIAN
ROCKIES/NA71–1636

Replacement of the Howe truss bridge across the Columbia River west of Revelstoke required strengthening the piers. Trains of flatcars brought boulders that were dumped into the river to provide additional protection to the original supports, c1888.

National Archives of Canada/PA25048

Hydraulic filling at Mountain Creek bridge, 1890. This method eliminated the need to transport fill from other areas, although not all locations possessed terrain suitable for hydraulic filling. Note the brace tower supporting the middle of the Howe truss span, and the considerable filling that has already taken place on the opposite side of the creek.

PROVINCIAL ARCHIVES OF BRITISH COLUMBIA/77638

The first Vancouver station at Burrard Inlet, 1888. This structure soon proved to be far too small for the volume of traffic.

Extensions and Branch Lines

The CPR built extensions to the main line and several new branch lines before the turn of the century. The initial western terminus was found to be unsatisfactory, "owing to the inadequacy of the harbour at Port Moody, and the unfavourable topography of the surrounding lands."[37] Vancouver, fourteen miles to the west, was selected as the new terminus, although the extension was not completed until 1887 because of litigation.

Beginning in the 1880s, the discovery of silver, copper, and later lead ores in the southern Kootenay and Boundary districts of British Columbia led to the construction of a number of small railways to move ore from the mines to shipping on the large lakes and the Columbia River. Many of the chartered companies, such as the Columbia and Kootenay Railway, the Nicola, Kamloops and Similkameen Coal and Railway Company, and the Shuswap and Okanagan Railway, neither built nor operated the lines themselves. They were either purchased or leased by the CPR. Van

Horne explained that the control of such railroads was important, "to prevent the invasion, by foreign lines, of the Kootenay District,"[38] a fear that was well-founded, since J.J. Hill and the Great Northern were making serious efforts to build lines into southern British Columbia. For many reasons, especially those involving finance, most railroad companies chartered during this time never laid a rail or turned a wheel.[39] Some were built and operated independently for a time, such as the Nelson and Fort Sheppard, an extension to Nelson of an American line originating at Spokane Falls; the Columbia and Western, a small mining line between Rossland and Trail; and the Kaslo and Slocan. While the Nelson and Fort Sheppard was built to standard gauge, the other two, in the interest of economy, were narrow-gauge lines.[40] The Kaslo and Slocan was particularly worrisome to the CPR, as it was considerably north of the international border, and was under the control of the Great Northern. The CPR concluded that it not only had to control as many lines in the Kootenays as possible, but that it had to construct an east-west line of its own to cut off further

Fort Macleod station on the Crowsnest Pass line, c1900. Fort Macleod's importance as a larger centre and as a junction with the Calgary and Edmonton Railway earned it a larger station building than most other locations on the Crowsnest Pass line.

NATIONAL ARCHIVES
OF CANADA/C5259

incursions from the south. Moreover, extensive deposits of coal had been discovered in the vicinity of the Crowsnest Pass, and in the light of this, Van Horne warned, "Any delay in securing your interests in that direction will be extremely dangerous— that unless your Company occupies the ground others will." The CPR desired "the immediate construction of a line from Lethbridge to a connection with your Columbia and Kootenay Railway at Nelson, a distance of 325 miles, and anticipating your approval they have already taken steps towards commencement of the work."[41]

The Crowsnest branch was constructed with liberal cash subsidies and land grants from the dominion government, but these came with a price. The rate charged to transport particular commodities, especially grain, was fixed, seemingly in perpetuity. The line, under the direction of Chief Engineer P. Alex Peterson, travelled from Lethbridge (on the former narrow-gauge line taken over by the CPR), through the valley of the Belly, Oldman, and St. Mary's Rivers, through the Crowsnest Pass to Kootenay Landing on the southern tip of Kootenay Lake. The heaviest grading and bridge work was within the first seventy miles west of Lethbridge, where twenty-four Howe truss spans were required, with a total length of more than two and a half miles. As with initial construction on the main line, this portion of the line was considered to be temporary, although most grades were no more than 1 percent, considerably less than on the 1885 main line.[42] Grading began in July 1897, and the line was completed by October 1898. Although it would be several years before the CPR reached Nelson directly by rail, the Crowsnest Pass line forestalled any concerted efforts of American lines to expand in southern British Columbia and Alberta.

Tourist Transport

Ever mindful of ways in which the CPR could make more money, Van Horne was interested in establishing a tourist trade, transporting tourists to great sights along the line, remarking, "Since we can't export the scenery, we shall have to import the tourists."[43] The CPR's service was designed much along the lines of the rapidly expanding Compagnie Internationale des Wagons-Lits in Europe.[44] Like the Wagons-Lits, the CPR purchased its own sleeping- and dining-cars, with most of the first passenger rolling stock being ordered from the Barney and Smith Manufacturing Company of Dayton, Ohio. Both dining-cars and the railway hotels boasted fine linen and special china, from firms such as Limoges in France and Minton in England, as well as silver-plate cutlery. Van Horne insisted that service and comfort be so good that it would become renowned, and as early as 1888, one traveller remarked that the CPR's passenger service was "the best on this continent." Although the sleeping-cars (first class, at any rate) were palatial, with plush upholstery and a spacious bathroom with a tub, the dining-car had one disadvantage: the menu was so large that it made selection difficult.[45] Not all passengers travelled first class, and less well-appointed coaches accommodated those travelling by either Tourist or Colonist class. Tourist sleepers contained a kitchen and stove at one end, where individuals could prepare meals using their own food. Colonist cars were the most Spartan of all, with simple wooden seats and berths without bedding. As the name implies, these cars were intended to transport immigrants from their port of entry to wherever they wished to settle, usually on land reached by the CPR.

Interior of a CPR tourist-class car, c1914. Sleeping accommodation was in berths. The seats folded down to make the lower berths, while the compartments above opened to comprise the upper berths. The leather-covered seats gave some comfort, but were not as well-appointed as first-class cars.

NATIONAL ARCHIVES OF CANADA/PA48407

The interior of a CPR dining-car, c1900. Each table was laid with a fine linen tablecloth, CPR china, silverware, and a crystal water carafe.

GLENBOW ARCHIVES/NA–3026–14

A shower and model
in a CPR first-class sleeping
car, c1920; more comforts
than home.

NATIONAL ARCHIVES OF
CANADA/PA48420

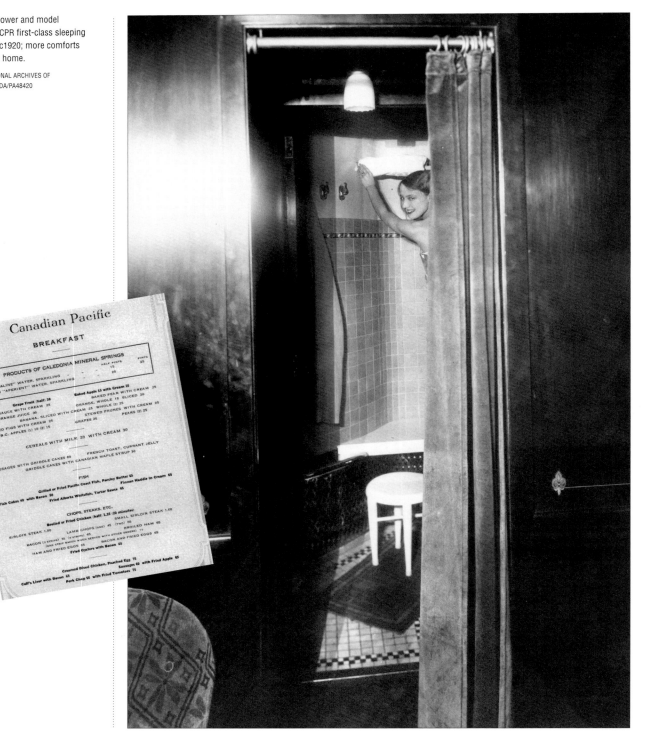

From the beginning of transcontinental service, travellers enjoyed viewing mountain scenery in the Rocky and Selkirk Mountains. While a view was available from the rear platform of the last car, few people could be accommodated there. Consequently, three cars were modified in 1890; their windows were removed and they were fitted with bench seats for up to seventy passengers. While certainly gaining a wider view, passengers were also subject to rain and to cinders from the locomotives. Designers took a novel approach to the problem in 1902, with the construction of an observation car with large windows on each side and caboose-like cupolas on each end of the roof. Benches and swivel chairs arranged on two levels in the main part of the car, and benches in the cupolas, seating fifty people altogether, afforded clear views to the sides, but the tops of the mountains remained obscured. Three additional observation cars built in 1906 had glass panels added to the central portion of the roof. While protecting passengers from weather and cinders, these enclosed cars became oppressively hot in sunny weather, and when it was cold outside, visibility was often obscured by condensation on the glass. These unusual cars were gradually shifted to the Esquimalt and Nanaimo line, but all were withdrawn from service by 1913.[46]

The Atlantic Express, shown here at Glacier House c1905, was equipped with one of the first enclosed mountain observation cars (without glass panels in the roof). This train will soon proceed through the snowsheds visible above, and then carry on through Rogers Pass.

MOUNT STEPHEN HOUSE, FIELD, B.C.

The popularity of Mount Stephen House led
to its expansion in two stages. Both additions
were designed by Rattenbury, and they
dwarfed Sorby's initial hotel, shown at the
left, c1905. The small log station for Field can
be seen at the right.

NATIONAL ARCHIVES OF CANADA/PA32025

Hotels

Unlike the Wagons-Lits Company, which simply fed and sheltered their charges en route, Van Horne also wanted the CPR to accommodate tourists at their destinations. To this end, a series of hotels were constructed in British Columbia beginning in 1886. The first were wooden buildings resembling Swiss chalets, designed by Thomas Sorby of Montréal. Examples were built at Field (Mount Stephen House), a divisional point, at the bottom of the Big Hill; Glacier (Glacier House), near the Illecillewaet glacier on the west side of Rogers Pass, just before the Loops; and North Bend (Fraser Canyon House), another divisional point, with a spectacular view of the Fraser Canyon. Each building contained fifteen bedrooms, some of which were used by staff initially. In spite of their diminutive size, these hotels had spacious dining-rooms, and at first were used to supplement the dining-car service. The problems of moving trains up and down the Big Hill and on the grades through Rogers Pass prompted the CPR to dispense with hauling heavy dining-cars in the area and instead to make meal stops at the hotels, usually of no more than half an hour.[47]

Rattenbury's pet project was the Empress Hotel in Victoria, shown here in 1908. Although he left the project before its completion, the exterior reflected his style. The Empress became one of Victoria's landmarks and remains one of the city's première stopping places.

COLLECTION OF THE AUTHOR

The CPR constructed larger hotels with some of the proceeds from the sale of town lots to immigrants. The first was the Hotel Vancouver, completed in 1887, and the second was the Banff Springs Hotel at the new national park in Alberta, finished in 1888. The Hotel Vancouver, an austere, six-storey brick and masonry structure, was designed by Thomas Sorby, but the much larger (250 rooms), mainly wooden Banff Springs Hotel was designed by Bruce Price of New York in the style of French châteaux.[48] The hotel received its name because of its proximity to several hot springs thought to possess great therapeutic value, yet another drawing card for tourists. The hotels were so popular, especially Glacier House, that additions and improvements were planned almost immediately. Bruce Price designed the first addition to Glacier House, which more than tripled the number of bedrooms available; it opened in 1892, just four years after the initial structure had been built. The smaller hotels were improved by the addition of electricity, plumbing, and hot and cold running water.

The CPR also exploited more remote locations, building in 1890 the Lake Louise Chalet, a small log cabin at the north end of the lake. A fire in 1893 led to the erection of a slightly larger structure, also immensely popular, even though it was not easy to

An early view of Mount
Stephen House at Field,
c1890, showing some of the
patrons enjoying the view
and air from the verandah.

VANCOUVER PUBLIC LIBRARY/31073

The first Hotel Vancouver
as it appeared shortly after
it opened, c1888.

PROVINCIAL ARCHIVES OF
ALBERTA/B9924

Amid spectacular scenery, Bruce Price's Banff Springs Hotel, c1890, was designed to provide the traveller with every modern luxury, while preserving the rustic setting of the Rocky Mountains.

COLLECTION OF THE AUTHOR

Thomas Sorby's Glacier House Hotel, c1888, with a decorative fountain imported from Montréal. Note the bear cub, which was appropriated by the hotel staff as a tourist attraction and a novelty.

PROVINCIAL ARCHIVES OF ALBERTA/B5359

Francis Rattenbury designed the rather unusual Hotel Sicamous, on the southern shore of Shuswap Lake, in 1898. A popular location for fishing and boating, the hotel soon proved to be inadequate for demand.

COLLECTION OF THE AUTHOR

Rattenbury also designed a large replacement hotel for the log chalet at Lake Louise, shown here c1905. Now travellers could enjoy the lake in the style to which many had become accustomed.

COLLECTION OF THE AUTHOR

1477. LAKE LOUISE CHALET, LAGGAN.

get to and there were minimal amenities. The nearest station was Laggan, nearly three miles distant, renamed Lake Louise in 1913. During this time, another small chalet was constructed at Emerald Lake, a short distance from Field.[49]

By 1896, the CPR had engaged another consulting architect, Francis Rattenbury, famous for his design of the Parliament Buildings in Victoria. Rattenbury's first CPR project was the small Hotel Revelstoke, completed in 1896. To serve those interested in hunting and fishing, he designed a combination station and hotel—the Hotel Sicamous—on the shore of Shuswap Lake in 1898. And the popularity of the Lake Louise Chalet led Rattenbury to design a large hotel for the site in the pseudo-half-timbered style reminiscent of Tudor England. The new hotel was opened in 1899. By the early 1900s, the CPR was importing Swiss guides for service at most of the alpine hotels. Less exotic local guides were also available for extended pack trips through the mountains. Rattenbury was also responsible for a fifty-four-room addition to Glacier House, which included an electric elevator, two large additions to Mount

The popularity of the château style for railway hotels was extended to some large stations as well. The Maxwell brothers designed the imposing Vancouver station, which opened in 1898, replacing a modest wooden station and platform.

GLENBOW ARCHIVES/ NA–3688–14

Stephen House, a new wing for the Hotel Vancouver, and a ninety-four-room addition to the Banff Springs Hotel, all constructed between 1900 and 1906.[50]

Rattenbury's crowning glory for the CPR was his design for the famous Empress Hotel in Victoria, named in keeping with the names of the railroad's expanding fleet of steamships in the Pacific. The site selected was James Bay, a tidal mud-flat to the east of the Parliament Buildings and bridged by a causeway. Although awarded the commission in 1902, Rattenbury's plans for the large, multistorey hotel in the Château style, containing 175 rooms, were not finished until 1904. After much negotiating between the CPR and the City of Victoria for tax concessions, construction began in 1906, but progress was slow because of disagreements over who was responsible for reclaiming and landscaping the surrounding land. After several changes, the Empress opened on January 20, 1908, although Rattenbury had resigned late in 1906 because his plans had been altered by Walter Painter, another CPR architect, and Catherine Reed, wife of the railroad's superintendent of hotels, Hayter Reed.[51]

With additional floors to accommodate more guests, Rattenbury's modifications to the Hotel Sicamous, shown here in 1924, reflected the pseudo-half-timbered style that characterised his later hotel designs for the CPR.

NATIONAL ARCHIVES
OF CANADA/PA122001

In keeping with the sylvan surroundings, the CPR erected rustic log stations at several points in the Rockies. Laggan, which was also the nearest stopping place to Lake Louise, initially had a small log station, shown here c1890. It was later replaced by a much larger log and frame building, although the original station remained at the site as a storage building.

CANADIAN PACIFIC CORPORATE ARCHIVES/A–1658

Stations

The increase in passenger traffic, combined with the desire to offer more luxurious facilities for tourists, led to the CPR replacing many original stations with larger and more elegant buildings. The brothers Edward and William Maxwell designed an imposing station and office complex for Vancouver. Opened in 1898, the building resembled the front of an enormous château. Although not considered an important enough place to warrant a station in the Château style, Calgary was a booming centre and its wooden station was replaced by an elegant masonry structure in 1893. When business exceeded expectations, an almost identical addition was erected in 1908. Stations at smaller centres were also replaced; the log stations at Banff and Laggan, for example, gave way to larger structures before the First World War, as did buildings at other locations where traffic increased.[52]

With additional means of income, improvements to the line, construction of new branches, and control of many feeder lines, the Canadian Pacific Railway was in an enviable position in Alberta and British Columbia. Although various concerns had tried, with little success, to threaten its dominance in these areas, concerted competition was about to begin.

The Grand Trunk Pacific:
A Titanic Effort

I n 1879, six years before the completion of the CPR, Sandford Fleming said that he believed another transcontinental railroad across Canada would be necessary to colonize those areas not served by the Canadian Pacific.[1] But no one expressed any interest in such a project until 1895, ten years after the CPR was finished.

The Trans-Canada Railway

Colonel George Church, an American who lived in London and who was also the vice-president of the Royal Geographical Society, led a group of English and Canadian investors to incorporate the Trans-Canadian Railway Company, later shortened to Trans-Canada Railway, in 1895. As envisaged, the TCR would run from Roberval, north of Québec City, in a northwesterly direction, passing south of James Bay and north of Lake Winnipeg. From there the line would travel north of Edmonton and continue either through the Yellowhead Pass, or a more northerly pass through the Rocky Mountains, and then follow the Skeena River, where the line would terminate at either Port Simpson or Port Essington. It was thought that the route would be sufficiently north not to compete with the CPR, a sentiment allegedly agreed with by Van Horne.[2] Unfortunately, the projected railroad ran from nowhere to nowhere, via nowhere. Nothing happened with this venture until 1902, when the dominion government gave a subsidy for the construction of the first sixty miles in Québec, and the company awarded a provisional contract for the construction of four hundred miles west from Roberval. By this time it was decided that the route to the Pacific Coast should be through the Pine Pass (near present-day Dawson Creek, B.C.) and that the western terminus should be Port Simpson. Construction was dependent upon a sizeable subsidy from Ottawa, which, unfortunately, was not forthcoming. The Grand Trunk Railway had finally launched its own plans for the construction of a second transcontinental railroad, and that company seemed to have the ear and the indulgence of the prime minister, Sir Wilfrid Laurier. Without large subsidies, the TCR was unable to proceed, and the venture collapsed in

1903. Its efforts were soon forgotten in the tumult surrounding the proposed western extension of the Grand Trunk.

The Grand Trunk Pacific

By the mid-1890s, most shareholders of the Grand Trunk Railway believed that a mistake had been made by not heeding the advice of Edward Watkin to expand westward, given the success of the CPR and the growth of other railroads. The Grand Trunk was hemmed in, and the CPR was proving to be a formidable competitor in eastern Canada. At the Grand Trunk's annual meeting in October 1895, Sir Henry Tyler, who had championed the fight against western expansion, was removed as president and replaced by Sir Charles Rivers Wilson, who was also elected chairman of the board. Although he had no practical experience with railroads, Wilson had considerable experience with the finances of various modes of transportation, including the Suez Canal in Egypt and the Central Pacific Railroad in the United States. A long-standing criticism of the Grand Trunk was that it was administered primarily from England, since most of the board and shareholders resided there. Sir Rivers changed the old policy by visiting Canada at least once every year, not just to see the offices, but to inspect the lines and interview staff. Under his leadership, responsibility for many decisions was shifted to individuals in Canada. From observing the CPR, Sir Rivers realized that for North American conditions, American principles of railroad operation were superior to British methods. Copying the CPR, therefore, Wilson hired a successful and innovative American railroader, Charles Melville Hays, as the Grand Trunk's new general manager.[3]

Hays, an egocentric, but an effective executive, was permitted to hire his own assistants—most of them Americans—and by the turn of the century, the fortunes of the Grand Trunk had improved greatly. To compete against other railroads successfully, Hays came up with a grand idea that, while risky, would result in high returns should it prove successful. He proposed to extend the Grand Trunk's main line westward from North Bay, Ontario, to Winnipeg, with a branch to a grain port at Fort William (part of present-day Thunder Bay). From Winnipeg, the line would head northwest to a good harbour on the Pacific, with the gentlest grades of any railroad in North America. At first, choices for the western terminus were similar to those of the CPR's original plan—Bute Inlet or Port Simpson—and it was thought initially that either the Pine or Peace River Pass would furnish the lowest grades through the Rocky Mountains. By constructing a trunk line designed primarily for the high-speed movement of goods from port to destination, Hays reckoned that the Grand Trunk could capture much cross-continent shipping, especially from the CPR:

C. Rivers Wilson

The dynamic Sir Charles Rivers Wilson, in 1905, president of the Grand Trunk Corporation, and one of the main proponents of the bold venture west, the Grand Trunk Pacific, of which he became first chairman of the board.

COLLECTION OF THE AUTHOR

Charles Melville Hays, in 1910, first president of the Grand Trunk Pacific, an experienced railroader who had the determination and skill to take on the CPR in western Canada. By a cruel turn of fate, Hays died in the *Titanic* disaster, leaving his western railroad unfinished.

COLLECTION OF THE AUTHOR

GRAND TRUNK PACIFIC

THE ONLY ALL CANADIAN TRANSCONTINENTAL ROUTE

TIME TABLES

Fort William
Winnipeg   Regina
Saskatoon
Edmonton
Yellowhead Pass
Melville
Yorkton   Canora
Camrose   Mirror
Prince Rupert East

Subject to Change without Notice

W. P. HINTON
GENERAL PASSENGER AGENT
UNION STATION
WINNIPEG

W. J. QUINLAN
DISTRICT PASSENGER AGENT
260 PORTAGE AVE.
WINNIPEG

FOLDER A, No. 15

June 15th, 1913

Our Directors feel, that in view of the apparent need for additional railway facilities and in order to guarantee to the present Grand Trunk System direct connection with that very important and growing section of Canada, the only wise policy is to take active steps towards this extension, which, I may add, will be commenced as soon as the necessary legislation has been obtained from the Government.[4]

A formal announcement of the plan was made on November 24, 1902, at which time it was revealed that the line would be constructed by a separate corporation, the Grand Trunk Pacific Railway Company (GTP), of which Hays would be president. Since the GTP would undoubtedly open up northern areas for colonization, both Wilson and Hays made it clear that they expected the dominion government to provide subsidies and land grants of the proportion given to the CPR during its construction. Frank Watrous Morse, third vice-president, added that the GTP would "expect the same treatment from a subsidy standpoint as had been meted out to the Canadian Pacific."[5] This sentiment was not shared by Sir Thomas Shaughnessy, president of the CPR, who contended, "The conditions have changed enormously since the pioneer road was constructed and circumstances which made Government cooperation absolutely essential no longer exist."[6]

Although news of the Grand Trunk Pacific was greeted with enthusiasm generally, Prime Minister Laurier was reluctant to fund it as proposed, since he was under pressure from members of his party to build railways in Québec and to the east coast of Canada, rather than to allow the Grand Trunk to use its existing facilities in Portland, Maine. Like Macdonald more than thirty years previously, Laurier said:

We lay it down as a principle upon which we are to be judged by friend and foe that we are to have a [second] trans-continental railway, that its termini must be in Canadian waters, and that the whole line, every inch of it, must be on Canadian territory.[7]

Instead of just expanding westward, Laurier and others in his government believed that the Grand Trunk should be part of a new transcontinental railway from Moncton, New Brunswick, to the Pacific Coast, passing through Québec City and Winnipeg, but running far north of the existing Grand Trunk lines. After much acrimonious debate both within Parliament and outside, an agreement was reached on July 29, 1903, whereby the dominion government would construct the eastern section, referred to as the National Transcontinental Railway (NTR), from Moncton to Winnipeg, and the Grand Trunk Pacific, incorporated finally on October 24, 1903, would build the western portion from Winnipeg to the Pacific Ocean, as well as the branch line to Thunder Bay. Upon completion, the NTR would be leased to the GTP for fifty years, at which time the NTR could be purchased outright.[8] Unfortunately, this proposal meant that the Grand Trunk Pacific would be separated from the Grand Trunk by a railroad outside its direct control.

Many Grand Trunk shareholders and some board members were not at all happy with the government's proposal, because much more capital was required than what was first believed. Moreover, what had begun as a westward extension to the Grand Trunk system ballooned into a commitment to construct and operate a transcontinental railroad largely through uninhabited and undeveloped country. To mollify the shareholders, Wilson met with Laurier frequently in late 1903 and early 1904 to obtain a supplemental agreement that would reduce the financial obligations and time constraints in the original agreement. Although Laurier accepted the new arrangement, Grand Trunk shareholders remained unconvinced. At the annual meeting on March 8, 1904, in an effort to bring them onside, many directors gave eloquent speeches on the necessity of constructing the Grand Trunk Pacific, even in its amended form. Perhaps the most convincing speech came from Sir Rivers, who said:

> Surrounded on all sides by elements of progress, it is absolutely impossible for our company to stand still. We must either continue to advance or we must recede and yield the offered advances to more enterprising and far-seeing competitors.[9]

A serious competitor was the Canadian Northern Railway, under the control of Mackenzie and Mann, who were intent on constructing a railroad to the Pacific by bits and pieces, and were well on the way to doing so. Mackenzie, initially at least, appeared hardly concerned about the GTP, claiming that the Canadian Northern possessed the rights of way through the Peace, Pine, and Yellowhead Passes. The possibility of the GTP-NTR competing with a Canadian Northern transcontinental line was something that neither Sir Rivers nor Prime Minister Laurier wanted. During 1903, Sir Rivers developed the idea of amalgamating the GTP with the Canadian Northern, and the prime minister held several meetings with representatives from both companies. Amalgamation did not appeal to either Hays or Mackenzie and Mann, with Mann stating publicly:

> We will have nothing to do with the Grand Trunk people, and what is more, we have no need. We control 85 per cent. of the stock and the interests of our enterprise and mean to hold on to our property and manage the Railway ourselves.[10]

In the end, no deal was reached. To avoid the political consequences of imposing amalgamation, or of showing blatant favouritism, Laurier indicated that his government would support each venture as equally as possible.[11]

Shareholders finally approved the modified form of the Grand Trunk Pacific, and it was up to Parliament to ratify the agreement. Much criticism of a second transcontinental came from the Conservative Opposition, whose leader, Robert Borden, argued that if Canada needed additional transcontinental lines, then the government should build them itself to ensure that money spent would remain in Canada. This idea of a nationalized rail system was unpopular at the time with most people. The federal election of October 1904 returned the Liberals to power with an increased majority, thus ensuring that the GTP would proceed as a private enterprise. And although it was to be built primarily with GTP money, the government agreed to guarantee the first $50 million worth of bonds. Sir Rivers was not satisfied with this arrangement, however, because the GTP did not obtain the same land grants as the CPR: "I am bound to say that we failed to secure from them [the dominion government] the same material assistance, in the form of enormous land grants, which has been one of the main causes of the prosperity of that corporation."[12] But the government was resolute, and the situation remained unchanged.

The GTP faced another difficulty that the CPR had been spared. In February 1904 Ottawa established a Board of Railway Commissioners to evaluate and decide upon all matters relating to the construction, operation, and modification of railroads in Canada. Approval had to be sought for everything from line location to the type of fencing used to keep livestock away from the tracks, and the commissioners had the power to reject requests, make modifications, order construction, delay approval, and to fine severely for offences.

Meanwhile, Hays was not idle. He had sent survey crews out in 1903 to ascertain the best route, and in the summer of 1904 he personally visited centres in Alberta and British Columbia, although most of his travel was by the CPR. Early in 1905, Hays announced that Edmonton would be the GTP's main divisional point between Winnipeg and the Pacific Coast, news that was most welcome in the city that the CPR had forsaken, and which was soon to become the capital of the new Province of Alberta. A grateful Edmonton also pledged many concessions to the new railway, and the GTP constructed an eighteen-stall roundhouse and extensive shop facilities on the north edge of town during 1909.[13] On August 3, 1905, the GTP announced that its Pacific terminal would be Kaien Island, just off the mainland about twenty-five miles south of Port Simpson. The island's natural harbour had been overlooked by Fleming's surveyors years earlier. Although a route through the mountains had not been decided upon, construction began near Portage la Prairie, Manitoba, in August 1905, with a projected completion date of September 1911. Such a short-time line seemed unrealistic, but even as late as 1908, with construction far behind schedule in the east, and no rails laid from the west, Hays insisted that the line would be complete on time: "I see no reason to doubt that by the Autumn of 1911 our first train will pass through the country from the Atlantic to the Pacific." Exaggerated claims of this sort encouraged some to refer to Hays

An example of the ubiquitous Plan A GTP station, located at Stony Plain, Alberta, c1914. The section crew has been levelling the track by jacking it up and shovelling ballast underneath the ties. The tapered wooden object lying across the tracks is a track level, which works the same way as a carpenter's level.

and the GTP as the Grand Trafficker of Promises.[14] Yet in spite of the delays and cost overruns, the board's confidence in Hays's leadership did not waver. On August 3, 1909, Sir Rivers Wilson stated:

> Mr. Hays has an absolutely free hand. We have such respect for him—so thoroughly has he impressed us with his great intelligence, ability and power—that any difference arising between him and the Board in London seems out of the question.[15]

To help keep costs down, the GTP, like the CPR before it, used standard designs for most buildings. Sidings were placed at intervals of every eight to ten miles where possible, and way stations, usually built to Plan A, grew up around most of them.[16] Townsites were laid out in a standard fashion, using a rectangular grid pattern. The avenues, running parallel to the tracks, were numbered from first upwards; streets ran perpendicular to the tracks. Main Street was aligned with the back of the station, with named streets on both sides. The naming of the streets also followed a prescribed format. Looking towards the front of the station, and proceeding left, streets were named Queen, Alberta, Québec, etc. To the right, streets were named King, Dominion, Young, etc. The naming of stations along the main line, to Edmonton at least, was somewhat in keeping with Fleming's route map of the original CPR line. But instead of letters of the alphabet, names were selected that followed the alphabet, hence Butze, Chauvin, Dunn, Edgerton, as the line entered Alberta. The sequence was not rigidly adhered to, and many names were altered and intermediate stations created at later dates.

Divisional points were special. With larger stations, roundhouses, and other facilities for locomotive and car servicing, they were usually named for GTP and Grand Trunk administrators, and for members of the board. Wainwright, Alberta, for example, was named for William Wainwright, the GTP's second vice-president, while Smithers, B.C., was named for Alfred Waldron Smithers, who became chairman of the board upon the retirement of Sir Rivers Wilson. Jasper was initially named Fitzhugh, after Earl Hopkins Fitzhugh, vice-president of the Grand Trunk, but local outrage caused the name to be changed back to Jasper, the traditional name of the location.[17]

To gain popular exposure, the GTP ran a contest in 1906 for naming its Pacific terminus. A $250 prize would be awarded for the best submission that did not exceed ten letters or three syllables. The entries that appealed to the judges were Prince Rupert and Port Rupert. Although Prince Rupert had too many letters, it was selected, and the two entries for Port Rupert, which was thought to be too similar to Fort Rupert on Vancouver Island, were also awarded the full prize. By the end of November 1906, Prince Rupert was sufficiently established to have its own post office.[18]

Interior view of the Wainwright roundhouse, c1911. The crew is responsible for routine maintenance such as boiler washouts, engine startup, and minor repairs.

GLENBOW ARCHIVES/NA–544–22

In 1905, Frank Morse, now first vice-president, exclaimed that the GTP would have the "lowest grades and least curvature of any transcontinental railway."[19] Bartholomew B. Kelliher was appointed chief engineer, and was charged with constructing the GTP with grades of no more than four-tenths of 1 percent (twenty-one feet to the mile). Most of the location work was undertaken by C.C. Van Arsdol, nicknamed "Four-Tenths Van." While the main consideration was finding a route that did not exceed the stipulated grade, surveyors discovered rich coal-bearing areas southwest of what would become the divisional point of Edson, as well as east of Jasper. To exploit the coal, it was thought advantageous to locate the main line as close to the deposits as possible. Despite initial statements to the contrary, the GTP, through a subsidiary, the Grand Trunk Pacific Branch Lines Company, fully intended to construct branch lines to reach lucrative markets and natural resources. Considering these factors, railroad officials submitted a plan in December 1906 for their line to be located through the Yellowhead Pass, keeping to the stipulated gradient except for one small portion, where the grade would be one-half of 1 percent. In a report to Hays, Kelliher said of the Yellowhead Pass, "There is no other break in the mountains that will admit of a 0.4% grade."[20] Notwithstanding the Canadian Northern's claim that they had first right to the Yellowhead through the charter of the Edmonton, Yukon and Pacific Railway, the GTP route was approved. And in the style that enabled him to outlive Sandford Fleming in government service, Collingwood Schreiber, in deference to a new minister of Railways and Canals, approved amended plans for the Canadian Northern to run a line through the pass as well. The GTP's attempt to gain prior approval for a branch line from the Yellowhead Pass to Vancouver via the Thompson and Fraser Rivers, however, was refused.[21]

Unlike the CPR, which constructed its main line as cheaply as possible, the GTP built its main line to top-class standards from the outset. Instead of using sixty-five-pounds-per-yard rail as initially proposed, heavier, more expensive rail at eighty pounds per yard was used for main-line construction. With a substantial roadbed and gentle grades, the GTP was able to use relatively small locomotives. Its first were thirty-six Moguls (2–6–0) built in the 1870s, and purchased from the Grand Trunk, which later supplied seven newer Moguls, built in 1895 and 1896, as well as ten Consolidations (2–8–0) built in 1898. While the old locomotives were adequate for construction trains, service on unfinished sections of the line, and for yard service, they were inadequate for high-speed hauling, anticipated at up to fifty miles per hour, on the completed line. With this in mind, the GTP ordered seventy-six new locomotives in 1908–09 with a 4–4–0 wheel arrangement, commonly called Americans but referred to as 8–wheel by the GTP. These locomotives, purchased from the Montréal Locomotive Works and from the Canada Foundry Company, were equipped with large-diameter (sixty-nine-inch) driving wheels and were capable of reaching main-line speed on the prairies while pulling either freight or passenger cars. In 1910, the GTP ordered thirty larger locomotives with a 4–6–0 wheel arrangement, called 10-wheelers, followed in 1911 by fifteen Pacifics (4–6–2) with seventy-three inch diameter driving wheels for main-line service primarily in British Columbia. Fifty Consolidations (2–8–0) for long, heavy freight trains joined the fleet in 1911–12, the largest, and last, locomotives ordered by the Grand Trunk Pacific.[22]

In spite of all the precautions taken against it, rolling stock would sometimes derail. In collisions, or in a serious derailment, such as the one here, at Irricana, Alberta, c1913, heavy cranes were required to lift the equipment back onto the rails. Grand Trunk Pacific Number 395302 is a typical example of a heavy, steam-powered wrecking crane that was used by most larger railways in western Canada.

COLLECTION OF THE AUTHOR

Construction was divided into two sections. Winnipeg to Wolf Creek, Alberta, was called the Prairie Section, and Wolf Creek to the coast was called the Mountain Section. While several contractors worked on the former, construction on the latter was largely undertaken by the well-known American firm of Foley Brothers, Larson and Company, later renamed Foley, Welch and Stewart.

Several mechanical devices helped speed construction. Steam shovels, rare when work began on the CPR, were used to move large quantities of material and to load ballast trains. Animal-powered graders also made their appearance, displacing the small and inefficient Fresnos. And once the grade was prepared, a mechanical track layer, usually called a Pioneer, after the manufacturer, the Pioneer Track Layer Company, laid both ties and rails. A Pioneer consisted of a wooden-framed derrick and several steam engines bolted to a specially fitted flatcar. A trough supported by a jib on the front deposited the ties, and when a sufficient number were laid, a length of rail would be unloaded from another trough, and crews would bolt it to the rail laid previously, and spike it to about every third tie. A separate crew behind the track layer would finish aligning and spiking the rails. The Pioneer and its attendant flat-

One of the old Moguls operating on the Grand Trunk Pacific, c1911, Number 20 is heading a small local passenger train that has just arrived at the divisional point of Fitzhugh, later renamed Jasper.

Animal-drawn grader at work on the preparation of the GTP grade west of Edmonton, 1910.

CITY OF EDMONTON ARCHIVES/EA–10–1296

A remarkable photograph taken at the eastern end of Wabamun Lake during the construction of the GTP main line west of Edmonton, in 1910. The Pioneer track layer is advancing along the completed grade, laying both ties and rails.

NATIONAL ARCHIVES OF CANADA/C6099

cars could carry enough material to lay about a mile of track at a time. Several men were required to operate the steam engines, bolt angle bars to the rails, and move ties and rails into the troughs. With all the moving parts and steam engines, the noise produced by a track laying train was deafening.[23]

While clearing and settlement began at Prince Rupert in 1906, no rails were laid until 1908. There were a number of reasons for this. Initial construction consisted of blasting out progressively larger areas for the railroad, yards, port, and a floating dry dock, and a major delay occurred when rock removal swelled from the original estimate of forty thousand cubic yards to more than a hundred thousand, incurring considerable time and expense. The port was essential to railroad construction, since supplies had to be brought in by ship. Another problem was that roadbed preparation was much slower on this section, requiring thirteen tunnels through rock, with an aggregate length of more than one mile.[24] In addition, construction was also taking place at locations removed from the main line. The GTP had acquired two charters that entailed subsidies from the B.C. government, contingent upon a particular amount of construction being undertaken.[25] After sufficient construction took place, the lines

Although the Pioneer reduced much of the heavy lifting associated with track laying, a large number of workers was still required. Here we see the rail conveyor, 1910. The two men standing on the platform

place angle bars on each end of the rail segments, so that the ground crews can simply place the rail and connect it to previously laid sections quickly.

CITY OF EDMONTON ARCHIVES/EA–500–64

The makeshift dock at Prince Rupert, in 1908, showing the stockpile of rails unloaded recently. With the delivery of such essential supplies, construction of the GTP could proceed from the western terminus.

COLLECTION OF THE AUTHOR

were abandoned. There were employment difficulties, too. Racist sentiments against Chinese ran high, and the GTP was prohibited from importing any Chinese labourers. In consequence, the railroad was forced to pay higher wages to attract workers to Prince Rupert.[26]

Many European immigrants and itinerant workers came to Canada, some believing they could make a quick fortune. In spite of the better pay, working conditions were often as deplorable as they had been on the CPR when Chinese labourers were used. In consequence, many workers died or were seriously injured. A notable example is Joachim Ribbentrop, who later became Hitler's foreign minister. In 1912, after holding other relatively low-paying jobs in Canada, Ribbentrop and his brother worked on the NTR, gradually making their way west to the higher-paying GTP. Although they reached Winnipeg, their tenure was cut short, when they both contracted tuberculosis. The severity of the disease combined with poor initial medical treatment resulted in lasting health problems for Ribbentrop, and the premature death of his brother in 1918.[27]

Besides constructing a high-speed line, which required expensive roadbed preparation, the GTP used mainly steel bridges, which added to the expense of construction and delayed progress in many instances. The railroad's innovative bridge engineer, Jacques Legrand, was responsible for designing most of them.

Grading of the Prairie Section proceeded quickly, but bridge construction impeded track laying. Steel had reached Alberta by July 1908, for example, but could not get to Edmonton until two large steel bridges were completed to the east of the city—one across the Battle River near Fabyan and the other across the North Saskatchewan near Clover Bar. Grading and other bridge construction did continue farther west, however. The Clover Bar bridge had the dubious distinction of having the tallest concrete piers of any bridge in North America at that time—124 feet from footing to top, not including the bridge superstructure. Parts for the superstructure, fabricated by the Canadian Bridge Company in Ontario, were shipped via the Canadian Northern, which had reached Edmonton in late 1905, and which obligingly built a spur from their main line to the site of the Clover Bar bridge.[28] The first GTP train did not pull into Edmonton until July 1909.

Financial matters did not go well for the GTP. While the CPR had received a blanket exemption from import duties on rails for its main line, the dominion government imposed duty on imported rails in 1906, which added another $4 million to the cost of the GTP, not including the extra cost of purchasing heavier rails.[29] Low estimates and cost overruns resulted in the GTP issuing more bonds and debentures, and borrowing heavily. The venture fast became a black hole for money. The poor financial situation was exacerbated by Hays, who constructed elaborate docks at Victoria, Vancouver, and Seattle, established a steamship service between these points and Prince Rupert, ordered millions of dollars worth of freight and passenger rolling stock, as well as progressively larger and more expensive locomotives, and began a chain of hotels to compete with the CPR for the tourist trade.

Ex-CPR architect Francis Rattenbury was intrigued with the GTP from its beginnings, and eventually became a consulting architect. In 1906, he designed a modest, three-storey wooden hotel for Prince Rupert, completed in 1907 and named the Grand Trunk Pacific Inn. By 1910, he had prepared preliminary designs for a large hotel in Victoria to compete directly with the CPR's Empress, although subsequent financial difficulties ensured that it would never be built.

In 1911, Hays announced that the GTP was embarking on the construction of a chain of hotels, some with hydrotherapy, to accommodate the anticipated tourist trade. The Montréal architectural firm Ross and MacFarlane designed a 250-room masonry hotel for Edmonton, to be named the Macdonald. Construction began in 1912, and the hotel was opened on July 5, 1915. Equipped with silver plate and china emblazoned with an elaborate Grand Trunk Pacific crest, the Macdonald afforded patrons luxurious accommodation equal to that of any CPR hotel. Although estimated to cost $1 million, the final bill was slightly more than twice that much.[30]

Rattenbury prepared designs in the Château style for the other hotels. The Château Miette, with 250 rooms and a spa, was to be built near the Miette Hot Springs, east of Jasper. The Mountain Inn was to be a large log complex on the shore of Lac Beauvert near Jasper (the future site of Canadian National's Jasper Park Lodge). The Château Mount Robson, a much larger masonry edifice with 500 rooms, was to be constructed on the plain facing the tallest mountain in the Rockies. The crowning glory was to be the Prince Rupert, a ten-storey brick and masonry structure with 600 rooms and provision for two, six-storey annexes. Rattenbury estimated that this hotel would cost only $1 million, a gross underestimate, given the cost of the Macdonald.[31] Before construction could commence on any of the hotels, however, the GTP suffered a series of unanticipated setbacks.

The retirement of Sir Rivers Wilson in 1910 led to Alfred Smithers becoming the new chairman of the board. While Smithers had supported and voted for the Grand Trunk Pacific in 1904, he lacked Wilson's enthusiasm and cunning. Smithers also tended to waver on financial plans and equivocate on policies. And when Laurier's Liberals were defeated in the federal election of 1911 by Robert Borden and the Conservatives, who were not friendly towards the GTP, it ensured that money would be harder to obtain from the dominion government. Realizing this, Hays made repeated excursions to England and Europe to raise further capital. Returning to Canada from one such journey, Hays was booked on the maiden voyage of the *Titanic*, and he was among the 1,522 individuals who perished when she sank on April 14, 1912. There were rumours that Hays was carrying plans on his person, and that if his body had not been lost, the plans would have saved the GTP from financial ruin.[32] Hays's body was, in fact, one of 328 found floating near where the *Titanic* sank;

The Clover Bar bridge, immediately east of Edmonton, was the last major obstacle to the GTP reaching that city. An east-bound ballast train, with an auxiliary water car for the locomotive, crosses the two-month-old bridge in early September, 1909. The auxiliary water car was necessary because water facilities along the line had not yet been completed.

CITY OF EDMONTON
ARCHIVES/EA–143–1

Dominating the Edmonton skyline, the newly completed Macdonald Hotel, shown here in 1915, afforded patrons luxurious accommodation equal to that offered by any CPR hotel.

COLLECTION OF THE AUTHOR

Growing from rock and trees, Prince Rupert soon became a boom town, its fortune tied to that of the GTP. Francis Rattenbury's hotel for the new town is shown prominently here, in 1907. Although intended as a stopgap until a more grandiose masonry structure could be built, the Grand Trunk Pacific Inn outlasted the corporation it was named for.

COLLECTION OF THE AUTHOR

One of Rattenbury's sketches of the proposed hotel at Miette Hot Springs, 1913, which was intended to compete directly with the CPR's Banff Springs Hotel. Financial problems combined with the loss of Charles Hays's dynamic leadership, resulted in the GTP's Château Miette remaining a "castle in the air."

NATIONAL LIBRARY OF CANADA/NL–13574

it was clothed and the pockets contained no special documents. His pocket watch was recovered, stopped by the action of sea water. The body was shipped to Canada, where it was interred in Montréal.

Hays's successor was Edson J. Chamberlin, general manager of the GTP. By 1913, as the financial picture worsened, Chamberlin tried to reduce peripheral building while maintaining speedy construction of the main line, so as to beat out the Canadian Northern's transcontinental line. Although work on the Macdonald Hotel continued, largely because of tax concessions promised by Edmonton, construction stopped on the remainder of the hotels, including the Prince Rupert, where a basement had already been dug.

Chamberlin's attempt to be fiscally responsible only gained him the ire of the dominion government. On November 17, 1913, the last spike was driven on the National Transcontinental Railway. But with the GTP's finances stretched to the limit, Chamberlin and the board refused to lease it, as stipulated in the original agreement. The GTP was able to avoid assuming the NTR lease because although all the track was laid, the railway was not constructed or finished according to specifications, and would not be so for several years because of problems with a large cantilever bridge over the St. Lawrence near Québec City. Chamberlin stated, "It is our intention to live up to our obligation within the meaning of the letter."[33] The dominion government was consequently forced to operate the NTR itself, something it did not want to do.

The GTP constructed several branch lines even before its main line was completed, largely to capture provincial subsidies and land grants. Although not built to as

The massive trestle north of Duhamel, on the GTP's branch line to Calgary, 1912. The bridge was the largest wooden structure in the British Empire at that time, and its cost contributed to the GTP's rocky financial condition.

G.T.P.R. Camp
at Big Eddy on Trout River

high a standard as the main line, they were usually better constructed than the main line of the Canadian Northern. Instead of erecting wooden water tanks to service locomotives, the GTP favoured more expensive steel tanks, which were erected on the main line and on most branch lines as well. Most of these steel water tanks were fabricated by the Chicago Bridge and Iron Works, to specifications for operation in cold climates. The Canadian Special had a large stove in its base, with three heating pipes that passed through the tank to prevent water from freezing in winter. This type of tank was also purchased, in smaller quantities, by the rival Canadian Northern Railway.[34]

While some branches were lucrative, others paralleled lines of competing railroads and did not generate much revenue. Plans for branches to Lethbridge from Calgary, along Vancouver Island with a possible bridge link to the mainland, and from New Hazelton to Dawson City in the Yukon were dropped altogether. In a desperate attempt to gain traffic and revenue, the railroad tried to interest other parties in constructing feeder lines with exclusive connections to the GTP. The Pacific Great Eastern, which was to be built from North Vancouver to Prince George, was one such venture. Another was the Edmonton, Dunvegan and British Columbia Railway,

To speed construction and help keep costs down, several temporary wooden trestles were built instead of larger steel bridges. One example was near the siding of Ansell, west of Edson. The so-called Big Eddy trestle spanned a large valley, and in a matter of months, carried the GTP over the main line of the Canadian Northern Railway. The construction took considerable time, so workers were housed in tents and temporary log structures visible in this view, c1911.

PROVINCIAL ARCHIVES OF ALBERTA/A21162

After the ceremonies at Finmoore, the train carrying dignitaries and GTP officials arrived in Prince Rupert on April 9, 1914. Besides featuring a special train, the event was especially significant to the residents of Prince Rupert, as this was the first through train to reach their community.

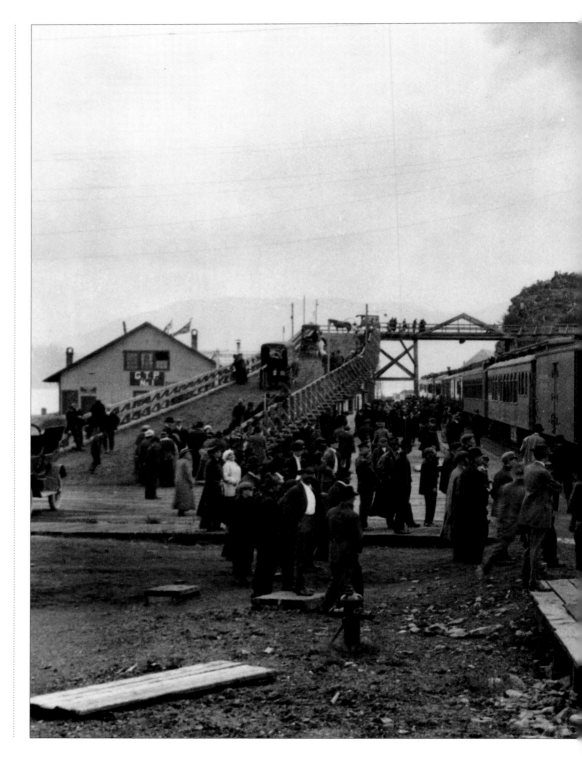

The last spike on the Grand Trunk Pacific was driven by Chief Engineer Bartholomew Brosnan Kelliher, April 7, 1914. Although there was much work to do before the line could be considered complete, the driving of the last spike signified that Canada had its second trans-continental rail line. The words "point of completion" were painted on the web of the last rail, which was subsequently removed and sliced up for keepsakes of the event.

NATIONAL ARCHIVES OF CANADA/C46483

which was to loop north of Edmonton through the Peace River district into British Columbia, where it would travel southwest to Prince George. Although both railroads began construction, neither was built rapidly enough to help the fortunes of the GTP.

Steel on the GTP's main line was connected on April 7, 1914, at Finmoore, B.C., and the last spike was driven at noon by Chief Engineer Kelliher.[35] Although the first west-bound train reached Prince Rupert two days later, the line was not considered finished until 1915, when ballasting and other work was completed. At that point, finances worsened because of a recession and the effects of the First World War.

Fires caused by sparks from locomotives were a serious problem in British Columbia, and the provincial government took steps to force all railroads operating there to minimize the hazard. The CPR had been using oil fuel in some of their locomotives since 1911, following litigation and a subsequent resolution by the B.C. Cabinet that steam locomotives in that province should burn oil. In February 1914, the Board of Railway Commissioners ruled that all steam locomotives in British Columbia were to use oil fuel by 1915.[36] In consequence, the GTP decided to convert nine Pacifics operating between Prince Rupert and Edmonton. Although the conversion required the construction of several large steel storage tanks and oil distribution facilities at divisional points, crude oil imported from California was less expensive than coal, something the GTP already knew, since it had converted its coast steamships from coal in 1912.[37] The conversion project was short-lived, however, for the regulation was rescinded during 1915 because of the demands of the First World War and heavy lobbying by the Canadian Northern Railway, which could not afford to convert its locomotives.

While the First World War suspended immigration and growth in western Canada, the GTP continued to function, although its finances became more and more precarious. The Canadian Northern was almost bankrupt, and in 1916, Prime Minister Borden ordered a royal commission to investigate the finances of both companies, since Smithers and the Grand Trunk Railway (he was also chairman of the Grand Trunk) wanted to divest themselves of the GTP and their financial obligations to it, because it was legally separated from the parent company. The findings, published in 1917 and known popularly as the Drayton-Acworth Report, found fault with the former Laurier government for funding two competing ventures and contributing to cutthroat competition instead of amalgamating the GTP with the Canadian Northern. The report also investigated several solutions, and recommen-

Troops of the Canadian army lifting rails on the Grand Trunk Pacific near the Yellowhead Pass in 1917. The rails were to be sent to France in aid of the war effort.

NATIONAL ARCHIVES OF CANADA/PA139827

ded that control of the GTP, the Grand Trunk, and the Canadian Northern pass to a new public authority at arm's length from the government.[38]

The need for rails in the battlefields of France led the dominion government to order the removal of rails from yards and sidings of the National Transcontinental Railway. When the demand for rails continued, the government decided in May 1917 to remove rails from different sections of the Grand Trunk Pacific main line west of Edmonton between Imre, Alberta, and Red Pass, B.C.—a distance of about a hundred miles. GTP rail was chosen because the holes for the angle bars were compatible with the rail already sent to France. Sections it was taken from ran conveniently close to the main line of the Canadian Northern Railway,[39] and since the GTP roadbed was generally superior to that of the other company, rail was lifted from portions of the Canadian Northern and relaid on the roadbed of its rival. In this way, parts of both lines comprised a new joint main line.

The consolidation of the Canadian Northern and Grand Trunk Pacific west of Edmonton in 1917 also entailed the sharing of some stations and divisional points. The Canadian Northern station at Jasper was abandoned in favour of the GTP facilities. On the left is the Canadian Northern's westbound transcontinental, which will soon depart for Vancouver. To the right is the Grand Trunk Pacific's transcontinental en route to Prince Rupert, pulled by one of the fast Pacific locomotives converted to use oil fuel.

PROVINCIAL ARCHIVES OF ALBERTA/A15974

Sections of both main lines were abandoned where they were distant from each other, and especially where there were problems, such as on the GTP line along the shore of Brûlé Lake in Alberta, where the wind caused sand to drift across the tracks almost constantly. Although rails were lifted, troops who undertook the work were ordered not to disturb the ties, bridges, buildings, or telegraph lines, as it was anticipated that abandoned sections would be rehabilitated after the end of the war. To prevent settlers from being isolated, wagon roads were constructed from towns along abandoned sections to portions of the line in service. Joint operation west of Edmonton impeded both railroads, but affected the GTP more, since it had to reduce loads on the lighter Canadian Northern rail, which could accommodate neither the heavy loads nor the faster speed of the GTP trains.

There is some question as to whether the rails lifted from the GTP were ever sent to France. When the Board of Railway Commissioners ordered the rails lifted in response to an Order in Council, considerable debate occurred in the House of Commons, with the Opposition accusing the government and Prime Minister Borden of purposely wrecking the GTP, since other rail was available closer to Atlantic ports.

As late as September 1917, the rails lifted from the GTP had not left Canada, giving further credence to the Opposition's charge.[40] In spite of this tumult, the joint operation west of Edmonton continued beyond the demise of both the troubled railways.

While the Canadian Northern succumbed first, in 1917, the financial health of the GTP was also terminal. In March 1919, president Howard Kelley of the Grand Trunk Pacific informed the dominion government that because its revenues were no longer meeting its expenses, it would suspend operations as soon as funds were exhausted. Since the government had already taken over the Canadian Northern, and since many employees (voters) would be put out of work if something were not done, the GTP was placed in receivership and kept operating. At this point Sir Alfred Smithers, chairman of the board, issued an extensive statement that placed blame for the failure of the GTP squarely on the shoulders of the dominion government:

> The late Mr. Hays originally had it in his mind to build the Grand Trunk Pacific from North Bay to the Pacific Coast. Had this project been adhered to, not a mile of unnecessary line would have been constructed, but under strong political pressure it was decided to extend the line to Québec and, finally, under further political pressure, to Moncton ... In the subsequent years—and this is very important—the Canadian Pacific Railway was allowed to build branches and extensions right into the new territory the Grand Trunk Pacific was designed, with the consent and at the desire of the Government, to serve, but the Canadian Northern was not only allowed, but was actually subsidised year after year by the Canadian Government, to build lines competing with and paralleling the Grand Trunk Pacific. The result was an enormous increase in the cost of the National Transcontinental and of the Grand Trunk Pacific over and above the estimates of cost when the projects were introduced into parliament.[41]

Smithers's attack did nothing to change the financial situation, and the GTP was taken over by the dominion government on March 8, 1920. The final ignominy was that the directors were replaced by a government-appointed board that consisted largely of administrators from the defunct Canadian Northern. The Grand Trunk Pacific became part of Canadian National Railways in 1923, thus ending the Grand Trunk's bold dream of having the best transcontinental railroad in North America.

The Canadian Northern Railway: A Line of Many Masks

William Mackenzie and Donald Mann, two successful contractors who had enlarged their fortunes through their work for the CPR, formed a partnership in the 1890s largely dedicated to the acquisition and building of railroads in western Canada. In 1899, they formed the Canadian Northern Railway Company (CNoR), by amalgamating two railroads in Manitoba that they already owned and operated. The Canadian Northern served as an umbrella for many smaller subsidiaries and separate charters. Mackenzie and Mann's typical methods of expansion were either to buy small existing railroads and build connections between them; or to purchase existing charters and construct the lines, thereby gaining subsidies and land grants, and operate them using Canadian Northern equipment. In this way, they quickly established a haphazard network of lines. Their purpose in constructing a larger railroad in this fashion was, according to David Hanna, third vice-president, "to cover the most pro-

ductive [wheat growing] regions, and to be assured of the essential business which would carry, later, the more costly construction in the more sparsely populated, less productive territory."[1] Deviation from this policy later led, ultimately, to the ruin of the CNoR. The first manifestation of the Canadian Northern in Alberta was the construction of a small line under the acquired charter of an Edmonton-based railway company, but Mackenzie and Mann were already a force in Alberta, as the two were involved with the Calgary and Edmonton Railway.

The Edmonton, Yukon and Pacific

In 1896, a group of entrepreneurs incorporated the Edmonton District Railway Company to construct a line from Edmonton to South Edmonton (Strathcona). Another line could be extended from Edmonton to the settlement about twenty miles to the west called Stony Plains (later changed to Stony Plain).[2] No work was done, and in 1899, Mackenzie and Mann obtained the controlling interest in the company. They had the charter altered to permit the company to construct a line to the Pacific Coast by either the Yellowhead or Peace River Pass, and another line to the Yukon River. In light of these new dreams, the company name was changed to Edmonton, Yukon and Pacific Railway (EY&P).[3]

Sir William Mackenzie and Sir Donald Mann, c1915, the risk-taking partners who created the Canadian Northern empire and who eventually suffered the ignominy of bankruptcy and rejection.

COLLECTION OF THE AUTHOR

In 1901, a four–and-a-half-mile line was constructed from the CPR-controlled Calgary and Edmonton Railway, down a circuitous 1 percent grade along the Mill Creek Valley, to the steel through-truss bridge on the North Saskatchewan River. On the north side of the bridge, the grade travelled west a short distance, where it switched into two tracks that straddled a small, single-storey wooden station. Possessing no rolling stock of its own, the EY&P used Canadian Northern equipment. Before operations could begin, however, the equipment had to reach the EY&P. The CPR wanted nothing to do with the railroad and tried to stop it from being linked to the Calgary and Edmonton Railway by running a locomotive continually back and forth on the section of track where the EY&P wanted to make a connection.[4] In spite of such crude measures, the CPR could not legally stop the EY&P from being linked to the C&E, since the latter favoured the connection. The lines were eventually brought together, and the first train, consisting of Canadian Northern locomotive 26, a flatcar, a boxcar, and a day-coach, reached the Edmonton station at 4 p.m., October 20, 1902. Regular passenger service was soon established between Edmonton and Strathcona; there were four trains a day, with the one-way fare being 25¢.[5]

Construction continued in May 1903, with the preparation of a grade west of the Edmonton station that gradually rose out of the valley of the North Saskatchewan and turned north into the Groat Ravine. After a short distance it turned east and approached the site of the Canadian Northern station in central

The first train into Edmonton on the EY&P, October 20, 1902. Although travelling on tracks laid under the authority of the Edmonton, Yukon and Pacific, Canadian Northern rolling stock was used exclusively. Number 26 was an old Mogul that served the Canadian Northern for many years. The bridge in the background is the Low Level, built by the dominion government in 1900, and the first permanent bridge across the North Saskatchewan River at Edmonton.

PROVINCIAL ARCHIVES OF ALBERTA/A15485

Edmonton, which was to be reached by their main line approaching from Saskatchewan.[6] The rails were laid by June, but the construction was crude, with little or no ballast. Without ballast the track shifted and crept easily, giving a rough ride and risking derailments unless the trains moved very slowly.

With the advent of the Grand Trunk Pacific and the building of new branch lines by the Canadian Pacific, the Canadian Northern either had to be content as a feeder railroad, delivering grain to railroads with trunk routes to coastal waters, or build a route of its own. By 1904, it was clear that Mackenzie and Mann wished to construct a transcontinental railroad, both to compete with the CPR and to prevent the GTP cutting off the Canadian Northern from routes to the West Coast. William Mackenzie stated, "You know, we expected at one time to be the favoured people to build this new transcontinental road. Now we must go along as best we can and it may take a little longer than it otherwise would."[7] In 1906, after the arrival of the Canadian Northern main line in Edmonton, a roadbed was graded west to about twelve miles beyond Stony Plains. Rails were laid as far as this small community, although, as was

For many years, the EY&P route was the Canadian Northern's sole means of linking the south side of Edmonton with the north. The grades were steep, and trains passed through residential areas. The two little boys in the foreground are Jack and Jim Barford, sons of Alberta educator Vernon Barford. The locomotive is one of the Canadian Northern's ubiquitous ten-wheelers, and the two-strand telegraph line permitted communication between the Strathcona station and the main station in downtown Edmonton, 1913.

PROVINCIAL ARCHIVES OF ALBERTA/A2017

the custom on the EY&P, no ballast was used.[8] The Canadian Northern built a standard third-class station at Stony Plains—a two-storey frame structure consisting of a freight shed, operator's office, waiting-room, and dwelling space in the upper storey (plan 100–3)—and the line was considered open for traffic June 16, 1907.

Although the EY&P submitted plans to the dominion government in 1906 for a transcontinental line through the Yellowhead Pass, the government favoured the Grand Trunk Pacific's proposal, and rejected the EY&P's because it was incomplete.[9] While several parties hoped that the GTP and the Canadian Northern would collaborate on plans for a second transcontinental railroad, Mackenzie and Mann were not interested in selling out to the Grand Trunk Pacific, or buying into it, so they renewed their efforts, with success, to obtain permission to extend the EY&P through the Yellowhead Pass. Although they anticipated grading the line beyond Stony Plains to the McLeod River in 1910, obtaining a subsidy for this extension proved difficult.[10] The best that could be accomplished was a subsidy for an extension south to the coalfields near the Brazeau River, on condition that the EY&P was amalgamated with the Canadian Northern. Amalgamation occurred on May 7, 1909, and it was now up to the Canadian Northern Railway to construct a transcontinental line.[11]

The Canadian Northern: The Main Line

After the creation of the Grand Trunk Pacific, the Canadian Northern made plans to extend its main line west into Alberta and to Edmonton as quickly as possible. Although the primary purpose of the line was to capture grain traffic, it was also intended to facilitate the movement of settlers, such as the Barr Colonists, who travelled the CNoR and settled in the vicinity of what would become the town of Lloydminster.[12] The CNoR used mechanical devices such as steam shovels and track layers, but the construction of its line was not to the high standards adopted by the GTP. The rail was only sixty pounds per yard, and the line tended to wander, following the contours of the terrain. The maximum grade westbound was 1 percent (52.8 feet per mile), more than twice that of the GTP on the prairies. This meant, however, that the CNoR was able to construct the line less expensively than the GTP. The railroad economized even more by building very few steel bridges, preferring wooden trestles that could either be filled or replaced with more substantial structures, if and when finances and traffic warranted. Only one steel bridge was required between the Saskatchewan border and Edmonton—the crossing of the North Saskatchewan River at Fort Saskatchewan. Although the line had to make a jog to the north to reach Fort Saskatchewan, crossing the river at this point was advantageous, since the valley was narrower and shallower than at Edmonton. The site also permitted the construction of a temporary wooden trestle to enable track-laying crews to continue on to Edmonton while the steel bridge remained under construction. The deck truss bridge, 874 feet long, was completed in 1906. The top of the truss carried the single-track main line, while a road deck sat on the bottom.[13] The CNoR main line reached Edmonton on December 17, 1905, where the steel was linked to that laid under the auspices of the Edmonton, Yukon and Pacific Railway. Lieutenant-Governor George Bulyea drove the last spike, and since a main-line railroad had finally reached Edmonton, there was considerable celebration. The Canadian Northern proper did not begin construction to the west immediately. Instead, Mackenzie and Mann built branch lines using other charters under their control.

Completed in 1906, and replacing a temporary wooden trestle, the Canadian Northern's steel truss bridge across the North Saskatchewan River accommodated a road deck as well as the main line. The eastbound passenger train has come from Edmonton and will soon be stopping at the station in Fort Saskatchewan, c1910. By crossing the river at this point, the Canadian Northern avoided the expense of having to build tall piers for a bridge closer to Edmonton.

COLLECTION OF THE AUTHOR

On a cold, wind-swept November 24, 1905, the first Canadian Northern train from the east, the track layer, arrived in downtown Edmonton. It would not be until the next year that the attractive brick and masonry station would be finished. For a time, the station also accommodated GTP passenger trains, but by the 1920s it proved too small for the volume of business. It continued to be used as a freight office, however, until the 1950s.

CITY OF EDMONTON ARCHIVES/EA–10–2289

The Edmonton and Slave Lake Railway Company

This company was incorporated in 1899 to construct a railroad from Edmonton to Peace River, via Athabasca Landing (now the town of Athabasca) and Lesser Slave Lake. It was distracted, however, by the discovery of particularly rich coal deposits just north of Edmonton, near the town of Morinville. In 1906, using provisions of the Edmonton and Slave Lake charter, the Canadian Northern constructed a twenty-three-mile line from the EY&P at Edmonton to Morinville, via St. Albert.[14] As with the EY&P, the Edmonton and Slave Lake Railway existed in name only, and used Canadian Northern equipment. Although the line was supposed to reach Athabasca Landing, construction did not continue until further subsidies were obtained. The dominion government granted one in 1911, at which point the Edmonton and Slave Lake Railway Company was amalgamated with the Canadian Northern, disappearing as a separate entity. The line eventually reached Athabasca Landing in August 1912, thirteen years after the original charter.

The Alberta Midland Railway Company

Always desiring more provincial subsidies, Mackenzie and Mann tried to acquire or incorporate as many railway companies as possible, and anxious to construct a branch from their main line to Calgary, they incorporated the Alberta Midland Railway Company in February 1909. The charter permitted the construction of several lines, including one from Edmonton to Peace River; another from Strathcona to Lethbridge via Calgary; and a third from Red Deer to the Brazeau coalfields via Rocky Mountain House. As with other charters of this sort, the company was empowered to amalgamate with the Canadian Northern, and did so in July 1909. Under the provisions of the charter, construction started that year on a line from Vegreville to Drumheller and its coalfields, via Camrose and Stettler.[15] Construction was extremely difficult in the badlands near Drumheller, although the line was open by the end of 1911. In 1914, the Canadian Northern extended the line from Drumheller to Calgary, and built another line from Strathcona to Camrose. To maintain a workable grade through the badlands to Calgary, the line crossed the Rosebud River more than fifty times, and was consequently both expensive and slow.[16]

Finances were limited by the time the Canadian Northern reached Calgary. Showing initiative, the railroad purchased a convent located near the centre of town, south of the CPR station. With a little modification, the masonry structure became the imposing, albeit unconventional Calgary Canadian Northern station, shown here c1914.

GLENBOW ARCHIVES/ND–8–07

The Canadian Northern's presence in southern Alberta was enhanced when its line from Saskatoon, sometimes referred to as the Goose Lake line, was extended beginning in 1912. Entering Alberta near Alsask, Saskatchewan, this grain and settlement line travelled west via Oyen, Youngstown, the divisional point of Hanna (named for D.B. Hanna), and connected with the branch from Vegreville to Calgary near the town of Munson. This 133-mile extension was open by the end of October 1913.[17]

Westward Extension of the Canadian Northern Railway

The CNoR required sufficient capital and a location for its line before it could expand westward from Edmonton to the Pacific Coast. In 1909, under provisions of the Edmonton, Yukon and Pacific charter, survey crews were sent to locate the best route to the Pacific. Having discovered a tree blaze made by one of Sandford Fleming's surveyors in 1877 near Tête Jaune Cache, west of the Yellowhead Pass, the CNoR surveyors followed Fleming's route closely and found for the most part that Fleming's proposed route for the CPR provided the easiest grades.[18] The projected Canadian Northern line followed the Thompson and Fraser Rivers south and west, but would have to cross the Fraser near Cisco to avoid the heavy tunnelling required to remain on the western shore and also to avoid the CPR main line. In fact, the alignment of the Canadian Northern provided a maximum grade of seven-tenths of 1 percent, slightly less than that on the GTP.[19] Instead of terminating in Vancouver, which would have required extensive construction into the city, it was decided to build a terminus and port facility on the south shore of the Fraser River near New Westminster. This location became Port Mann, named for Mackenzie's partner, Donald Mann.

Although the Canadian Northern possessed the charter of the Edmonton, Yukon and Pacific Railway, it required a much larger subsidy to build west of Edmonton. To obtain sufficient money, a new company was incorporated in 1910, the Canadian Northern Alberta Railway Company, which was connected to the CNoR by a guarantee of securities, and which was considered a constituent company of the Canadian Northern by 1914. Under this charter, the CNoR received permission and a subsidy to construct a line from St. Albert to the Yellowhead Pass and the boundary with British Columbia.

The Canadian Northern Western Railway Company was also incorporated in 1910, enabling the CNoR to construct lines from Edmonton or Strathcona to either the Pine or Peace River Pass, as well as to the Brazeau coal fields from the Vegreville to Calgary branch line. By the time the Canadian Northern succumbed to financial difficulties in 1917, two lines had been constructed. The first, opened in August 1914, ran west from Warden to the Brazeau coalfields, sharing a section with the CPR near Rocky Mountain House. The second, completed in early 1916, ran from Camrose to Alliance, a grain producing area.[20]

The Canadian Northern Railway was faced with an interesting problem in British Columbia; the name had already been used and a charter granted. This had occurred in 1892, when some local entrepreneurs incorporated a B.C. company called the Canadian Northern Railway. The charter authorized them to construct a line from the eastern boundary of the province to the northern terminus of the Esquimalt and Nanaimo Railway, via bridges from Bute Inlet, much along the lines of the original CPR route. In 1910, to avoid litigation and confusion, Mackenzie and Mann incorporated the Canadian Northern Pacific Railway Company in British Columbia. The terms of this charter enabled the construction of the line from the Yellowhead Pass to Port Mann. In addition, the Canadian Northern Pacific could build a line on Vancouver Island from Victoria to Barkley Sound, near the northern end of the island.[21] Like the Canadian Northern Alberta and Canadian Northern Western companies, the Canadian Northern Pacific was considered an integral part of the Canadian Northern Railway Company by 1914. With the subsidies provided under these charters, the CNoR was able to commence building its line to the Pacific Coast.

To minimize the potential loss of traffic to the Grand Trunk Pacific, which was advancing rapidly towards Prince Rupert, it was in the best interests of Mackenzie and Mann and the Canadian Northern to have the line constructed as quickly as possible. Work began late in 1910, with anticipated completion within four years.[22] Explaining the project publicly on September 7, President Mackenzie said:

> It is our intention to link Edmonton and the Pacific Coast with all possible despatch consistent with building a standard line having the lowest gradients of any transcontinental railway. If any delay occurs it will not be our fault … There at present exist no reasons why we should not have the British Columbia end finished and in operation before the middle of 1914.[23]

Crews worked their way east from Port Mann and west from St. Albert to the Yellowhead Pass, with much of the contracting being done by the Northern Construction Company, a subsidiary of Foley, Welch and Stewart, the main contractors for the GTP. By the time CNoR grading crews reached the Yellowhead Pass, the GTP line had already been laid, and the narrowness of the pass meant that the Canadian Northern had to closely parallel the Grand Trunk Pacific. At Moose Lake, west of the Yellowhead, the terrain was so severe that the Canadian Northern had to be laid right next to the GTP along the northern shore of the lake, as if the two lines were a double-track railway. Farther west, the alignment of the Canadian Northern was at a higher elevation than that of the GTP. Because both railroads remained next to one another, and since the GTP had already been completed at this point, the Canadian Northern had to construct six special trestles over the GTP tracks, so that spoil could be dumped directly into the Fraser River.[24]

Like the CPR before it, the Canadian Northern experienced difficulties constructing its line through the Fraser Canyon, since much tunnelling was required. Fifteen rock tunnels, with a total length of 8,321 feet, were blasted out between Yale and Boston Bar. The salmon run up the Fraser River was disrupted when large boulders, dislodged by a blast near Hells Gate, blocked and diverted the watercourse. Much of the work in this section had to be done by hand, since it proved too difficult to move machinery into the area.[25] Although the Canadian Northern built wooden trestles wherever possible, ten steel bridges were required. One of the most spectacular was the large steel arch constructed across the Fraser River and over the main line of the CPR near Cisco. The bridge was designed by the engineering firm of Waddell and Harrington of Kansas City, Missouri, who also designed the other steel bridges, including the large deck girder lift bridge across the North Thompson River at Kamloops. The middle span of this bridge could be lifted fifty-three feet in a hundred seconds by a system of steel cables wound onto drums by a gasoline engine.[26] The lift span permitted large ships to pass underneath the bridge.

In 1912, President Mackenzie said of the Canadian Northern Pacific: "The line will also give access to an hitherto unknown section of the Canadian Alps, of which the scenic attractions are such as will divert a large volume of the transcontinental tourist traffic to the route."[27] Although the Canadian Northern did not plan an elaborate chain of hotels, as did the GTP, Mackenzie was determined to capture at least some of the tourist trade. To do this with any success, he believed that the railroad should reach Vancouver, where a tourist hotel could be constructed. After much negotiation, an agreement was reached with the City of Vancouver in 1913, whereby the Canadian Northern Pacific would enter the city via a tunnel designed for electric locomotives. The city would provide land for a large station to be built near the southern shore of False Creek, and the Canadian Northern agreed to construct a 250-room hotel within five years, but not on donated property. While the railroad accepted the land eagerly, financial difficulties prevented all the plans from being carried out. A magnificent masonry terminal was built in Vancouver, but there were insufficient funds to construct a tunnel approach, so the Canadian Northern negotiated running rights over the Vancouver, Victoria and Eastern Railway, a Great Northern subsidiary. Plans for the hotel were also abandoned.[28]

The Canadian Northern possessed much more motive power than the GTP. Its first locomotives, primarily Americans and Moguls, came from existing lines acquired by Mackenzie and Mann. In Alberta and British Columbia, the most common engines were ten-wheelers (4–6–0), more than three hundred of which were purchased between 1901 and 1913. The ten-wheelers, with sixty-three-inch-diameter driving

The rugged terrain in the Fraser Canyon had forced the Canadian Pacific to switch sides at Cisco. The Canadian Northern faced the same difficulties, and the large steel arch bridge shown here c1915 carried the Canadian Northern not only across the Fraser, but also over the CPR's main line. The building next to the CNoR line is a section house for track and telegraph maintenance crews. The design was common throughout the Canadian Northern Railway lines.

VANCOUVER PUBLIC LIBRARY/8373

wheels, had sufficient power for most freights and could reach speeds of up to fifty miles an hour while pulling passenger trains. Larger Pacifics (4–6–2) and Consolidations (2–8–0) were ordered for use on heavier trains between Edmonton and Vancouver. The Consolidations were touted as being the largest of the kind operating in Canada, with sixty-three-inch-diameter driving wheels and a wheel base of twenty-five and a half feet, not including the tender. By the time the Consolidations were being constructed in 1912, the CNoR was aware that British Columbia intended banning coal-burning locomotives, but the engines were built as coal burners, nevertheless.[29] Through intense lobbying, coupled with the effects of the First World War, the requirement for locomotives to burn oil fuel was rescinded by the time the CNoR ran trains into British Columbia. The average of about $8.5 million a year for locomotives and rolling stock added to the Canadian Northern's financial difficulties.

S.J. Hungerford, Canadian Northern's superintendent of rolling stock, who later became president of the Canadian National Railways, devised a system of locomotive classification for the CNoR in 1912, using an alpha-numeric code and a percentage rating for pulling power. This system became the standard used by the Canadian Northern and later the Canadian National. Hungerford also designed a standard tender that could be interchanged with several types of locomotives, so the engines would not be laid up while their tenders underwent repair. Because of this, locomotive numbers were not displayed on the sides of tenders, but rather, painted onto a removable metal plate held by brackets at the rear of the tender.[30]

The effects of an economic recession and the start of the First World War in late 1914 combined to retard construction on the Canadian Northern. Steel on the main line from Edmonton to Vancouver did not meet until January 23, 1915, when the last spike was driven at Basque, B.C., by Sir William Mackenzie. As on the GTP, work on the Canadian Northern was far from complete when the last spike was driven. Considerable bridge and track work remained to be upgraded from temporary standards. Regular service, as well as a ceremonial last spike re-enactment, were also delayed by the collapse of a tunnel in the Fraser Canyon in early February.[31] The CNoR's budget was being stretched further still, since lines were also being constructed on Vancouver Island.

On February 18, 1911, the lieutenant-governor of British Columbia turned the first sod near Burnside Road in Victoria on what was to be a line travelling northwest from Victoria to Port Alberni. It was to compete with the CPR's Esquimalt and Nanaimo Railway. Although the surveying and partial grading of the line occurred rapidly, little track was laid, since the priority for rail was the transcontinental line. Rails were difficult to obtain even later because of scarcity caused by the First World War. By 1913, most effort on Vancouver Island was concentrated on the construction of a sixteen-mile line between Patricia Bay on the Saanich Peninsula and Victoria. A dock and ferry terminal built at Patricia Bay would allow the transport of passenger and freight cars from Vancouver, thus permitting rail travel from the mainland. By April 1916, sufficient rails had been laid for the first Canadian Northern locomotive—number 105, a Mogul—to be unloaded on Vancouver Island, although the line could not be opened until a suitable bridge was erected over the navigable Selkirk Waters in Victoria. Following the installation of a steel single-bascule bridge with trestle approaches, the line opened for service at the

While the Canadian Northern Railway reached Vancouver by sharing track with the Great Northern subsidiary Vancouver, Victoria and Eastern, each concern had its own terminal. The Great Northern station, built in 1916 and located immediately to the left of the CNoR terminal, was a smaller yet just as elegant building as the CNoR structure, c1938.

VANCOUVER PUBLIC LIBRARY/19670

An example of the common Canadian Northern ten-wheeler that was the workhorse in western Canada, 1915. While the placement of the Canadian Northern logo on the side of the cab was not a universal practice, the alpha-numeric classification below the locomotive number was. The H–6 series comprised most of the ten-wheelers, with the final letter suffix indicating which order the unit came from.

PROVINCIAL ARCHIVES OF ALBERTA/FS557

end of April 1917. The movement of transcontinental passenger trains to Vancouver Island from Port Mann did not occur, however, since the special car ferry was still under construction in Québec. The Canora (the name derived from the first two letters of CAnadian NOrthern RAilway) did not arrive until December 1918, and in the meantime, service on the Patricia Bay line was supplied by a gas-electric car—number 500—built by the General Electric Company and previously used elsewhere on the Canadian Northern. Unfortunately, with the Canadian Northern's expansion west and east, the company was left in such a desperate financial condition that it could not afford to proceed quickly with construction on Vancouver Island, and the line from Victoria to Port Alberni remained largely unfinished until September 1918. By that time, the demand for Sitka spruce for aircraft construction prompted the dominion government to second sufficient rail from the Pacific Great Eastern Railway to enable about fifty miles of the line to be placed in service. Four dignitaries, including Premier Oliver, drove four last spikes, and a Canadian Northern ten-wheeler, number 1018, drew the first train to the end of steel.[32] The end of the First World War and the consequent collapse of the aircraft industry delayed further construction until the Canadian Northern's economic problems were dealt with.

The economic health of the Canadian Northern continued to deteriorate in spite of the completion of its transcontinental line, and further loans and bond guarantees from a friendly dominion government did little to offset the precarious financial situation. The consolidation of the main line west of Edmonton with the Grand Trunk Pacific in 1917 did not help matters either, since the little traffic that existed was slowed down by having to share a common line with the GTP. The findings of the Drayton–Acworth Report combined with further requests for money convinced the dominion government by mid-1917 that the Canadian Northern either had to be taken over or be allowed to fall into bankruptcy. Since there was no end in sight to the First World War, and it was generally believed that railroads were essential for the war effort, bankruptcy was not an option. Lord Shaughnessy, president of the CPR, offered to take over Canadian Northern lines that would be of use to the CPR, but wanted nothing to

The interior of a Canadian Northern Railway first-class coach, taken shortly after the completion of the main line to Vancouver, 1915. This advertising shot was intended to show off the well-appointed equipment and suggest that the CNoR was the railroad to take. The claim of being Canada's second transcontinental was technically correct, as the Grand Trunk Pacific had refused to take over the National Transcontinental Railway, which was being run by the dominion government, even though the line was connected to the GTP.

NATIONAL ARCHIVES OF CANADA/C34292

do with the remainder. This alternative was not well received by the government, which did not wish to be saddled with the portions that stood little chance of turning a profit. Moreover, in a speech given on May 15, 1918, Prime Minister Borden envisaged a total nationalization of railways in Canada, including the CPR:

> It may be possible, indeed, it is probable, that at some later date, but not in the immediate future, all the land transportation facilities of Canada in the shape of railways, may, so far as operation at least is concerned, be amalgamated into one system carried on under one management.[33]

As far as the moribund Canadian Northern was concerned, the Borden government first appointed three directors to oversee the running of the system, and in May 1918, a new board of directors, without Sir William Mackenzie or Sir Donald Mann, assumed control of the day-to-day operation of the railroad, removing it from the direct control of the government. This decision was a hard, bitter blow to both men. In reaction, Mackenzie stated:

> The C.N.R. [CNoR] in my opinion, and in the opinion of the transportation experts who have examined the situation, is destined to be an essential factor in the development of the country, and will be particularly useful in the reconstruction days into which this country must soon enter. Sir Donald Mann and myself have devoted the best of our years in developing it to its present stage, and confidently rely upon the future to justify our work.[34]

The new board, under the leadership of David B. Hanna, a former vice-president of the Canadian Northern, was also placed in charge of the Canadian Government Railways, and in 1919, the Grand Trunk Pacific. For the sake of convenience, the name Canadian National Railways was used to refer to the government-controlled railway system. Although it was not clear at that time, the demise of the Canadian Northern and the Grand Trunk Pacific created a phœnix that would soon rise out of the economic ashes to challenge the CPR like no other concern before.

A common belief persists that the Canadian Northern succumbed because of its expansion in eastern Canada, coupled with its mad dash to the West Coast and the consequent duplication of lines with the Grand Trunk Pacific. As early as 1924, however, David Hanna disagreed with this explanation. The CNoR and the GTP were constructed for different purposes, he explained, the former as a colonization road and collector for grain, the latter as a trunk road for the rapid movement of commodities. Hanna believed the real cause of the Canadian Northern's demise was the effects of the First World War, which not only cut off immigration to Canada, but also halted foreign investment and much demand for the movement of goods. "There were other contributing causes, of course, but the real overwhelmer was Armageddon."[35]

Meeting the Competition: Smaller Concerns and the CPR

mmigration to western Canada increased dramatically during the early years of the twentieth century. The Canadian Pacific Railway brought many of the immigrants west, and it experienced a surge in other passenger and freight traffic. The system had to be improved, however, if it wished to increase carrying capacity and speed. Competition was anticipated from the Canadian Northern and Grand Trunk Pacific Railways, although there was at first little threat to the dominance of the CPR. It was a fact, however, that the CPR possessed an inferior grade on its main line through the Rocky and Selkirk Mountains, and a difficult temporary grade on the Crowsnest Pass line west of Lethbridge. And other railroads, especially those under control of the Great Northern, were already making inroads into the vast areas with undeveloped natural resources. To improve its position and to diminish any operational edge its competitors might claim, the CPR undertook massive improvements to its infrastructure and a program of expansion.

The Lethbridge Viaduct

One of the first major works was the elimination of the temporary grade on the Crowsnest Pass line. By the turn of the century, most of the original Howe truss bridges were wearing out, and several smaller trestles were being washed out almost every spring. It would cost an estimated $1 million to replace the wooden bridges along the line. This cost, plus the fact that the line was exceedingly curvy and steep in places, led the CPR to re-survey the area in 1904–05 for a better alignment. A new one was discovered proceeding directly west from Lethbridge, with a grade of only four-tenths of 1 percent, eliminating thirty-seven curves, and requiring only two bridges. One drawback was that one of the bridges, spanning the wide, deep valley of the Belly (now Oldman) River, would exceed a length of one mile and be more than three hundred feet high.[1]

After much study, the CPR determined that the most economical structure would be a straight steel viaduct, consisting mainly of plate girder spans supported by thirty-three steel towers resting on substantial concrete pedestals supported, in turn, by deep concrete piles. The designer chose through-plate construction, where the rails are placed at the bottom of the span rather than along the top, as in deck-plate construction. Although more expensive, through-plate design, because of the thick sides of the deck, would prevent derailed equipment from falling off the bridge and damaging the legs of the towers. It was also believed that the deck sides would partially protect rolling stock from the strong cross-winds experienced in the area. A single, deck-lattice Warren truss was used near the western bank, because the terrain did not permit the erection of a tower.

The viaduct was designed primarily by C.N. Monsarrat, a bridge engineer for the CPR, but some consulting was provided by Charles Schneider, who had designed the original Stoney Creek bridge in 1885. The steel work was fabricated by the Canadian Bridge Company beginning in late 1906. Although work on the piles and pedestals began in October 1907, it was not completed until February 1909 because of delays caused by flooding in the spring of 1908, labour disputes, and because some piles on the east end sank, since they had been placed over an abandoned Galt Mines shaft. During this time, flatcars of bridge components were delivered to Lethbridge, and in late April 1908, the bridge company's men arrived and began the fabrication of two travellers. These were mobile derricks equipped with several hoists and engines, both to power the hoists and to propel the travellers. The larger of the two, the erecting traveller, moved along the tops of the deck on a system of rollers, and lowered tower components and bridge spans into position. It also held a steel cage that enabled workers to assemble the pieces of the bridge. The smaller unit, called the riveting traveller, supported moveable platforms for teams of riveters, which followed the erecting traveller. Work began on the Lethbridge side of the river in August 1908, and the superstructure was completed on June 22, 1909, although the first train did not pass over it until four months later, when the rest of the line was finished. Six people were killed during construction. Three were employees, but only one of these died by falling from the bridge; the other two were asphyxiated by gas escaping from an abandoned mineshaft encountered during pile construction. The other three fatalities were trespassers.[2]

Upgrading the Main Line

The main line also received a major upgrade at this time. The temporary 4.5 percent grade on the Big Hill east of Field, B.C., was slowing traffic so much that the cumulative delay limited the amount that the line could carry. Surveys carried out between 1902 and 1905 attempted to find a better route. Construction of the original grade as surveyed by Major Rogers was rejected, as it would bypass Field at a high elevation and be subject to rock-slides and avalanches. A series of loops, much like those at the

A view of the erecting traveller lowering a lattice girder on the Lethbridge Viaduct in 1908. It is fall, and the superstructure is being erected westwards from the Lethbridge side of the valley. Behind the erecting traveller is the riveting traveller, whose crew will finish securing each new piece of the bridge.

COLLECTION OF THE AUTHOR

CPR BRIDGE LETHBRIDGE ALTA UNDER CONSTRUCTION WHEN COMPLETED WILL BE 5327 FT. LONG 307 FT. HIGH

The enormity of the Lethbridge Viaduct can best be appreciated by viewing it from a distance. The photographer is standing on the Lethbridge side and shooting west, c1910.

western edge of Rogers Pass, was also considered and rejected because of frequent avalanches. Instead, the CPR decided to reduce the grade to 2.2 percent by building two spiral-shaped tunnels. The upper, or Number One, encountered first approaching from the east, would curve through 234° in 3,255 feet, and would drop the line by forty-eight feet. The lower—Number Two—curved 232° in 2,921 feet, and would drop the line by forty-five feet to the valley of the Kicking Horse River. The line would then pass through a shorter, straight tunnel before rejoining the existing grade to Field. Construction was contracted to Macdonnell, Gzowski and Company, and work began in September 1907. The tunnels and grade revision were finished two years later, in August 1909.[3]

Although easing the grades helped to speed traffic on the line, equipment was becoming heavier and rolling stock larger. In consequence, heavier rails had to be laid and some bridges had to be strengthened or replaced. The cantilever bridge across the Fraser River at Cisco was dismantled in 1909 and re-erected across the Niagara Canyon on the Esquimalt and Nanaimo Railway on Vancouver Island in 1910.[4] At Cisco, the original piers were retained, although steel pedestals were installed to extend their height. The replacement bridge consisted of three steel through-trusses.

The Connaught Tunnel

Another problem on the main line was Rogers Pass and the Loops at the western approach. Although the grade through the pass had been realigned following the disastrous avalanche of 1899, and a further relocation with new yards was constructed in 1909, avalanches continued to disrupt service and take the lives of employees. Larger rotary snowploughs were built, some with massive steel frames, and a special cover was erected over the turntable at Rogers Pass to prevent it being buried by snow. A particularly bad series of avalanches in March 1910 killed sixty-two people.[5] Besides causing such dreadful loss of life, the pass was also unpopular because of the limited number of trains that could use the line per day. In 1912, President Sir Thomas Shaughnessy announced a multimillion dollar program to double-track the main line through the vicinity of Rogers Pass.[6] Although it was possible to duplicate the existing line, a relocation with a lower gradient and minimum exposure to avalanches was preferred.

By the end of 1912, the only solution seemed to be the construction of a double-track tunnel, twenty-nine feet wide at rail level, twenty-four feet high, and five miles long, beneath Rogers Pass. This would be, at the time, the longest tunnel in North America; it bypassed Rogers Pass and the Loops and reduced the westbound grade to less than 1 percent, a considerable improvement. With an estimated cost of $8 million, the design and execution were placed under the direction of John Sullivan, the CPR's chief engineer, and the contract was awarded to Foley, Welch and Stewart, contractors for the GTP, who also worked on the Canadian Northern.[7]

A crew somewhere in the main bore of the incomplete Connaught Tunnel, c1915. One of the pneumatic drills can be seen in the centre.

GLENBOW ARCHIVES/NA–1263–36

Since the tunnel and approaches would require about three and a half years' work, workers and their families would need to be accommodated at the site. Rogers Pass was considered unsuitable because of the time that would be wasted moving workers to and from the ends of the tunnel. So a temporary camp was erected at each end, with a third established farther east near the Bear Creek station. About five hundred workers at a time were employed on the construction. The main camp was at the western end of the planned tunnel, between the Loops, not far from the Glacier House Hotel. Outfitted with a power plant, a kitchen, and accommodation for men and their families, the camp was designed by Walter Painter, the former chief architect of the CPR. Temporary spurs connected the eastern and western portals to the main line. Construction began in September 1913 from both ends, and one of the first tasks was to build a permanent diversion of the Illecillewaet River, moving it to the south, away from the western portal. Most of the diversion consisted of a reinforced concrete trough.

A novel method adopted from Europe enabled crews to speed tunnelling by working on more than two faces at once. At each end, a small tunnel called a pilot drift was driven along the line of the main tunnel to roughly the midpoint, but fifty feet to the left. Cutting side drifts to the main tunnel line, crews could excavate at several points simultaneously. Pneumatic drills bored a ring of holes that were then filled with dynamite; when the ring was detonated, an entire section of tunnel would be excavated. Air-powered shovels and cars on a temporary track were used to remove the spoil.[8]

The main bores met on December 19, 1915, with almost perfect alignment, and excavations were finished on July 6, 1916. On July 18, the governor-general, Arthur, Duke of Connaught, visited the tunnel, naming it the Selkirk Tunnel, but it was soon renamed the Connaught Tunnel in his honour. Although it was anticipated that electric locomotives would be used, their cost, plus shortages created by the First World War, led to the assignment of oil-burning steam locomotives. This necessitated the installation of a ventilation system, consisting of two squirrel-cage fans, twelve feet in diameter and eight feet wide, powered by two, five-hundred-horsepower, four-cylinder, four-stroke engines that burned the same fuel as the locomotives. The fans were on top of the western portal, with each engine enclosed in a small concrete structure. They forced air east through the tunnel by means of large nozzles.[9]

The diversion of the main line to the tunnel began in the east near Stoney Creek bridge, while Ross Peak station marked the beginning of the diversion to the western portal, where a new station named Glacier was established. The Connaught Tunnel came into service in December 1916, although it was almost a year before crews began the removal of materials along the old grade. The demand for rails and a shortage of dressed lumber meant that almost everything, including snowsheds and the steel bridges of the Loops, was salvaged.[10] Although the Connaught Tunnel was considered finished, pieces of rock soon began to fall from the sides and the roof, and the railroad decided in 1920 to line the entire length with concrete. The contract was awarded to the Sydney Junkins Company, and a large construction camp reappeared at the western portal. The old pilot drifts from the initial construction were used again for moving workers, equipment, and spoil, since portions of the tunnel had to be enlarged. Labourers built wooden forms to hold the concrete, and a twenty-seven-ton, gasoline-powered locomotive moved rock-scaling equipment and concrete mixers, which were loaded by means of a special trestle dock erected at the camp. Progress was slow, since the tunnel had to remain in use, but the lining was completed by the end of 1921.[11]

Arthur, Duke of Connaught, governor-general of Canada, in 1916. His Royal Highness was present at the completion of the new tunnel through the Selkirk Mountains, and named it the Selkirk Tunnel. It was soon renamed the Connaught Tunnel in his honour.

COLLECTION OF THE AUTHOR

The western portal of the Connaught Tunnel, c1930, showing the engine houses and large fans used to ventilate the tunnel. Number 5917, a large Selkirk-type locomotive, is pulling the westbound transcontinental. Trains usually entered the tunnel by the left track, as in the manner of vehicular traffic in the United Kingdom, to give the engineer, located on the right side of the locomotive, better visibility.

COLLECTION OF THE AUTHOR

The Glacier House Hotel was an unfortunate casualty of the Connaught Tunnel. It remained open, and a horse-drawn coach carried people to it from the new Glacier station, but its popularity waned. The hotel was closed in 1925, and although a larger and more up-to-date building was designed in 1926, nothing was done, and the buildings were demolished in 1929. The first casualty of the CPR's western hotels, however, had been Mount Stephen House. Patronage began to decline before the First World War and the hotel was closed in 1918, with the buildings being sold to the Field YMCA. The original Fraser Canyon House, designed by Thomas Sorby, survived until 1927, when it was destroyed by fire. Patronage had been high, however, so the CPR constructed a new building in 1928.

The new log station of Glacier, a short distance from the western portal of the Connaught Tunnel, 1920. The Glacier House Hotel is a considerable distance to the left of the new station, and at a higher elevation. The horse-drawn wagon is about to carry a load of luggage up the crude road, which used the old grade in part, to Glacier House.

VANCOUVER PUBLIC LIBRARY/12941

Motive Power

Larger trains and heavier rolling stock resulted in progressively larger, more powerful locomotives being built. Pusher locomotives continued to be needed on the Big Hill, in spite of the spiral tunnels. Instead of using several locomotives, each of which required its own crew, the CPR designed special locomotives for pusher service and had them built in their Angus shops in Montréal. Referred to as articulated compound locomotives, or Malléts, these units consisted of a large boiler resting on two separate sets of six driving wheels (0–6–6–0 wheel arrangement), each powered by its own set of cylinders. Each wheel-and-cylinder set could move independently, hence the term articulated. And the steam from one set of cylinders was exhausted into the other, thus using the power of the expanding steam twice, hence the term compound. The first Mallét, number 1950, was delivered in 1909, and was found to be satisfactory

The first of the special Malléts designed for service between Field and Laggan, shown at Field with an engineer and fireman. The rectangular object on top of the boiler, with a large pipe curving down to the right, is the special vertical superheater applied initially. It was soon found, however, that this type of superheater leaked, and so later versions of the Malléts possessed conventional horizontal models.

REVELSTOKE AND DISTRICT HISTORICAL ASSOCIATION/149

after several modifications. Five additional Malléts were fabricated in 1911 and 1912. The units were based in Field, assisting trains between Field and Stephen, and sometimes as far east as Laggan (Lake Louise). Although the locomotives functioned as expected, they proved difficult to maintain and required special parts. In 1916, therefore, they were withdrawn, rebuilt as rigid-frame Decapods (2–10–0), and returned to service, where most remained until the late 1950s.[12] Besides adding locomotives with large wheel arrangements, the CPR also added many ten-wheelers and Consolidations to its roster between 1910 and 1920, many of which were assigned to lines in western Canada.

Passenger Service

In order to capture more of the tourist trade, passenger service on the main line was improved as well. Beginning on July 2, 1907, the CPR introduced a new, faster transcontinental passenger train named the Trans-Canada Limited, which was run only during the summer months at first, with service ending on September 1.[13] Beginning in 1916, following the conversion of some passenger locomotives to oil fuel, the CPR tried a new type of observation car on its transcontinental trains. Because there were no cinders released by oil-fueled locomotives, it was not thought necessary to enclose passengers as before. Initially, the railroad converted four old colonist cars, removing their roofs and sides to the bottom of the windows, gutting their interiors, and replacing them with two rows of wooden seats. These open cars were placed at the rear of the trains in the summer months, affording an unobstructed view of the countryside. Twenty more cars of this type were prepared between 1917 and 1928, and while they proved popular at first, several problems appeared. Not all locomotives were converted to oil, and so coal burners continued to shower the cars with cinders; even the oil burners would deposit a sooty film on any exposed surface. In addition, the cars were unusable in rain or when it was cold, and they were excessively windy, especially while passing through tunnels. Realizing that some sort of enclosure was necessary, the CPR installed roofs and enclosed the central portion of the remaining cars between 1927 and 1929.[14]

Hotels and Stations

The hotel system was both improved and expanded. In 1911, Walter Painter, the CPR's chief architect, designed a new masonry structure for the Banff Springs Hotel. As the newer additions were still in good repair, and since the CPR did not wish to close the hotel entirely during reconstruction, only the central portion was replaced. The eleven-storey structure in the Château style, with hot and

One of the open observation cars bringing up the rear of a westbound Trans-Canada Limited, shortly after leaving the lower spiral tunnel on the way to Field, c1925.

COLLECTION OF THE AUTHOR

cool swimming pools, provided accommodation for about three hundred guests. The new portion of the hotel was opened in 1914, with the planned rebuilding of the wooden wings postponed until after the First World War.[15]

Painter designed a more simplified steel and masonry addition for Lake Louise, also in the Château style. The addition was built in 1912, next to Rattenbury's wooden hotel, at which time the name was changed from the Lake Louise Chalet to Château Lake Louise. To facilitate movement of hotel guests and their luggage between the hotel and the station, a forty-two-inch-width, narrow-gauge railroad was constructed from the station to the hotel, a winding route slightly longer than 3.6 miles. Since conventional locomotives and rolling stock were too large, the line, often referred to as the Lake Louise Tramway, used small, self-propelled passenger and freight cars instead. The first two, numbered 40 and 41, were each powered by a gasoline engine coupled directly to the wheels. Luggage was carried in separate motorized baggage cars, and a small shed and maintenance facility built near the hotel serviced and stored the equipment. Operations began in August 1912, with a telephone line between the hotel and the station ensuring that each passenger train was met on time. The tramway, run by the CPR's hotel department rather than the railroad itself, operated only when the hotel was open, and so no service was available during winter.[16]

A view of the new Château Lake Louise wing designed by Walter Painter, to the left of Rattenbury's pseudo half-timbered structure, 1914.

COLLECTION OF THE AUTHOR

To meet the competition of the Grand Trunk Pacific, which was planning to build several hotels in urban centres, the CPR announced the construction of a large hotel in Calgary in 1910. Two years earlier, Walter Painter had designed a four-storey station with two wings, which was under construction, although obtaining permission to demolish an older building on the site delayed the completion of the new station until 1912. The old station was dismantled carefully, with much of the salvaged stone used to construct new stations at Claresholm and High River, both in Alberta. Painter left the CPR's employ before designing the new hotel, so William Maxwell received the commission. He designed a 350-room hotel with three towers, but not in the Château style, as the CPR had decided that this style would apply only to resort hotels. Construction began in 1912,

The diminutive Lake Louise Tramway was an effective means of transportation between the station and the hotel complex at the lakeshore. The CPR main line is on the other side of the station. The tram cars are about to depart for the steep climb to the lake, c1925.

WHYTE MUSEUM OF THE CANADIAN ROCKIES/NA–71–97

The new Hotel Vancouver, designed by Painter and Swales, c1920. It replaced the original Hotel Vancouver designed by Thomas Sorby, with later additions by Francis Rattenbury. The new hotel was equipped with a roof-garden to afford guests a respite from the hustle and bustle of Vancouver.

COLLECTION OF THE AUTHOR

William Maxwell's Palliser Hotel in Calgary reflected the CPR's new policy of not designing urban hotels in the Château style. Although located adjacent to both the main line and the station, the Palliser remained Calgary's premier hotel for many years, c1914.

COLLECTION OF THE AUTHOR

to the west of the station, and the hotel was opened in 1914.[17] Strangely, the hotel was named the Palliser, after the man who had warned against farming in the arid lands of southern Alberta, and whose advice Van Horne had chosen to ignore years later.

The capacity of the Hotel Vancouver proved inadequate over time, and there were complaints that some of the older rooms were uncomfortable. In consequence, a new building was designed by Walter Painter, now part of the Vancouver firm Painter and Swales, to replace the old hotel. Construction of the new fifteen-storey building began in 1912, and was finished in 1916 at a cost of more than $2 million.[18]

The CPR continued its policy of replacing station buildings once they were too small for the traffic. One of the sorriest victims of replacement was the magnificent Vancouver station designed by the Maxwell brothers. Although structurally sound and comparatively young, the building was too small for the burgeoning business in Vancouver, and so it was demolished after the new station and pier, designed by the Montréal firm of Barrot, Blackader and Webster, were completed in 1914.[19]

Number 522, an old American-style locomotive, was one of the first converted by the CPR to burn oil fuel in 1911. The locomotive is shown at the service facility at Golden, B.C, in 1912. The structure at the left is a forty-thousand-gallon water tank that is almost full, as shown by the position of the ball indicator on the staff attached to the roof. The square wooden structure to the right of the water tank is a sand house, used to dispense sand into reservoirs called sand domes on the top of locomotive boilers. The sand dome is the first cylindrical projection to the right of the smokestack. The cylindrical tank to the right of

continued on page 117

Fuel

While most CPR locomotives in British Columbia burned wood in the early years, coal was the preferred fuel, and by 1910, wood was rarely used. One disadvantage of coal is that hot cinders are expelled from the smokestack, even with the use of screens or other spark arresters, and sparks from locomotives caused many fires along the right of way. Although cause was sometimes difficult to prove legally, in 1911 the Supreme Court of British Columbia found the CPR guilty of starting a large conflagration that destroyed a lumber company's forest reserve, and ordered the railroad to pay $140,000 in damages. Because coal seemed to be responsible for most fires caused by the railway, the CPR began to investigate other fuels. From the 1890s, the Southern Pacific Railroad had been successfully burning a variety of crude oil, termed Bunker C, in many of its locomotives,[20] and in 1911, the CPR decided to convert several of its engines to burn oil fuel. Besides diminishing the risk of starting fires, oil fuel permitted larger locomotives to be fired more easily, since coal burners, until the perfection of the mechanical stoker during the 1920s, required the fireman to shovel coal into the firebox almost continuously. Although the use of oil burners was concentrated on the main line between Field and Revelstoke, large oil-storage tanks, smaller service

tanks, and oil-filling cranes were installed at these locations and at other divisional and intermediate points, including Calgary, Golden, Rogers Pass, Kamloops, and Vancouver. Oil fuel was also used for a time on Vancouver Island.[21] Although the British Columbia government and later the Board of Railway Commissioners stipulated that all locomotives in that province were to burn oil fuel, shortages caused by the First World War and objections from the railways resulted in the order being rescinded, and so complete conversion to oil fuel never took place.

Irrigation

Although Van Horne had insisted brusquely in 1884 that southern Alberta, especially the area east of Calgary, was not dry, nature deemed otherwise. If the CPR wanted settlers to farm the land, irrigation had to be made available, and by 1904, construction had begun on an elaborate canal system designed to irrigate about a million acres between Calgary and Strathmore on the main line. The headgate was built on the Bow River east of Calgary, and two main canals were formed, using both existing watercourses and new excavations. The canals could hold ten feet of water and their sides were sloped to permit easy access. To maintain a grade of 0.05 percent, about four and a half miles of the line west of Strathmore had to be moved. The headgate, flumes, and other structures were made of wood to minimize both cost of materials and labour, as there was a shortage of the latter.[22] This installation comprised the first part of a much larger canal system constructed by the CPR. A large dam later built near the town of Bassano was claimed by some to be the biggest irrigation dam in the world at the time. The dam and its connecting canal system were opened officially on April 26, 1914, by CPR president Sir Thomas Shaughnessy.[23]

Edmonton's High-Level Bridge

The CPR finally managed to extend the Calgary and Edmonton Railway into Edmonton proper, but only after the Canadian Northern and Grand Trunk Pacific railways had reached the city. Although the CPR had issued bonds in 1903 for the construction of a high-level bridge, it chose instead to obtain running rights for freight trains on the Canadian Northern's Edmonton, Yukon and Pacific Railway. Later in 1903, the CPR purchased land in Edmonton to the west of the city centre, north of Jasper Avenue, where the company erected a freight shed and laid a spur from the EY&P. Although it seemed that the construction of a bridge from Strathcona was imminent, there was controversy over whether there should be a traffic deck and provision for street railway tracks, and who was to pay for them. The CPR wanted hefty concessions from both Edmonton and Strathcona. To hasten a resolution, the CPR investigated the possibility of sharing the Grand Trunk Pacific's Clover Bar bridge.[24] After further wrangling and grants from all levels of government covering 45 percent of the estimated $1.5 million cost, the CPR agreed to construct a high-level

the sand house is an oil–service tank. The bunker C fuel oil was stored in a larger tank not visible in the photograph. Before being put into a locomotive tender, the oil was pumped through filters to remove solid objects and water, and then stored in a service tank. Gravity would feed the oil from the tank through the oil crane, seen immediately to the right of 522's tender.

PROVINCIAL ARCHIVES OF BRITISH COLUMBIA/CP–17

Edmonton's High-Level or 109th Street bridge, looking towards the south side, c1925. The bridge enabled the CPR, forty years after its initial construction, to finally enter Edmonton proper.

bridge across the North Saskatchewan River, including a traffic deck and provision for two street railway tracks, beginning in 1910. The bridge is 2,478 feet long, and about 160 feet above the river. Five large concrete piers support most of it on the north side and across the river, while nine steel towers complete the framework on the south side. Fabricated by the Canadian Bridge Company, the superstructure consists of three large Pratt trusses across the river, with smaller trusses for the approaches. The CPR track runs down the centre of the bridge along the top, with the street railway tracks on either side; the roadway and sidewalks are about nineteen feet below. Construction was completed by June 1913, with the first train crossing on June 2.[25] Continuing north between 109th and 110th streets, the line crossed Jasper Avenue on a steel overpass, where a two-storey masonry station was built on the north side. Alberta was burgeoning at the time, and both the provincial and dominion governments encouraged other concerns interested in constructing railroads.

The Alberta Central Railway

The first premier of Alberta, Alexander Cameron Rutherford, a Liberal, made it quite clear at the end of 1908 that his government favoured the construction of railways in the province and would provide what financial assistance it could for each endeavour. On February 5, 1909, a delegation of 150, the largest to that point, approached the provincial government to ask for a subsidy for a proposed railway, the Alberta Central (ACR).[26] Although it had been granted a charter in 1901, nothing had been done. The focus of this railway was to be the central Alberta town of Red Deer, and lines would travel west, over the Calgary and Edmonton Railway to Rocky Mountain House, the Brazeau coalfields, and the Yellowhead Pass beyond. A line southeast to Moose Jaw, Saskatchewan, was also planned, as well as a branch northeast to Saskatoon. An election was due in Alberta, and Rutherford ensured that the Alberta Central received a subsidy. Construction was to begin in 1910 on the line from Red Deer to Rocky Mountain House, to standards equivalent to those adopted by the Grand Trunk Pacific, although the Alberta Central was intended as a colonization rather than a trunk railway. The surveying and construction were under the direction of J.G. Macgregor, chief engineer, and the company hired its own workers. Track laying was planned to coincide with the visit in August of the prime minister, Sir Wilfrid Laurier, and the planning had a purpose beyond mere public attraction.[27]

The Canadian Northern was also constructing a line west from Red Deer, and did what it could to obstruct and squeeze out the Alberta Central, locating its line next to that of the ACR, and planning to cross it at least five times. ACR management hoped that Laurier's visit might result in the CNoR's line being relocated. Laurier was already well known as a promoter of railways, and he gladly took the opportunity of driving the first spike on the Alberta Central on August 10. Although the Canadian Northern's line was eventually relocated farther north, the Alberta Central found itself with little money, and work proceeded slowly. To accelerate construction to Rocky Mountain House, the ACR hired the contracting firm J.D. McArthur Company, which had built sections of the National Transcontinental as well as several GTP branch lines. The cost of building the concrete and steel overpass above the Calgary and Edmonton Railway and two large steel bridges west of Red Deer further depleted the Alberta Central's meagre finances, and by the end of 1912 the concern was almost bankrupt. In December, the CPR leased the line for 999 years, and completed construction to Rocky Mountain House by August 1914. Although located in Red Deer, the CPR station was named Lochearn, to distinguish it from the Canadian Northern's station in the same community.[28]

The Alberta and Great Waterways Railway

Premier Rutherford's aggressive policy of financing railways extended to ventures that larger railroads would not undertake. He was convinced that vast areas of north-

August 10, 1910, probably
the most auspicious day
in the short history of the
Alberta Central Railway.
No less a person than the
prime minister, Sir Wilfrid
Laurier, is about to drive the
first spike of the line that
was projected to reach
Rocky Mountain House and,
ultimately, the West Coast
via the Yellowhead Pass.

PROVINCIAL ARCHIVES OF
ALBERTA/A1802

Thomas, Lord Shaughnessy, president of the CPR,
1899–1918. Brought into the company by Van Horne in 1882,
Shaughnessy proved his worth as chief purchasing agent by
wresting as much value from each meagre penny as possible. Born and raised in the United States, Shaughnessy
lacked the physical presence and ebullient personality of Van
Horne. Nevertheless, he presided over an ever-expanding and
prestigious transportation company. His efforts at increasing
colonization in western Canada earned him a knighthood in
1901. Although a survivor of the CPR's lean construction
years, Shaughnessy detested competition, and he intrigued
politically to undermine the expansionist efforts of the
Canadian Northern and the Grand Trunk Pacific Railways.

Lacking the subtlety of his predecessor, Shaughnessy's
efforts had little effect, as he was too outspoken and often
backed the losing political party. A strong patriot, he com-
mitted the CPR's resources to Canada's cause in the First
World War, and was granted a peerage in 1916. Saddened by
the loss of his son in the war, bothered by failing health, and
distracted by an increasing interest in Irish politics,
Shaughnessy relinquished the presidency in 1918 and played
an increasingly minor role as chairman until his death in
December 1923. This photograph is c1912.

COLLECTION OF THE AUTHOR

ern Alberta would be excellent for farming, and all that was required were railroads, constructed by independent companies, to open up the area. William R. Clarke, a banker from Kansas City, led a consortium that applied for a charter to build a railway from Edmonton to Fort McMurray, through Lac La Biche. The Alberta and Great Waterways Railway Company (A&GW) was incorporated in 1909, with the legislature approving a cash subsidy and guaranteeing large quantities of bonds. The promise of expansion to the north probably contributed to the reelection of the Rutherford government later that year.[29]

The first sod of the A&GW was turned on November 15, 1909, about sixteen miles north of Edmonton. Planning and construction were under the direction of Chief Engineer J.A.L. Waddell, an accomplished American railway engineer who had been decorated by the emperor of Japan in 1888 for his work in that country.[30] Clearing progressed quickly, and by the end of 1909, almost seven miles of the line had been graded. Shortly after Rutherford and his government were reelected, the minister of Public Works, John Cushing, resigned, alleging impropriety by other members of the government in matters related to the A&GW. There were further suggestions that some of the A&GW bonds had been sold above par, and the Opposition leader, R.B. Bennett, contended that the difference had been pocketed by William Clarke and perhaps members of the government. Rutherford called for a royal commission in March to investigate the allegations, but before the commission completed its work, Rutherford resigned as premier and was replaced by Arthur Sifton. Although the commission's majority findings, presented in November 1910, exonerated Rutherford and found no impropriety with the bonds, Sifton canceled the contract for the A&GW with Clarke. Litigation halted further progress until 1913, when the government received a letter from J.D. McArthur on September 22, stating, "I propose to take over the Alberta and Great Waterways Railway on terms satisfactory to representatives of bondholders and the Royal Bank, and propose to construct same between original terminals."[31]

The imposing John Duncan McArthur, c1914, a contractor who had garnered sufficient capital constructing parts of the National Transcontinental and Grand Trunk Pacific Railways to enable him to build railways of his own.

PROVINCIAL ARCHIVES OF ALBERTA/86.587/3281B

John Duncan McArthur had considerable success contracting for the National Transcontinental and the Grand Trunk Pacific, and was building his own railroads. After much debate in the legislature, the provincial government approved McArthur's deal. Construction began at the end of October, at Carbondale, about thirteen and a half miles north of the Edmonton terminus of McArthur's Edmonton, Dunvegan and British Columbia Railway.

Grading was done primarily with mechanical graders and steam shovels, and a Pioneer track layer was used to lay the ties and rail. Most rail was sixty pounds per yard, and ballast was used where available. Rails reached Lac La Biche in February

1915, but by March, crews encountered heavy muskeg and stretches of sand to the north, which provided little support for the roadbed, which promptly sank, pulling ties and rails down as well. Such problems delayed construction and the use of the line.[32]

Even before track reached Lac La Biche, McArthur had visions of building a tourist hotel next to the lake, one that would be comparable in style to those of the CPR and GTP. An Edmonton architect, Roland Lines, designed the hotel, called the Lac La Biche Inn. Although smaller than the hotels of his competitors, the inn was to be a three-storey frame and stucco building with a fieldstone foundation and chimney and a tall enclosed observation tower at one corner. Constructed during 1915, it cost more than $66,000 to build and outfit. There were twenty-two guest rooms besides bathrooms, a lounge, and a large dining-room equipped with custom-made china marked with an A&GW crest.[33]

Although not as grand as its counterparts on the transcontinental railroads, the Lac La Biche Inn, shown here c1915, was one of the most elegant structures to grace a feeder railway. The upper floor of the tower afforded guests a sheltered vista of the lake and surrounding countryside.

NATIONAL ARCHIVES OF CANADA/PA18819

Envisaging special trains carrying patrons to and from his new hotel, McArthur purchased two used self-propelled gasoline motor cars made by the McKeen Motor Car Company of Omaha, Nebraska, in 1914. The McKeen cars—retaining their old numbers of 709 and 711 on the Woodstock and Sycamore (Illinois) Traction Company—provided round-trip excursions for the first guests of the Lac La Biche Inn in 1916. Although more economical than a regular train, this second-hand equipment proved unreliable, especially when parts became difficult to obtain following the demise of the McKeen Company.[34] The career of the Lac La Biche Inn was also short-lived. A drowning mishap on the lake in August 1916 prompted McArthur to close the hotel until the 1918 season. Then a fire destroyed much of the community in 1919, and the A&GW's subsequent financial difficulties resulted in the hotel closing until 1937, when it was sold to an order of nuns, who converted it into a hospital.

Construction on the A&GW north of Lac La Biche was beset with problems: muskeg, shortage of workers, and lack of rails caused by the First World War. Completed sections of the line required almost constant maintenance or rebuilding, and delays caused by derailments were so common that the line was nicknamed Arriving, God Willing. Labour shortages after the end of hostilities continued to slow the progress towards Fort McMurray, although the track had been extended to within eight miles of the settlement by 1919. The point was named Waterways (now

A construction train on the A&GW, somewhere north of Lac La Biche, c1914. Money was so limited that watering facilities sometimes consisted of a pipe placed in a creek or slough. A steam-driven pump drew the water and filled the tender. The white deposits on the side of the driving wheels indicate that the water was heavily laden with minerals, which caused severe problems in the boilers of the locomotives.

PROVINCIAL ARCHIVES OF ALBERTA/A18528

A soft roadbed and poor ballast contributed to frequent mishaps along the Alberta and Great Waterways. While many tourists are photographed pushing against the leaning tower of Pisa in Italy, engine crews on the A&GW were usually delighted to be photographed preventing their locomotives from falling over, c1914.

PROVINCIAL ARCHIVES OF ALBERTA/A10177

Draper), and this was the end of the line until November 1925 because of difficulties constructing the line down a steep hill to the site, at the confluence of the Clearwater and Athabasca Rivers, opposite Fort McMurray.

The A&GW's financial condition, never very sound, became critical in 1920. Losing money and showing little prospect of generating much revenue, the railroad was, however, important to settlers and the inhabitants of the northern part of the province. And as neither the dominion government nor a larger railway was interested in taking over the A&GW, the provincial government was obliged to sustain it. An agreement was signed on July 23, 1920. The premier of Alberta, Charles Stewart, became the nominal president, replacing J.D. McArthur, who had the option of regaining control up to 1927 if he could muster sufficient funds to cover the railroad's debt.[35]

The Edmonton, Dunvegan and British Columbia/ Central Canada Railways

J.D. McArthur's other main venture in Alberta was the line he hoped would open up the Peace River districts of Alberta and British Columbia. Although the Edmonton, Dunvegan and British Columbia Railway (ED&BC) had been incorporated in 1907 by a group of entrepreneurs, no construction occurred. Taking advantage of the provincial government's enthusiasm for railroads, McArthur gained control of the charter in late 1911 and duly received financial backing from the province. He also gained favourable shipping rates from the GTP for pledging to ship with them exclusively. The line would run northwest of Edmonton to the border with British Columbia and on to Dawson Creek, passing south of Dunvegan.

The Alberta terminus was north of the GTP's main line on the outskirts of Edmonton. Called Dunvegan Yards, the area had ample provision for an extensive marshalling yard, and soon a station, water tank, a four-stall engine house, and other buildings had been erected. The line proceeded northerly to the confluence of the Athabasca and Lesser Slave Rivers, then turned west along the southern shore of Lesser Slave Lake.

This part of the route was a surprise to the residents of Grouard, a town near the western end of the lake. Many of them had thought that the ED&BC would take the north shore, since fewer watercourses drained into the lake on that side, and they had fully expected that the line would pass through Grouard. McArthur, however, owned several tracts of land along the southern shore, and preferred that the railroad pass through his land in spite of Grouard and a better route to the north. Bypassing Grouard, then, the line continued northwest along the southern shore of Kimiwan Lake and then turned west, passing south of Dunvegan to avoid a difficult crossing of the Peace River.

Although the terrain was relatively flat, construction was slowed by many watercourses and by ground composed of oozing, sticky clay called gumbo. Roadbed preparation and bridge construction took the most time, although progress was aided by the use of a Pioneer track layer to lay the ties and rails. Rails reached a point near Spirit River in early 1916, and by March, a branch had also been graded and laid south from Rycroft to Grande Prairie.[36] Spirit River was on the projected main line west, and although grading and some bridge construction was completed for several miles beyond, the shortage of rails caused by the First World War, and the demands of McArthur's other Alberta railroads, meant that construction could not proceed, and Spirit River would remain on the end of a short spur line. Although McArthur acknowledged that the ED&BC was not comparable to the transcontinental railways, the standard of construction and the alignment of the grade was considered by many

so substandard that the line soon earned the nickname Exceedingly Dangerous and Badly Constructed. This view was supported by the incidence of frequent derailments in spite of the slow speed of trains, the subsidence of the tracks into the ground, and an inability to keep to published schedules.

Several divisional points and many sidings were established as construction of the ED&BC progressed, and it was hoped that most of these would develop into new towns. While two-storey stations were built at divisional points and sidings where there was already considerable settlement, portable combination freight and passenger shelters were constructed on flatcars in Edmonton and moved to sidings with little development. Should the location grow and traffic increase, the portable could be replaced with a permanent structure.

Motive power and rolling stock for the McArthur lines consisted of a variety of locomotives and cars, many coming from the J.D. McArthur Company, some purchased second-hand from other concerns, and a few ordered new. Most were lettered for the Edmonton, Dunvegan and British Columbia or the Alberta and Great Waterways, with only a few pieces of rolling stock, a baggage car, and two boarding cars being lettered for the Central Canada.[37] Most of the locomotives—which were primarily Moguls—were purchased used from the J.D. McArthur Company; only two, A&GW Numbers 27 and 28, both ten-wheelers, were purchased new, in 1915. Most of the second-hand engines were retired and scrapped in the 1920s and early 1930s.[38]

In the early stages of construction, with the ED&BC line projected to pass well

The divisional point of Smith on the Edmonton, Dunvegan and British Columbia Railway in 1915. Although not a centre for heavy locomotive maintenance, Smith was an important point for crew changes and became a focal point for mercantile trade in the area. Number 1, the only American-type locomotive on the ED&BC roster, had been purchased second-hand by the J.D. McArthur Company some years before being sold to the ED&BC. The train is unloading baggage and freight, and will soon depart for Slave Lake and the end of steel. The age and small size of Number 1 contributed to its retirement during the early 1920s.

GLENBOWARCHIVES/NC–6–1564

It is a rainy day in 1917, as Number 5, an old Mogul in its third incarnation, having been purchased second-hand by the J.D. McArthur Company, pulls a Peace River-bound passenger train across the large steel Heart River bridge. Built to a high standard, the new bridge seems incongruous with the small, old rolling stock being used on the line. It was expenses such as steel bridges, however, that intensified the dire financial straits of the Edmonton, Dunvegan and British Columbia Railway.

GLENBOW ARCHIVES/NA–1044–35

Number 7 of the Edmonton, Dunvegan and British Columbia was a Mogul purchased by the J.D. McArthur Company in 1908 from the Canadian Foundry Company of Toronto. This locomotive possessed sloped cylinder banks, so that the valve gear was located on the centre driving wheel axle, between the driving wheels. While this arrangement protected the valve gear from external hazards, it made lubrication difficult and added to the problems of maintenance. Shown here in 1929, Number 7 remained in service until the late 1930s, when it was retired and scrapped.

GLENBOW ARCHIVES/ND–3–4627E

south of the Peace River, many settlers in the area lobbied for a branch line. Following the example set by the Canadian Northern, McArthur incorporated the Central Canada Railway in 1913 and obtained a provincial subsidy for it. The line was to run from the ED&BC main line west of McLennan to the settlement of Peace River Crossing (now Peace River). Construction, including a large steel bridge across the Heart River, began in 1915 and was completed the following year. McArthur also used the charter to construct a branch on the Alberta and Great Waterways Railway called the Egg Lake branch, or the St. Lina line. Starting from Dewar, between Hylo and Venice, the Egg Lake branch was to proceed southeast to Prince Albert, Saskatchewan. While the line was graded for about thirty miles, only eleven miles of track was laid, primarily to enable McArthur to harvest the softwood in the area. Track laying continued no farther, since rails were scarce and the finances of the McArthur railways were in sorry shape. The Egg Lake branch came to an ignominious end. The fire of 1919 that destroyed most of Lac La Biche swept south, where it burned most of the ties and bridges on the branch. When time permitted, crews salvaged the rails for use elsewhere.

The final blow to the ED&BC and Central Canada Railways came in 1918 with the extension of the Central Canada beyond Peace River Crossing. To continue west, a 1,736-foot steel bridge was constructed across the Peace River, but rails continued only half a mile beyond, as the supply of rails and funds for construction were both exhausted. Nevertheless, Norman Harvey, acting deputy minister of railways and telephones in Alberta, gushed about the bridge:

> This fine structure constitutes one of the most important links in the colonization chain of the Province and in bridging yet one more of the barriers that Nature has flung ... has brought into homogeneity with the rest of this Province and in contact with the transportation systems of an entire continent, a territory of vast extent and unmeasured potentialities of minerals and growth.[39]

Both railways continued to operate at a loss. By 1920, it was evident that McArthur's lines could not survive as they were, and although he had approached both the GTP and the CPR for assistance, the former was unable and the latter was unwilling to assist. The problem became acute when there were insufficient funds to repair damage caused by several slides on the Central Canada line to Peace River. But the provincial government considered the ED&BC and the Central Canada, like the A&GW, too important to forsake. The young Canadian National Railways could not afford to nationalize McArthur's lines, but the CPR was willing to manage them, with the exception of the A&GW, if the provincial government would supply money

The poor condition of the roadbed on the Alberta and Great Waterways Railway north of Lac La Biche, and the need to maintain service, prompted the McArthur administration to install flanged wheels on a Packard car. Besides performing inspection duties, the car could carry several passengers and pull a small trailer for baggage. The large single headlight and white flags indicate that this was an extra train. In this way, at least some form of passenger service was maintained on the northern reaches of the A&GW.

NATIONAL ARCHIVES OF CANADA/PA18316

to help upgrade the lines. A five-year agreement was signed with the Canadian Pacific in July 1920. As with the A&GW, McArthur could recover control of the Edmonton, Dunvegan and British Columbia and Central Canada Railways up to 1927 if he could raise capital to cover the lines' debt, a task that he never accomplished with any of his Alberta lines.[40] Although only as the manager, the CPR had gained control of yet another railroad in western Canada.

The Peanut Special

Perhaps the most unusual motive power in Alberta during this period was found on a short railway with a long name. It was incorporated by a group of local business-men and farmers in 1909 as the Lacombe and Blindman Valley Electric Railway

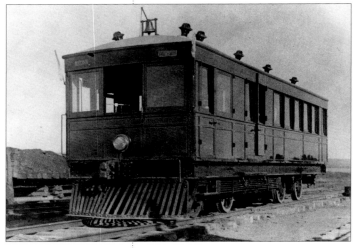

(L&BVER). They wanted to construct an electric railway between the Calgary and Edmonton line at Lacombe, and Rimbey, about thirty-five miles to the northwest, through Bentley, another farm-ing community along the route. Disagreements and an absence of government money delayed construction until 1913, when grading began with the assistance of a provincial subsidy. By the outbreak of hostilities in 1914, rails still had not reached Bentley. Operations did not com-mence until 1917, when the province provided additional cash and engineering assistance to enable rails to get as far as Bentley. As with most other small railroads in Alberta, the Lacombe

The Baguley/McEwan, Pratt hydraulic car at Lacombe, shortly after the commencement of service on the Lacombe and Blindman Valley Electric Railway, c1917.

PROVINCIAL ARCHIVES OF ALBERTA/70.206/5

and Blindman Valley Electric was in poor financial condition, and the operation was taken over by the provincial government in 1918. While not as important as McArthur's lines, the L&BVER passed through heavily settled farmland, and thus served many voters. The track was extended to Rimbey in 1919, and the name of the company was changed to the Lacombe and North-Western Railway. Three years later, the combination engine house and machine shop were moved to Rimbey as well.[41]

The euphoria associated with the start of construction in 1913 led the railroad to order motive power. The idea of using electric equipment was abandoned, probably because of the high cost of generating electricity and the related infrastructure. Instead, the railroad ordered two self-propelled passenger cars from the British-based Baguley Cars Company, which had absorbed McEwan, Pratt and Company, developer of one of the first hydraulic drive systems for railroad vehicles. Only one of the cars was completed in 1913, a thirty-two-foot vehicle with a steel frame, wood-en superstructure, and seating capacity for thirty-six. A six-cylinder inline engine, capable of consuming either gasoline or kerosene, and producing between eighty-five and a hundred horsepower, was coupled directly to a hydraulic pump, which drove four hydraulic motors, each powering a single axle of the running gear.[42]

Although the car was delivered in 1914, the railway was in no condition to operate it, and it is possible that it was leased to the Edmonton Interurban Railway, running between Edmonton and St. Albert. The second car was never finished because of the disruption caused by the First World War. When operations started on the Lacombe and Blindman Valley Electric Railway in 1917, service was provided by the Baguley/McEwan, Pratt car and a small steam locomotive (0–4–0) for freight, nicknamed the Peanut. At some point, the passenger compartment of the self-propelled car was shortened and the seating capacity reduced to twenty-four to allow for a baggage room. The L&BVER's unusual motive power survived until 1928, when it was scrapped by the CPR, who bought the line.[43]

The Pacific Great Eastern

The British Columbia government was also caught up in the railroad mania before the First World War. The premier, Richard McBride, had encouraged the growth of the CPR as well as the Grand Trunk Pacific and Canadian Northern Pacific. His government's support also extended to smaller railways. The one that caused the most problems, both politically and from an engineering point of view, was a railroad chartered in 1912 that was to be the Grand Trunk Pacific's link to Vancouver. Through efforts primarily by the Canadian Northern and Canadian Pacific Railways, the GTP's repeated requests for permission to build a line to Vancouver were invariably refused by Ottawa. President Hays searched for other ways by which the GTP could reach Vancouver by rail, and revealing a certain cunning, or perhaps deviousness, he favoured the creation of a separate company that would receive GTP backing. Named the Pacific Great Eastern (PGE), the line was to run from Prince George to North Vancouver, and be completed by the end of 1915.[44]

The Pacific Great Eastern was not the first railroad to be built in that area. In 1907, the Howe Sound, Pemberton Valley and Northern Railway was chartered to construct a line from near Squamish on Howe Sound, north to Anderson Lake by way of the Cheakamus River. Construction began in 1909, and about seven miles of track was in operation the following year. At that time, the charter was amended to allow the railroad to build farther north to Lillooet, and the name was changed to Howe Sound and Northern Railway. Three small second-hand locomotives and various pieces of rolling stock were used on this primarily logging railroad. The line, charter, and rolling stock were purchased by the PGE in October 1912.

The railroad contractors Foley, Welch and Stewart, closely associated with the Grand Trunk Pacific, were the main partners in the Pacific Great Eastern, with John Stewart as president. This company also undertook most of the construction, assisted

by several former officers of the Grand Trunk Pacific, who assumed new positions with the PGE. The most noteworthy was D'Arcy Tate, the GTP's former solicitor, who became vice-president of the new company with Charles M. Hays's blessing. Premier Richard McBride, who had refused to fund any GTP line to Vancouver because it appeared that the railroad was simply trying to prevent the Canadian Northern's entry into B.C., did not realize that the Pacific Great Eastern was a creature of the GTP, and awarded the company a bond guarantee of $35 thousand per mile early in 1912.[45] If Hays's grand strategy of having the GTP enter Vancouver via the PGE had developed as he had imagined, the Grand Trunk Pacific might well have prevented the Canadian Northern from becoming a serious competitor to the West Coast.

Surveying began at both ends of the PGE, and it soon became apparent that considerable difficulties would be encountered constructing the line along the southern shore of Howe Sound. Nevertheless, construction began at North Vancouver in 1913, and by July 1914, track was laid to Whytecliff, on the shore of Howe Sound, a distance of 12.7 miles. Passenger service was provided by three self-propelled gas-electric combination passenger and freight cars manufactured by the Hall-Scott Motor Company of San Francisco. Additional service was supplied by one of the former

Conventional locomotives and trains plied the northern section of the Pacific Great Eastern. Number 54, a Consolidation built new for the PGE by the Canadian Locomotive Company of Kingston, Ontario, heads a mixed train (freight and passenger) north at D'Arcy, c1918. The station was named for D'Arcy Tate, a lawyer formerly in the employ of the Grand Trunk Pacific. To the right of the train is a water tank and the frame station, which also housed a dining-hall.

PROVINCIAL ARCHIVES OF BRITISH COLUMBIA/83103

Howe Sound and Northern locomotives, which also moved freight. The Pacific Great Eastern also ordered six large Consolidations, two from the Montréal Locomotive Works, delivered in 1913, and four from the Canadian Locomotive Company of Kingston, Ontario, received during 1914. All of them were intended to be used on the line north from Squamish.[46]

Construction also proceeded north from the Howe Sound and Northern's line near Squamish, and by October 1914, service was available from the docks at Squamish to Pemberton, a distance of fifty-seven miles. Although the track reached Lillooet on the east side of the Fraser River in 1915, the PGE's finances were becoming stretched and further funds were hard to obtain. A change of premier in December, combined with the realization that there was no way the PGE would be finished in 1915, resulted in the provincial government refusing to provide additional funding. The slowness of construction prompted some to call the railroad the Prince George Eventually. Other nicknames included Please Go Easy, Past God's Endurance, and after being taken over by the province, Provincial Government Expense, and Promoters Get Everything.

The government relented in early 1916 and provided the PGE with a $6 million

The front of the D'Arcy station included a large portico decorated with logs for a rustic appearance. The arrangement of the station name board followed the custom of the Grand Trunk Pacific, which listed mileages to the termini of the line. Unfortunately, neither terminus listed on the name board was reached by the PGE at this time, c1918.

VANCOUVER PUBLIC LIBRARY/9963

loan to sustain construction, but the Conservatives were defeated in the November election, and the new Liberal government began an investigation into allegations of corruption and fraud involving Foley, Welch and Stewart, de facto owners of the PGE, who had been charging the railway and paying themselves. Foley, Welch and Stewart and other officers of the Pacific Great Eastern offered little co-operation to the inquiry. One notable exception was John Callaghan, the chief engineer, who stated that Foley, Welch and Stewart had been overpaid for certain operations. In February 1918, when it appeared that the findings of the inquiry substantiated the allegations, Foley, Welch and Stewart announced that they were abandoning the enterprise. But as with the McArthur railroads in Alberta, the B.C. government could not afford to have the Pacific Great Eastern cease operations, especially since the government had already sunk millions of dollars into the venture. Reluctantly, Premier Oliver and his government entered into an agreement with Foley, Welch and Stewart in 1918, whereby the government acquired the stock and assets of the railroad and operated it with a board of directors appointed by the lieutenant-governor. In return, the government would cease all litigation against Foley, Welch and Stewart, and any former PGE officers.[47]

Work resumed by September 1918, but a shortage of labour continued to impede progress. After many delays and the construction of a large steel bridge across Deep Creek Canyon, the track reached Quesnel in July 1921. Unfortunately, the PGE was not generating much revenue, and the government decided it could no longer afford further construction. Early in 1922, a committee of three well-known railroaders (John

Sullivan, former engineer, CPR; W.P. Hinton, former traffic manager, GTP; and J.S. Dennis of the CPR) was hired to evaluate the PGE and advise on its future. The consensus was that even if the railway were to be extended to Prince George, there would be insufficient traffic to justify construction and sustain operations. In consequence, they recommended that the line be abandoned north of Clinton and the salvaged materials be used to construct a line southeast to Ashcroft. This was an unpopular recommendation, and at a political rally on September 30, Premier John Oliver declared, "I'll take my chances, I'll not abandon the road until I have taken stock and have satisfied myself that we cannot redeem the situation." The PGE continued to operate in this unfinished and disjointed state, from North Vancouver to Whytecliff and Squamish to Quesnel, through most of the 1920s.[48]

The Kettle Valley Railway

The CPR had perennial concerns about the possibility of the Great Northern Railway encroaching into southern British Columbia, and its concerns were not unfounded, as the Great Northern had managed to drive a few lines across the border. In 1909, despite heavy opposition by the CPR, the Great Northern reached Vancouver by its Canadian subsidiary, the Vancouver, Victoria and Eastern Railway and Navigation Company (VV&E), which had, in turn, purchased the Vancouver, Westminster and Yukon Railway running from New Westminster to Vancouver. The VV&E was backed initially by Mackenzie and Mann, but J.J. Hill of the Great Northern gained control of it in 1901. In addition, Hill was trying to buy coalfields in areas already served by the CPR, and another tentacle of the Great Northern, named the Morrissey, Fernie and Michel Railway, reached from Rexford, Montana, to Fernie and Morrissey, B.C. These actions were seen by John Houston, a member of the provincial legislature, to be more than mere competition: "The acquiring of the Crow's Nest coal lands by Mr. Hill and the capitalists behind him is simply the first step in acquiring the control of the Canadian Pacific Railway."[49] Publicly, the CPR put on a brave face and trivialized the significance of Hill's northern invasion. William Whyte, manager of the CPR's western lines, said in January 1906, "Our rates are cheaper than those of the Great Northern, so I do not think the new lines, which are simply intended to be feeders of the Great Northern, will take much Canadian trade." In April, Sir William Van Horne portrayed Hill and the Great Northern as anti-Canadian:

> People who do not think very deeply about railway matters are eager to welcome Mr. Hill's schemes, because they mean competition and thus they look upon unlimited railway competition as a good thing. They forget that every train-load of grain carried from Canada into the United States means a substantial loss to Canada.[50]

133

Privately, the CPR was gravely concerned, as the Great Northern's business was booming in southern B.C. There was also a comparatively large area from Hope east to Nelson that the CPR did not dominate, which it was feared would be entered by the Hill lines and lost to the CPR.

In the midst of this undeclared war between large corporations, the Kettle River Valley Railway (KRVR) was chartered in 1901 to build several lines near Grand Forks, primarily to serve mines and a smelter. Another line was also constructed south to Republic, Washington. Completed in April 1902, and called the Spokane and British Columbia in the United States, the Kettle River Valley Railway found itself competing fiercely with the Great Northern line. In fact, the KRVR tried unsuccessfully to block the Vancouver, Victoria and Eastern from crossing its line to gain entry to Grand Forks, parking a locomotive over the VV&E crossing, a method similar to that used earlier by the CPR to stop the EY&P from connecting to the Calgary and Edmonton Railway.[51] The KRVR was compelled to yield in this case, but other lines were planned from its proposed new headquarters at Penticton. Lines were to run from Midway to Penticton, Penticton to Osoyoos, and Penticton to the coalfields near Nicola Lake, northeast of Merritt. The CPR had already reached this area in 1907 through the charter of the Nicola, Kamloops and Similkameen Coal and Railway Company, which was leased to the CPR in 1905. The KRVR had been granted running rights along the projected line from Spences Bridge to Nicola Lake in 1904. Nevertheless, the company managed to obtain a large subsidy from Premier McBride for the proposed line from Penticton to Merritt. At the same time, the CPR planned to extend a line southeast to connect with the former Columbia and Western line, rebuilt to standard gauge and extended to Midway.[52] The CPR also wished to build east from Hope to Nelson, effectively capturing the business in the area before the Great Northern could arrive. While J.J. Hill's desire for expansion into Canada manifested itself as many, but relatively small, incursions, the goal of his son Louis, who took over the Great Northern in 1907, was Napoleonic:

If our Canadian plans do not miscarry, I expect within the next ten years, to have a railroad system there which will be almost an equivalent of the Great Northern system as it is today in the United States. The Great Northern will then touch Winnipeg, Brandon, Regina, Calgary, Edmonton and probably Prince Albert, and may traverse the Peace River country with a line several hundred miles further north than any Canadian line.[53]

The CPR's fears of an invasion were realized in part in 1909, when the Vancouver, Victoria and Eastern constructed a line from a Great Northern branch originating at Oroville, Washington. The new VV&E line travelled northwest to Princeton, and by 1911, the track was extended to Coalmont, where there were several coalmines. The

CPR had to act quickly to prevent further incursion. Reaching an agreement with the Kettle River Valley Railway, the CPR undertook to finance the construction of the KRVR lines in exchange for stocks and other securities. In addition, the company assigned Andrew McCulloch, an experienced civil engineer who had been involved with the planning and construction of most of the CPR lines in southern B.C., to oversee construction of the new lines. In view of these developments, the name of the company was changed to the Kettle Valley Railway Company in 1911.[54]

While the intent was to construct a line west to Hope through the Coquihalla Pass, the arrangement of the mountains and lakes meant that the line would follow three broad northerly arcs, roughly from Midway to Penticton, south from Penticton to Princeton, and from Princeton, through the Coquihalla Pass to Hope, where a bridge across the Fraser River would connect the line to the CPR main line. The construction, over difficult and often treacherous terrain, was a daunting task of engineering and perseverance, especially through the Coquihalla Pass, which Sandford Fleming had rejected as a possible route for the CPR main line because of narrowness, heavy snowfall, and avalanches.

Another obstacle threatened the project: the Vancouver, Victoria and Eastern Railway and Navigation Company. Both the VV&E and the Kettle Valley wanted to use the Coquihalla Pass, although initially, the VV&E had considered boring an eight-mile tunnel beneath it, which would have been extremely expensive and time-consuming. Since both railroads were similar in purpose, there was little justification for two separate lines. To compound the issue, the VV&E had a running rights agreement with the Canadian Northern, whereby it could use the CNoR line between Hope and its own north-south line from Seattle. An agreement finalized in July 1914 gave the Kettle Valley Railway rights to use VV&E trackage from Princeton to Brookmere, and the VV&E rights on the Kettle Valley through the Coquihalla Pass to Hope.[55]

Construction on the new KVR lines began in 1910, with the contracting firm Macdonnell, Gzowski and Company building twenty-nine and a half miles of track from Merritt south to Brookmere, reached in 1911. On July 1, 1911, the first sod was turned at Penticton, signifying the construction of the main line from Midway to Hope. Work also began at Midway, and later at Hope. The work was as gruelling and difficult as the construction of the CPR main line through the Fraser Canyon, with

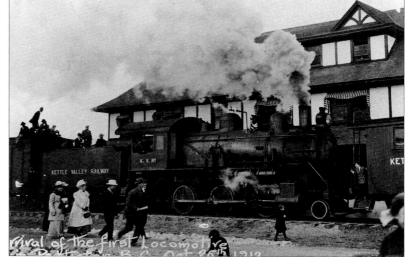

With much fanfare and excitement, the first Kettle Valley Railway train arrives in Penticton, B.C., on October 26, 1912. The locomotive and rolling stock arrived at Penticton by barge, tangible evidence of construction that would soon link Penticton to the Kettle Valley line being built from Midway. Number 3, a Mogul, was purchased second-hand by the KVR in July 1912 from the Chicago Iron Works.

NATIONAL ARCHIVES OF CANADA/PA177904

many solid rock tunnels and bridges required, and it was not until the end of May 1915 that the first train travelled from Midway to Merritt. During 1913, to ensure that the concern would not fall into unfriendly hands, the CPR leased the Kettle Valley Railway for 999 years. Like the Esquimalt and Nanaimo Railway, the Kettle Valley maintained its corporate identity, although most of its motive power and rolling stock was supplied by the CPR.

Construction through the Coquihalla Pass proved to be extremely difficult, requiring extensive snowsheds as well as many tunnels and heavy bridges. Perhaps the most spectacular example of railway engineering on the line were the so-called Quintette tunnels between the stations of Lear and Othello, about eight miles east of Hope. The tunnels, which eliminated the need to construct one, much longer tunnel, were five separate tunnels in quick succession, with some being separated by the Coquihalla River. Beginning in 1914, a combination road and train truss bridge was constructed across the Fraser River at Hope. It was one of the largest steel bridges on the Kettle Valley, with a total length of 955 feet. In contrast to most bridges of this design, the roadway was placed on top of the truss, while the track travelled along the bottom.

In deference to the military activities of the First World War, some of the new stations on the Kettle Valley lines from Penticton west were named after military leaders. The connection on the CPR main line with the Kettle Valley Railway, for example, was named Pétain, after the French Marshal; it has since been renamed Odlum. Jellicoe, about forty-six miles west of Penticton, honoured the commander of the British Grand Fleet. And in a whimsical manner, many of the stations on the Coquihalla subdivision from Brookmere to Pétain were named after Shakespearean characters, including Juliet, Romeo, Iago, Portia, Lear, and Othello. This portion of the Kettle Valley line was finished in July 1916, and its completion provided the CPR with another east-west route through British Columbia.

With competition from the Great Northern resolved, and with the subsequent collapse of the Canadian Northern and Grand Trunk Pacific Railways, it seemed that the Canadian Pacific Railway would emerge from the First World War as the only railway in western Canada with enough resources to capture most of the trade and any new immigration. In 1918, Lord Shaughnessy, who had joined the CPR at the behest of Van Horne before the main line was finished, retired from the presidency in favour of an ambitious young corporate lawyer, Edward Wentworth Beatty. Unlike any of his predecessors, Beatty had not risen through the ranks of the railroad and possessed no practical experience of railroading. An arrogant intellectual who was independently wealthy and who inherited a considerable amount of CPR stock, Beatty preferred a low-profile life of solitude and few public appearances. While he may have hoped to run the CPR quietly and with little competition, events would unfold to prevent this from occurring.

The difficulties of constructing a railroad through the Coquihalla can be appreciated by this photograph of the Quintette tunnels a few miles east of Hope, c1929. Not only was extensive tunnelling required at this location, but a bridge had to be installed as well.

CANADIAN PACIFIC CORPORATE ARCHIVES/7865

The Battle of the Giants

fter the dominion government took over the Canadian Northern and the Grand Trunk Pacific Railways, David B. Hanna assumed the unenviable task of trying to consolidate all the existing government railways into an organization to be called the Canadian National Railways. Besides contending with different management structures, varying standards of motive power and rolling stock, and tenuous financing from the dominion government, Hanna also struggled with infrastructure that had been neglected during the First World War and was in immediate need of upgrading:

The life of a tie and of a wooden trestle is from seven to ten years. On the Canadian Northern, the National Transcontinental, and the Grand Trunk Pacific, there were many trestles which must be replaced either by fills or steel bridges.[1]

The construction of several branch lines started by predecessor companies, such as the CNoR's line on Vancouver Island, had to continue if they were to generate any revenue. There was also the matter of the joint Canadian Northern/Grand Trunk Pacific main line west of Edmonton. Although it had been the intention to restore both lines after the First World War, economics did not justify a two-track main line. Decisions had

to be made as to which portions of each line would be retained, and which abandoned. Unfortunately, abandonment did not entail simply the removal of rails and steel bridges. Several divisional points were affected, where many people had already settled and established homes and families. Displaced personnel would also include track sectionmen and telegraph linemen located along the line. As Hanna said:

Wherever possible, trestles were filled with earth transported from other locations. Unloading the spoil usually entailed the use of a special piece of equipment called a Ligerwood, consisting of a small steam engine that rotated a drum attached to a steel cable. The cable was connected, in turn, to a wheeled plough that travelled along the bottom of the special Hart cars, the sides of which were hinged along the tops, so the bottoms could be opened. As the plough passed, it pushed spoil out of the cars and into the chasm below. Operating a Ligerwood was extremely dangerous, as the plough could snag and suddenly break loose, or the steel cable could snap. The Ligerwood in this photograph is filling a trestle near Obed on the consolidated (CNoR and GTP) main line west of Edmonton, c1921.

GLENBOW ARCHIVES/NA–471–5

How many people realize that every water tank must be heated, night as well as day, from fall to spring, and that in most cases the water supply must be maintained by a man who patrols perhaps fifty miles of line on a gasoline-driven jigger, doing nothing but pumping and warming water?[2]

The former Grand Trunk Pacific main line was considered superior at most locations, and after much debate, the Canadian Northern divisional points of Tollerton, Alberta (south of Edson), and Lucerne, British Columbia (on the south side of Lake Lucerne), were abandoned, and operations consolidated at Edson and Jasper in 1923. Portions of the GTP grade where rails had been removed in 1917, such as the section near Hinton, were rehabilitated, while those requiring heavy maintenance, such as between Dyke (Entrance) and Pocahontas, were abandoned. The consolidation of lines resulted in improvements to service and revenue generation. The western main line possessed the speed capability of the Grand Trunk, and maintained much of the Canadian Northern's local service. While steel bridges were removed from the abandoned grades, most trestles remained, and portions of the abandoned grades were later used as a road between Edmonton and Jasper.

A portion of the former Canadian Northern main line west of Edmonton in use as a road, 1922. Although passable, it appears that there was little traffic.

To save money, several new water tanks using streams and gravity for supply were built along the consolidated main line west of Jasper. Prior to this time, most water tanks were supplied by gasoline-driven pumps that drew water from wells. The groundwater was frequently hard, and the dissolved minerals caused the water to foam inside the boilers of steam locomotives. The steam became saturated with water, washing the lubricating oil from the cylinders and accelerating their wear. And the boilers quickly filled with mineral deposits and scale, with resulting poor performance and frequent maintenance. To alleviate these problems, special water cars had been hauled behind the tenders of steam locomotives. Besides displacing revenue loads, the water cars themselves were costly. The new tanks filled by water from streams eliminated most water cars and the additional expense of supply pumps.

David Hanna believed that much of the dominion government's ill-will towards the Grand Trunk Pacific and the Canadian Northern was attributable to the personal animosity between the presidents of these companies (Edson Chamberlin of the GTP, and William Mackenzie of the CNoR) and President Shaughnessy of the Canadian Pacific. Hanna noted, "The personal equation sometimes enters prejudicially into the larger responsibilities confided to individuals."[3] He tried to be as cordial and accommodating as possible to the new CPR president, Edward Beatty, even though he was inexperienced and egotistical. In fact, Beatty did not hold back on his criticism of the CNR, nor on the dominion government's ownership of railways:

Serious and continuing blunders in railway policy have resulted in the Government being required to assume the ownership at present of 11,400 miles of railway, with the prospect of an additional 6,400 miles … I have no fear of Government ownership, but Government ownership apparently has some fear of private competition under equal conditions.[4]

Without referring to Beatty or the CPR directly, Hanna tried to insist that the CNR was run independently of the government:

We all recognize the supremacy of Parliament. We must go to them when we require money. But I do not admit, and I won't admit, that any Cabinet Minister or member of Parliament should come to any of our Directors and say they want this done, and that done.[5]

His credibility in this regard suffered in October 1920, when several CNR employees desired to run for political office and were immediately fired for doing so. In a curt communiqué, Hanna said:

Under no circumstances can an employee as such with the Canadian National Railways become a candidate for Legislature—Provincial or Dominion. The moment he does he automatically severs his connection with the Railway. The reasons are too obvious for discussion.[6]

Some, including Beatty, suggested that Hanna's actions proved that the government controlled the CNR directly, a charge Prime Minister Meighen denied on November 28: "The action taken by the Directorate of the Canadian National Railways was in no sense taken at the instance of or by any information from the Government."[7] Many employees were not happy with what became known as the Hanna Order, which barred them from politics, and Liberal leader Mackenzie King made it clear that he would do something about it if he were to become prime minister. Hanna's inability to shake the image of being sympathetic to the Conservatives, the unpopular Hanna Order, and his reluctance to compete strenuously with the CPR were seen by the Liberals as weaknesses. The election of December 1921, which put Mackenzie King and the Liberals into office, meant the end of Hanna's administration.

Since 1911, the dominion government had been dominated by the Conservatives, allies of the CPR since the days of Sir John A. Macdonald. The Liberals, although not enemies of that company, were more inclined to favour other enterprises. And keenly aware that many westerners did not like the CPR, because of its monopoly position and what many perceived to be high freight rates, Prime Minister Mackenzie King continued this Liberal tradition. The Liberals also soon prepared changes to the fundamental administration of the CNR. The board of directors and many of the old Canadian Northern administrators, including D.B. Hanna, were to go. A new board and a new president would take charge of a reconstituted nationalized railway, including the remaining Grand Trunk lines, and retaining the name Canadian National Railways. After announcing his retirement, Hanna remarked, "The future success of the Canadian National Railways depends on one thing, and on one thing only. That one thing is to keep out of politics."[8]

There was considerable debate as to who should succeed Hanna as president. Although names of many experienced Canadian railroaders were put forward, the government felt that to avoid allegations of political patronage, a foreigner should be chosen. An outstanding railroader was selected in 1922 to be the new president and chairman of the board. An American by birth, Sir Henry Worth Thornton had established an excellent reputation as a railroad administrator by 1914, when he became general manager of the Great Eastern Railway in England. His reputation was further enhanced during the First World War, when he performed near miracles while responsible for rail transportation of British forces in France. In gratitude, Thornton was knighted in 1919. With such credentials, Sir Henry seemed the ideal candidate to take on the CPR. Initially, Thornton and Edward Beatty were cordial to each other, with the latter stating in the 1922 annual presidential address to CPR shareholders:

> If the Chief Executive of the National Railways and his tried and able assistants are permitted to administer the properties as a private enterprise would be administered, the people of this country will, in a short time, know exactly what prospects of success confront their venture into public ownership. If, on the other hand, political considerations prevail and a free hand is not given to these administering officers, there can be but one result, namely, the increasing of the financial burdens of the country.[9]

The personalities of the two men, however, were entirely different. This, and Beatty's mistrust of government ownership, led inevitably to discord. While Beatty preferred solitude and tended to distance himself from the daily operations of the railway, Thornton delighted in attracting publicity and in being involved with all aspects of the railroad, including socializing with employees of every rank.[10]

Much to Beatty's, and the CPR's, dismay, Thornton soon proved himself capable of transforming the CNR into a serious competitor. One of his first acts, which ingratiated him with most employees, was to revoke the so-called Hanna Order, which prevented workers from entering politics.[11] Besides creating a high morale in the company, Thornton was responsible for the improvement of existing lines; the expansion and upgrading of motive power to take advantage of modern technological developments, such as automatic stokers and feedwater heaters; and the modernizing of passenger equipment. Much of the motive power the CNR inherited from its predecessors was either obsolete or too small to handle larger and heavier trains. Thornton

The charismatic Sir Henry
Thornton at Jasper Park
Lodge shortly after his
appointment as president of
the Canadian National in 1923.
Unlike his counterpart in the
CPR, Thornton enjoyed being
involved with every aspect of
railroading, including surveying for a new addition to one
of the corporation's hotels.

PROVINCIAL ARCHIVES
OF ALBERTA/A1480

Some of the log cabins built along the shore of Lac Beauvert as part of the CNR's Jasper Park Lodge complex, c1925. Although rustic in appearance, these cabins boasted every convenience and luxury of the time.

not only urged the board of directors to approve the purchase of many heavier locomotives, he also instructed his vice-president, S.J. Hungerford, to investigate other forms of motive power that might be more economical than the traditional steam engine and train.

After considerable investigation, especially of motive power used by European railways, it was decided that a diesel-electric form of propulsion was the most economical and efficient. In 1925, the CNR built two self-propelled passenger cars, each equipped with a diesel engine imported from Scotland. Extensive testing, including a transcontinental run by one of the cars, proved that diesel-electric equipment was indeed less expensive to operate and required less maintenance than a regular train with its steam locomotive. The self-propelled cars were thought well suited for operation on branch lines with light traffic. Although it did not undertake a wholesale change to diesel-electric locomotives at that time, the CNR continued to experiment with this type of motive power, and in so doing, gained a considerable lead on the CPR, whose chief of motive power, Henry Bowen, considered the diesel engine to be a passing fad.[12]

In a bold move, Thornton introduced several innovations intended to make CNR passenger travel more appealing than that offered by the CPR. A radio department was established in 1923 to provide entertaining broadcasts to passengers and patrons of the system's hotels. Aerials were installed on parlour and lounge cars, and console radio sets placed in prominent locations, many with special operators. Although availability was limited at first, the system expanded quickly, with radio-telephone service and an early facsimile (fax) system introduced by 1930. Sir Henry commented, "The administration believes that in the establishment of a radio department it has taken a unique and constructive step in railway operation."[13] Thornton also had barber-shops, libraries, and live entertainment added to transcontinental trains.

The hotel system also became a tourist draw. Besides improving the existing hotels inherited from the Grand Trunk Pacific, Thornton established new resorts. Although the GTP had planned to build a hotel on the north shore of Lac Beauvert near Jasper, its financial demise prevented construction. Under Hanna's administration, several cabins were opened in 1922, under the name Jasper Park Lodge. While the Spartan cabins were functional, they were thought unlikely to attract high-paying tourists. A greater attraction would be a large rustic hotel similar to the one planned by Rattenbury for the GTP, but not a tall structure that would overwhelm the natural beauty of the site. A new design for a single-storey log structure with well-appointed log cabins adjacent to it was prepared by John Schofield, the

Jasper Park Lodge was a considerable distance from both the CNR station and Jasper townsite. To transport guests to the lodge in style, the railway assembled a fleet of luxury motor cars and chauffeurs. Number 5 is a large McLaughlin-Buick, a Canadian-made automobile, pictured in front of the fieldstone garage located near the main lodge, c1925.

COLLECTION OF THE AUTHOR

CNR's chief architect, formerly with the Canadian Northern Railway.[14] The lodge and cabins, although made almost entirely of wood, were outfitted with every modern convenience, including electricity, telephones, hot and cold running water, and steam heat. Wood-burning fieldstone fireplaces were also installed for those interested in "roughing it." Initially, the lodge could accommodate 350 guests. Like Van Horne with his hotels, Thornton became involved with the Jasper Park Lodge personally, visiting the site during construction, suggesting improvements, and residing there during the regular season. An excellent eighteen-hole golf-course was an added attraction, along with a fleet of chauffeur-driven limousines to transport guests and their luggage between Jasper station and the lodge. The new lodge cost under $1 million to construct, much less than the European-style hotels built by the CPR, and it became popular immediately. The high demand for accommodation resulted in a considerable expansion of facilities in 1927-28.[15]

In response to a suit launched by the City of Vancouver, the CNR began to fulfill

The operation of a railroad, even a branch line, was a labour-intensive enterprise. This photograph taken at Smoky Lake, Alberta, on one of the CNR's secondary east-west lines, c1935, shows some of the personnel required to operate and maintain the railway. From left to right, we see the fireman, the conductor, the station agent, the trainman, engineer, brakeman, and section foreman. They are gathered to set their watches, a necessary step in the days before two-way portable radio communication. By maintaining accurate time, crews knew where a train was likely to be at a particular time, and could minimize the chance of mishaps.

PROVINCIAL ARCHIVES OF ALBERTA/G3740

one of Mackenzie and Mann's unkept promises to obtain land from the city for a hotel. The long-awaited construction of a CN hotel in Vancouver was announced in 1927, and the next year, construction began on a five-hundred-room hotel, estimated to cost $3.5 million, to be named The British Columbia. While it was anticipated that the building would be ready for occupancy by the end of 1930, the effects of the Great Depression meant that construction was suspended that year, and the project was cancelled in 1933. Costs to that point had exceeded $9 million because of problems building a stable foundation and other cost overruns.[16]

Besides augmenting the hotel system and improving the speed of existing rail lines by laying heavier rail, Thornton launched a vigorous campaign of branch line construction in western Canada. While many of the branches in Alberta were extensions of existing lines, intended to serve grain-growing areas better, some were built to cut off projected CPR branch lines. In 1925, the CNR constructed 111 miles of branch lines, as opposed to the CPR's 67. Many of these generated little or no revenue, and while it might appear at first that the branch line construction was foolish, it must be kept in mind that the CNR and CPR were competing to develop agricultural areas and natural resources.

Silk Trains

Competition also extended to more lucrative endeavours. Thornton announced in 1924 that the CNR intended to secure contracts to ship raw silk from Vancouver and Prince Rupert to New York by means of special trains; moreover, the CNR would do it faster than the CPR. This was the sort of traffic that Hays had hoped the GTP would carry on its high-speed main line. While the CPR had already established silk trains before the First World War and held a monopoly in Canada, Thornton did not share the view that the CPR deserved exemption from competition because it was Canada's first transcontinental railway and had been shipping silk before anyone else. The first CNR silk train, made up of eight baggage cars lined with wood to protect the burlap-wrapped bales of silk, and pulled by a fast, oil-burning Pacific locomotive (4–6–2), left Vancouver on July 1, 1925, and took little more than eighty-seven hours to reach New York, beating the CPR's time by almost two hours. Since the silk was perishable, the saving in time was considered advantageous. Silk trains could not make the trip without stops, as the locomotives had to be watered and fueled, the running gear lubricated, and the coaches inspected. To protect the shipments from pilfering or looting in the event of a derailment, at least two CNR police officers were assigned to each train.[17] Melvin Marshall, who began his railroad career with the GTP and worked in the CNR claims department in Edmonton by the mid-1920s, recalls that the silk trains were given priority over all others on the line, and travelled at the maximum speeds possible, stopping only at divisional points except for emergencies. Operators at each station contacted the next divisional point when the silk train passed. Occasionally one would derail, requiring a rapid response by crews. If the train could be re-railed in less than half a day, the shipment continued on its way, but if the delay was longer, then the insurance was paid, as the silk would soon begin to spoil. Claims department personnel would then sell as much as they could of the salvaged shipment to recoup some of the loss.

While silk trains were lucrative, they did not comprise the CNR's only priority freight shipments. The railway obtained contracts for transporting perishable commodities such as lily bulbs, fresh fruit, meat, and fish. In most instances, the CNR was able to better the time taken by its rival.

A CPR silk train with special wood-lined steel boxcars for the silk bales is about to leave Vancouver for its rapid journey east to New York. The gentleman to the left of the locomotive is a CPR police inspector who is making sure that no unauthorized personnel are riding the train.

VANCOUVER PUBLIC LIBRARY/15641

During the height of competition between the CPR and the CNR, branch lines were constructed by one company into the territory of the other. Vegreville had long been a town associated with the CNR, having been moved to its current location following the arrival of the Canadian Northern Railway in 1904. It was not until 1930, the date of this photograph, that CPR rails reached the community. The new line was intended to travel southeast from Vegreville to link with the CPR line at Paradise Valley. But the Great Depression and the established client base of the CNR ensured that Vegreville would only be a minor stopping place at the end of a tiny branch off a secondary CPR line.

PROVINCIAL ARCHIVES OF ALBERTA/A10682

Beatty and Thornton extended the competition between their respective railroads to a personal level. Thornton's behaviour, wide public exposure, and early successes annoyed Beatty, who responded by making disrespectful and inappropriate public remarks about Thornton and the CNR. Thornton managed to make Beatty's life unpleasant by other means. Beatty owned a palatial house in a quiet, exclusive neighbourhood of Montréal, and enjoyed relaxing in his yard in the evening, and then retiring early. Discovering this, Thornton rented the house directly across the street in 1926, and in keeping with his outgoing nature, entertained a near-constant stream of visitors and held many loud parties that generated much noise well into the night, no doubt disturbing Beatty and disrupting his routine.[18]

The CPR Rises to the Challenge

Beatty spent vast sums to upgrade the CPR both to meet and beat the CNR competition. From the end of the First World War, the CPR had begun retiring wooden freight and passenger rolling stock. The new equipment, mainly steel, was heavier and required more powerful locomotives to haul trains of economical length, so progressively larger locomotives, including 2–10–2s, were added to the roster. Beginning in 1929, the CPR also acquired larger oil-burning units called Selkirks, which had a 2–10–4 wheel arrangement with a two-cylinder booster steam engine connected to the second axle of the trailing wheels. This additional power assisted the locomotives when starting, or along grades at slow speed. These massive locomotives were necessary because the grades of the CPR main line through British Columbia were much steeper than those on the Canadian National. The larger locomotives enabled the CPR to operate heavier and longer trains, but at a stiff price. Many of the bridges between Golden and Revelstoke were not designed for such heavy loads, and had to be either strengthened or replaced.

In some instances, such as the Stoney Creek bridge, no alternate route could be found, so the bridge was strengthened while remaining in service. Beginning in 1928, and completed the following year, the work entailed adding a second arch outside the original, joining the two arches, and replacing the lattice deck with a more substantial plate deck. A truss bridge resting on concrete piers replaced the arch over Surprise Creek. As at Stoney Creek, the old bridge remained in use while the new one was constructed, but on January 28, 1929, the Warren deck truss at the east end of the old bridge collapsed as a pusher locomotive passed across it. Besides killing the crew and wrecking the locomotive, the main line remained closed until the new bridge was finished on February 17.[19] Several other bridges on the main line, including the arch across the Salmon (Nahatlatch) River, were replaced at this time as well.

Improvements were also made to other lines, including the Esquimalt and Nanaimo and the Kettle Valley Railways. The long-delayed, thirty-four-mile extension between Kootenay Landing and Procter, continuing west to Nelson, was finally built, both speeding service and cutting costs by eliminating the need to transport trains across Kootenay Lake by barge, and to maintain an expensive fleet of stern-wheeled steamboats.

Several branch lines were constructed in Alberta. While they were intended to develop new areas, most were placed in close proximity to CNR lines in the hope of taking business away, and to forestall further CNR extensions. Like many of the CNR's branch lines, however, most of the CPR's new lines, such as that into Vegreville from Willingdon, or the westward branch to Cremona from the Calgary and Edmonton Railway, did not make money.

Several hotels were also improved. Additional floors were added to the Palliser Hotel in Calgary, and additions were made to the Empress in Victoria. Improvements were sometimes dictated by unforeseen circumstances. A fire on July 3, 1924, destroyed the wooden portions of the Château Lake Louise, and construction of an extension to Painter's masonry wing began almost at once. The new addition opened during the 1925 season. Likewise, a fire in the north wing of the Banff Springs Hotel during 1925 prompted the replacement of the old wooden portions. Work was completed in 1928.

To cater to those interested in more rustic accommodation, and to counter the CNR's Jasper Park Lodge, the CPR constructed several bungalow camps near their lines during the 1920s. The plan consisted of a large main building containing the kitchen and dining-room, with small frame or log cabins, most with fieldstone fireplaces, in the vicinity of the main building. Although purported to be rustic, the CPR's advertising claimed, "No camping was ever like this—a spacious house all your own, hardwood floors, screened windows, a verandah, a clothes cupboard, an

Banff Springs Hotel, Banff, Alta.

The prosperity of the 1920s and the consequent increase in tourism, plus a fire in one of the wooden wings during 1925, encouraged the CPR to complete the modernization and expansion of the Banff Springs Hotel. Finished in 1928, a large brick hotel following Walter Painter's design was the result, pictured here about two years later.

COLLECTION OF THE AUTHOR

insomnia-proof bed, electric light, running water." Bungalow camps, with accommodation ranging from nine to sixty-four, were constructed at Wapta Lake, near the eastern end of the Big Hill; Lake O'Hara, about eight miles south of Hector station; Yoho Valley, about eleven miles north of Field; Moraine Lake, nine miles southeast of Lake Louise; Castle Mountain; and Radium Hot Springs. The camps were accessible by trails or roads in some cases, and smaller tea and rest-houses were built along the way as added convenience, with light meals and sleeping accommodation provided.[20]

The CPR also competed aggressively with the CNR for passengers, each trying to outdo the other in anticipating customer needs. Since they tended to travel during the high season and often in groups, teachers were especially sought after, usually through extensive advertising campaigns in their professional magazines. The competition reached a climax in 1924, when the annual convention of the Canadian Teachers' Federation was to be held at the Empress Hotel in August. The CPR put on a special train to carry participants to Vancouver. As soon as the arrangements were known, the CNR also put on a special train, but at a lower fare. Similarly, each railroad tried to outdo the other in having the fastest transcontinental trains. In general, both systems took about eighty-three hours to travel between Vancouver and Montréal. When the CNR announced that it was slashing its time by four hours, the CPR retaliated by cutting four and a half hours off its schedule. The CNR countered by cutting another hour off. The CPR then tried to match the CNR's time, but to no avail, primarily because trains had to travel through the spiral tunnels at low speed.

The train was the main means of overland passenger transportation during the 1930s. Here the CNR's crack transcontinental passenger train, the Continental, is seen steaming west past Mount Robson, the tallest peak in the Canadian Rocky Mountains, c1930. Although using heavyweight steel rolling stock, the CNR line had gentler grades than the CPR and so could employ lighter motive power.

NATIONAL ARCHIVES OF CANADA/PA49847

By the end of the year, the CPR admitted that it was beaten in the passenger train speed war. After this capitulation, both railroads agreed to revert to the original schedule.[21] The cutthroat competition did neither railroad any good, since such rapid speeds meant greater wear on equipment and track, resulting in losses rather than profits.

The war of attrition between the two railroads did not lead to the bankruptcy of the CNR, as Beatty had anticipated. In 1929, with a large share of the silk traffic and

increased business generally, Thornton reported that for the first time ever, the CNR had earned an operating surplus—$58 million—a much larger profit than that reported by the CPR.[22] Sir Henry's accomplishment was remarkable. In just seven years he had taken a disjointed system of decrepit, near-bankrupt railways and transformed them into a cohesive, money-making competitor to the CPR. Although publicly owned, the CNR did not receive unlimited funds from the dominion government. Nevertheless, neither railroad was making a profit on passenger service or hotels, and both concerns were mounting heavy debts by building miles of branch lines of doubtful return.

Like the CPR, the Canadian National prepared special observation cars to enable patrons to see more of the mountain scenery along the route. Although open at the ends, the cars were fully roofed. The bars along the open sections, to prevent individuals leaning too far outside, led to this type of car being referred to by railroad personnel as hayracks. The black bear and her four cubs, disregarding signs to the contrary, are trespassing on railroad property, a dangerous practice, 1928.

COLLECTION OF THE AUTHOR

The Northern Alberta Railways Company

While the giants were busy battling each other, the smaller railways in Alberta and British Columbia were struggling to survive. The Edmonton, Dunvegan and British Columbia and the Central Canada Railways were maintained under the management of the CPR between 1920 and 1926. The general manager was D'Alton Coleman, a CPR vice-president who became the president of the company following the resignation of Sir Edward Beatty. With money from the provincial government, the CPR extended the Central Canada from Peace River to Berwyn and Whitelaw, the latter of which was reached in 1924. And the ED&BC was extended fifteen miles west from Grande Prairie to the new town of Wembley, with the line opening in 1924. In spite of funding from the Alberta government and the CPR's claims to be an efficient railroad operator, the ED&BC and Central Canada continued to operate at a loss. The Alberta deputy minister of railways and telephones, John Callaghan, contended that the CPR was not only unnecessarily bureaucratic, but was skimping on maintenance and quality of construction, allegations that Coleman and the CPR angrily denied.

Meanwhile, the provincial government was managing the Alberta and Great Waterways and the Lacombe and North-Western Railways. In 1921, John Callaghan, who had been the chief engineer of the Pacific Great Eastern under the Foley, Welch and Stewart administration, was hired as new general manager and deputy minister of railways and telephones. Callaghan was a railroader of the same temperament as Van Horne, and by the end of 1921, he had terminated several contracts and fired individuals he thought were slack and inefficient. Not pleased that he had to share Dunvegan Yards with the CPR-run ED&BC, Callaghan hinted that when the lease with the CPR expired, the ED&BC would become more efficient if he were to oversee its operation.

The cold, hard visage of John Callaghan, 1930, general manager of the railroads owned by the Alberta government, and later the first general manager of the Northern Alberta Railways. One of the few individuals untouched by the financial shenanigans affecting the Pacific Great Eastern, Callaghan had his own inimitable style of building and running railways. A confirmed bachelor, Callaghan resided in Edmonton's Macdonald Hotel, preferring that others took care of his domestic needs.

The government built several northerly extensions to the Lacombe and North-Western during the 1920s, adding twelve miles from the end of steel in 1922 to a new town called Hoadley at the terminus. A further extension of twenty-two and a half miles beyond Hoadley was constructed in 1926–27 to another new town named Breton. New, large motive power was purchased for both railways—a Consolidation (2–8–0) for the L&NW and a Decapod (2–10–0) for the A&GW. Although smaller than the CPR's Selkirks, the Decapod wheel arrangement distributed the weight of the boiler over a lengthy area, minimizing the possibility of spreading the rails, while hauling larger trains than the older locomotives inherited from J.D. McArthur.

In 1926, the provincial government chartered a new railway, the Pembina Valley, to build a line from Busby, on the ED&BC, twenty-six and a half miles to the northwest, where a townsite named Barrhead was laid out. Construction could not be completed, however, before a sizeable bridge was built across the Pembina River near Manola. To minimize costs—despite the fact that they were considered an obsolete design—the railroad built two wooden Howe through trusses resting on concrete piers. The line opened in October 1927.

The lease of the ED&BC to the CPR had been extended in 1925, but was terminated in November 1926, when John Callaghan assumed control of it and consolidated the administration and operations of all government-run railways, at considerable savings. His allegations that the CPR had skimped on maintenance were borne out by evidence uncovered after the railway relinquished control of the ED&BC. Callaghan reported that seventy-five bridges required extensive rebuilding, "due to insufficient repairs during previous seasons, and also to the use of jackpine piling driven by the former management [the CPR], this piling, owing to its limited life, requiring extensive renewals in 1927 whenever it had been used."[23] To improve service on the ED&BC and the A&GW, an agreement was reached with the CNR for passenger trains to originate and terminate at its Edmonton station. This was welcome news to the CNR, which was constructing a new station at the end of 100th Street, about where the planned GTP station would have been built.

In 1927 and 1928, the Alberta government purchased seven more Decapod locomotives and three Consolidations, all coal-burners, from the Canadian Locomotive Company of Kingston, both to replace older locomotives and to expand service.

While the consolidation of the A&GW, Central Canada, and ED&BC Railways under one management made sense, the inclusion of the Lacombe and North-Western did not, since it was isolated from the other Alberta government lines, and was wholly dependent upon the CPR for the interchange of traffic. The CPR was also interested in securing the mail contract for the towns along the line, and so made an offer to purchase. After hard negotiations, the CPR paid $1.5 million for the Lacombe and North-Western, recovering $37,000 through the sale of the L&NW Consolidation back to the Alberta and Great Waterways Railway.[24] The CPR promptly began a twenty-mile extension of the line east towards Thorsby. From Lacombe, on the Calgary and Edmonton Railway, the line made a large loop to the northwest, then turned east. An extension to Leduc in 1933 gave the CPR a northern connection, thus closing the loop.

The ED&BC and Central Canada Railways were extended farther in 1928, the former reaching twenty-five miles to Hythe and the latter fifteen miles to Fairview. Although the operation of the lines was becoming more efficient and resulted in more settlement of northern areas, the Alberta government was anxious to sell its remaining railways, so as to minimize its debt load. The CPR was interested, but not if it had to buy the A&GW as part of the deal, and the CNR wanted too many concessions. Premier John Brownlee, standing fast in his resolve that all the lines, including the A&GW, would be sold as a package, suggested that the CPR and CNR purchase the railways jointly. At first reacting with disdain, Sir Henry Thornton later agreed, with some provisos. True to his nature, and concurring with the sentiments of the Alberta government, Thornton insisted that John Callaghan, who had been critical of the CPR when it operated the ED&BC, but who proved repeatedly that he was an honest railroader, remain as general manager. This was agreed to, and a board of directors, consisting of three CPR and three CNR appointees, would oversee the new company. Referring to the arrangement, and making a slight dig at Beatty and the CPR, Sir Henry exclaimed, "The CPR and CNR, when they decide to co-operate, do so as enthusiastically as when they decide to differ and fight one another."[25]

To minimize the confusion caused by the many different names of the component railways, a single name was chosen—the Northern Alberta Railways Company (NAR). The new company was incorporated in June 1929, the parent companies paying more than $26 million for the railroad, and committing themselves to extending lines and expanding service. By the end of the year, construction had begun on two extensions. The former Central Canada line was extended from Fairview to Hines Creek, with construction completed in 1930. A longer extension was built from Hythe to Dawson Creek, B.C., and the first train reached the new town on January 12, 1931. The remains of McArthur's ED&BC had finally reached British Columbia.

Numbers 101 and 102 were the last new steam locomotives purchased by the Northern Alberta Railways. Slightly larger than the older Decapods, they were designed to spread their weight over several small driving wheels, thus distributing stress on the rails and roadbed over a larger surface. It was anticipated that many of the derailments that had bedeviled the older McArthur locomotives could be avoided by this improved design. Number 101 was photographed at Dunvegan Yards, Edmonton, c1935, waiting its next assignment.

PROVINCIAL ARCHIVES OF ALBERTA/A14935

Two additional Decapods, the last new steam locomotives purchased by the NAR, arrived in 1930 from the Canadian Locomotive Company. Although the Great Depression halted further extensions of the NAR, the lines required considerable maintenance, especially the former ED&BC along the south shore of Lesser Slave Lake, which frequently flooded and washed out the line. The NAR continued to operate during the 1930s with only minor improvements to the infrastructure.

The Pacific Great Eastern

The Pacific Great Eastern (PGE) did not fare as well. Although operated by the government of British Columbia, it had little money to continue with construction. During the mid-1920s, several proposals were made for completing the line to Prince George, and then building northeast to connect with the ED&BC. But limited funding and other projects that received higher priority from the B.C. government prevented these new developments from taking place. It was rumoured that Sir Henry Thornton and the CNR showed interest in buying the railroad in 1928, but no serious offer was made. The CNR had a much better route to Vancouver anyway. That same year, the PGE's southern line, from North Vancouver to Whytecliff, was abandoned, since there was little traffic and few employees would be affected. Traffic on the northern line increased during the 1930s, largely through the opening of more mines along the route, and the increased revenue prompted the provincial government to resume construction north from Quesnel to Prince George. Although he was managing several railways in Alberta, John Callaghan was also hired by the PGE to advise

156

on the route the line should take. He reported that construction would be much easier if the line were moved several miles east of Quesnel. After much dithering, the provincial government decided in September 1931 to proceed with the extension if the dominion government would underwrite half the cost. Prime Minister Bennett agreed to this, but further political wrangling in British Columbia and a provincial election delayed the start of construction. Although the revenues of the PGE continued to increase, with an operating surplus of more than $73,000 in 1934, the financial state of the dominion government grew worse, and Prime Minister Bennett withdrew his government's offer of assistance. Without this money, the B.C. government concluded that the cost of extending the line to Prince George was too expensive, and it would be many years after the Second World War before "the railway with a personality" (an oblique reference to the many trials and tribulations of the line and the people associated with it) reached Prince George and linked with the NAR at Dawson Creek.[26]

The Final Showdown

The tough competition between the CPR and CNR ended, at least temporarily, due to the effects of the Great Depression and a change in the dominion government. Even before the election of 1930, Sir Henry Thornton had suffered a personal setback in the form of a mild heart attack, and his problems and those of the CNR were made worse by the election of R.B. Bennett and the Conservatives. Bennett, who had been involved in Alberta politics and contributed to the downfall of the Rutherford administration, had also been a corporate lawyer for the CPR. Popular sentiment was that Bennett would hand the CNR over to his old pal and fellow corporate lawyer Edward Beatty. At first, Bennett and his minister of transport, R.J. Manion, hotly denied the possibility, but at the same time it was made clear that the Conservatives did not favour government ownership of corporations such as railroads. Trying desperately to accommodate Bennett and Manion, Thornton was as cordial to the Conservatives as he had been to the Liberals. The financial picture became dismal, however, and Thornton instituted a series of cutbacks, including halting the construction of branch lines and cancelling many passenger trains, such as the transcontinental Confederation, a train run in addition to the Continental. Resisting mass layoffs, Thornton met instead with many workers and urged them to agree to lower wages, thus ensuring that more people would remain employed. His tactics, while greatly appreciated by his staff, were regarded dubiously by many Conservatives, and in November 1931 the government established a royal commission to investigate railways and transportation in Canada. A select standing committee on government-owned railways and shipping also investigated Thornton and the CNR. Perhaps thinking he could intercede on Beatty's side in the feud between the two railways,

"Another CPR wreck," or so claimed Bob Edwards, editor of the Calgary *Eye Opener*, referring to Prime Minister Richard Bedford Bennett, formerly the general solicitor for the CPR, pictured here in 1931. Hailing from New Brunswick, Bennett had been a school teacher before heading west to become a lawyer and politician. He tried his hand at provincial politics in Alberta, becoming leader of the Opposition, and playing a major role in the fall of the Rutherford administration.

Ambitious, he entered federal politics, where he defeated the Liberal Mackenzie King in 1930. Like John Callaghan, Bennett was a confirmed bachelor, who made his residence in a railway hotel, the CPR's Palliser in Calgary. His close association with the CPR prompted many citizens to conclude that he would have few qualms in handing the CNR over to the CPR, either free, or at fire-sale prices.

CITY OF EDMONTON
ARCHIVES/EA–43–39

Epitomizing the fear that Bennett would forsake the CNR, *Winnipeg Free Press* political cartoonist Arch Dale compared Bennett and Beatty to the Walrus and the Carpenter, fictitious characters in Lewis Carroll's *Through the Looking Glass*. Indeed, the final verse of the poem quoted in the cartoon indicates the conjected fate of the CNR: "'O Oysters,' said the Carpenter, 'You've had a pleasant run! Shall we be trotting home again?' But answer came there none—And this was scarcely odd, because they'd eaten every one," February 8, 1935.

COURTESY OF THE *WINNIPEG FREE PRESS*

Prime Minister Bennett said that he hoped that the CNR and CPR could co-operate so that both railways might do better financially. Thornton was willing to do so, but much to Bennett's chagrin, Beatty was not.

While Manion and others accused the CNR of mismanagement, by using public money freely to compete with a private concern that was "paying its own way," the fact remains that the CPR had received enormous government handouts and land grants earlier on, and the CNR and its predecessor companies had received much less. And the CPR was also in rocky financial shape. By 1931, Beatty had increased the railroad's funded debt by $133 million and had added largely useless branch lines that enlarged the CPR's fixed charges to $22 million a year.[27] As chairman of the board as well as president, Beatty did not tolerate much criticism of his initiatives, and fortunately for him, the CPR was not under government scrutiny. Beatty believed that the CPR should once again become the dominant railroad in Canada, taking over the profitable parts of the CNR and amalgamating them into one large concern. This view was not popular with many people in western Canada, however, some of

THE COMING FEAST?

The Great Depression threw thousands of individuals out of work. Although blamed for much of the general suffering, Bennett did little initially to alleviate such personal hardship. In many instances, men searching desperately for employment would travel across the country illegally on freight trains. The railroads discouraged hobos and transients from riding freights, as the practice is extremely dangerous. This photograph, showing several men travelling on top of freightcars in 1932, was taken on the CPR at Hope, a commodity that became scarce during the Depression. Nevertheless, the kindness of many railroad people alleviated the hardships of a transient life. Steve Hunka, the son of a CNR section foreman, recalls his mother bringing sandwiches and water to the back door of the Three Hills, Alberta, section house to feed anyone who came by and asked for food. The prevalent attitude was that if one were lucky enough to have plenty, then it should be shared with those who were less fortunate.

whom blamed the CPR for their personal misfortunes. As a resident of Alberta himself, Bennett eventually tried to distance himself from Beatty.

The degree to which the royal commission and the House standing committee investigated the CNR and Sir Henry Thornton approached the level of an inquisition. Officials scrutinized everything from motive power and branch lines to the purchase of wild strawberry preserves from Québec farmers. But Thornton was able to defend himself well when attacked by committee members. When criticized for spending the surplus of 1929 on new rolling stock, when he should have been anticipating an economic downturn, for example, Thornton replied:

If money had been plentiful, this scene would likely have not occurred. It is the summer of 1937 and Castor, Alberta, has lost its station to fire. Instead of building a new station, a less-expensive alternative for the CPR was to move the station at Loyalist along the line to Castor. Although a large station had been built at Loyalist in 1918, the town did not grow as anticipated, so the station was jacked up and slid on a wooden frame onto flatcars, and then moved to Castor.

GLENBOW ARCHIVES/NA–3685–18

The railway had one very large problem on its hands, and that is it had to deal with a large amount of wooden-underframe freight cars [inherited from predecessor companies] which were rapidly becoming obsolete and would be shortly refused in inter-change with other railways. That is a problem which has been concerning us ever since January 1923 ... how we were going to replace this equipment without placing too great a burden on capital expenditures in any one year.[28]

Criticized severely for competing with the CPR hotels, Thornton reminded the committee that he had inherited many hotels and that to prevent them from losing even more money, he had to make some effort to compete, and added that if he had had his way, the CNR would not have had any hotels at all. In an action typical of the meanness for which the Bennett government became notorious, Robert Manion hinted that the CNR was not ruthless enough in eliminating jobs, and was retaining workers simply to give them employment. Edward Beatty echoed similar sentiments: "Reductions in staff were not, in the case of that company [CNR], considered advisable and that the Government system would maintain men in employment at the public expense under conditions which demand measures of retrenchment in the case of a commercial corporation." Beatty's comments were unfair, as he minimized job loss in the CPR by imposing wage cuts, the same method used by the CNR.[29] In rebuttal, Thornton pointed out that eliminating too many workers would interfere not only with the daily operations of the railway, but would impede the training of new workers when required. In spite of the responses, Bennett and the Conservatives pressed hard for Sir Henry Thornton's resignation. Attacked scurrilously by members of the standing committee and the royal commission, a dispirited and ill Thornton resigned in July 1932. He died the following March of cancer. Though Beatty and the Conservative government did their best to paint him as a villain, many thought otherwise, and perhaps the greatest testament to Sir Henry's accomplishments were the bronze memorial plaques placed on several stations across Canada by CNR employees.

Samuel J. Hungerford, a former Canadian Northern machinist who had risen through the ranks, became acting president after Thornton's resignation. As vice-president, Hungerford had been largely responsible for the CNR's investigations of innovative types of motive power, namely the diesel-electric system and small self-propelled vehicles. The dominion government emasculated the presidential position, however, and Bennett made it clear that he wished to divest the government of the CNR so as to concentrate on the elimination of the accumulated public debt.

One of the royal commission's significant findings was that the CNR and CPR should co-operate as much as possible. And as a result of the commission's recommendations, Parliament passed the Canadian National–Canadian Pacific Act in 1933, establishing a board of trustees to oversee the CNR and to ensure the prudent spending of public funds: "The policy of the Trustees must, of necessity, continue to be one of rigid economy, consistent with safe operations and service to the public."[30] The three-person board was headed by Justice C.P. Fullerton, a man with no experience of railways except in his former position as the chairman of the Board of Railway Commissioners. The board of trustees along with three CPR directors formed a joint executive committee to investigate ways in which the two systems could co-operate. Among the first recommendations were suggestions to abandon lightly used branch lines, especially those that duplicated other lines, and to construct any new branch lines as joint ventures. Although Manion and Bennett greeted the recommendations with much fanfare, Beatty was not pleased: "Control by a tribunal constituted as proposed should not be imposed upon any privately owned railway company operating in competition with the Government railways."[31] Later, Beatty cast further aspersions on the act, and returned to his old argument that the CNR should be amalgamated with the CPR: "No scheme of co-operation between competing companies, however far it may be pursued, will effect these essential economies without risk to the integrity of one property or the other and corresponding damage to Canadian credit."[32] In consequence of the CPR's reluctance to co-operate under these terms, few existing branch lines were abandoned, few new branch lines were planned, and few of those already under construction were completed. A twenty-five-mile CNR branch line in Alberta, running from Bulwark northeasterly to Airways, was graded during 1931, but no further work occurred. In response to an angry member of Parliament from Alberta, who insisted that the line was necessary to new farmers in the area, both the minister of transport and the prime minister replied that construction would resume shortly.[33] The failure of this to occur reinforced the view of many Albertans that Bennett and the Conservatives did not care much for the needs and wishes of ordinary citizens.

The hotel systems of both railroads had not been profitable for some time, and it was recommended that operations and further construction be consolidated where possible. Under the act, construction resumed in 1935 on the long-dormant CNR hotel in Vancouver. Showing its age, the CPR's Hotel Vancouver was due for replacement, so the project was an ideal candidate for co-operation. Both railroads provided money, and the new Hotel Vancouver was finished in 1939 and operated jointly. Also under the auspices of the CNR-CPR Act, the Patricia Bay line on Vancouver Island was abandoned in 1935, as was part of the Alberta Coal branch from Foothills to Lovett. The following year, a remaining portion of the old Canadian Northern main line from Peace River Junction to Darson Junction was abandoned as well. Although the line carried holidayers to several popular lakes, the traffic was too light to justify continued operations. Plans to pool passenger and freight service on most lines was dismissed as impractical because of disparities among rates and because considerable money would have to be spent to make facilities compatible for different equipment. Nevertheless, several connections were constructed between the main lines of the two railways in the Thompson and Fraser Canyons to enable traffic to be exchanged or diverted from one line to the other.

Following the desires of the Conservatives to dismember the CNR and sell off the pieces, the board of trustees sold the CNR radio network, established for its passenger trains and hotels, to the dominion government at a great loss. The network comprised the basis of what would become the Canadian Broadcasting Corporation. Believing that the minister of transport was privatizing the CNR too slowly, Edward Beatty launched his own campaign to influence public opinion, much to the disapproval of Bennett and Manion. Although Beatty did not enjoy public appearances, he forced himself to speak before various organizations. He also wrote long harangues, excerpts of which were printed in newspapers, condemning the public ownership of railways, criticizing the questions asked of the CPR by Manion, and often ignoring or changing facts. Besides claiming that the CPR had paid its way solely through entrepreneurial initiative, conveniently forgetting the enormous land grants given to the railroad, some of Beatty's claims were so incredible as to be outrageous. In the manner of a mediocre businessman beaten by a competitor, Beatty portrayed the CPR as a victim: "It [the CPR] saw territory, which it had nursed and developed, invaded by a competitor with all the resources of the nation behind it … It saw novel and extraordinary publicity methods used to divert traffic from it."[34] Beatty failed to mention the CPR's branch line running from Edmonton to Lloydminster, completed in 1929, and the branch from Willingdon to Vegreville, completed in 1930, both in territory first occupied and developed by the Canadian Northern Railway. Critical of the dominion government's imposed compulsory co-operation, Beatty contended that the best future for Canadian railways was to have them unified, under his and the CPR's governance. While reflecting a popular and deep-seated distrust of public ownership, Beatty's speeches and newspaper articles were largely ineffective in convincing citizens that public ownership of a competitive railway system was bad for the country. To many, the CPR was seen as a corporation desiring to become a monopoly, and the bad situation referred to by Beatty would simply be replaced by another and possibly worse one—total ownership by one corporation controlled by comparatively few individuals. In response to Beatty's ideas of unification, Hungerford remarked:

> The consolidation of practically all railways into one system would inevitably result in a serious decline in the energy, initiative, and enthusiasm of the officers and employees which is now at a remarkably high level and which has been largely developed and sustained by vigorous competition … Competition has very largely created the existing morale of the staff and only competition can maintain it.[35]

The Draconian plans for the CNR came to an abrupt end following the election of October 1935, in which the Conservatives were soundly defeated. Through his ill-conceived and seemingly uncaring policies, Bennett was reviled by many. Insults and sometimes objects were often hurled at him whenever he was seen in public. A hurt and hated man, Bennett left Canada permanently in 1938.

The return of Mackenzie King meant that the Canadian taxpayer would not make a gift of the CNR to the CPR. The new minister of transport was C.D. Howe, an experienced civil engineer. While he urged the continuation of CNR-CPR co-operation, he fought to eliminate the partisan board of trustees, finally having to resort to legislation, as Justice Fullerton refused to leave voluntarily. Following the removal of the board of trustees, Samuel Hungerford was confirmed as president and also as chairman of the new board. Although lacking Sir Henry Thornton's brashness, Hungerford was capable of both running the CNR and standing up to Edward Beatty, who was knighted in 1935.

With an increased office staff, Sir Edward continued his campaign against the public ownership of the CNR, but in deference to Mackenzie King and the Liberal government, who were not friendly to the CPR, he backtracked on his negative views of the CNR-CPR Act, stating, "In periods of intense competition the railways do fight—sometimes rather against their wishes; most of the time—especially in recent years—we are more interested in how to co-operate than how to score against each other."[36]

While not acquiescent like David Hanna, S.J. Hungerford was not as competitive as Sir Henry Thornton, and simply ignored most of Beatty's accusations and criticisms. To Beatty's frustration, the CNR's financial picture began to improve, and he eventually stopped attacking the railway in public, diverting his vitriol instead to other publicly funded modes of transportation. In the 1937 report to shareholders, he noted:

> The Canadian railways, which are subject to strict regulation, are still exposed to the unrestrained competition of other forms of transport both by highway and water. The commercial motor vehicle continues to be subsidized jointly by the taxpayers at large and the owners of private pleasure vehicles. Shipping, particularly on the Great Lakes and connecting waterways, is still permitted to operate with no regulation of rates and without any contribution to the tremendous capital and maintenance cost of these waterways.[37]

The sparring with Thornton and the CNR had taken its toll on Sir Edward's health, contributing to his resignation as president in 1942 and his death of a stroke on March 23, 1943, ten years and nine days after the death of Sir Henry Thornton.

Modernization

There were some improvements to railroads in Alberta and British Columbia during the 1930s, and both the CNR and the CPR investigated new ways of making rail transportation more efficient. The difficulty of pulling trains through grades along the main line in the Rocky and Selkirk Mountains continued to be a problem for the CPR. Although the Selkirk locomotives helped, they were not cost-effective because they consumed large quantities of fuel and water. A more efficient engine would reduce costs. While the CPR's chief of motive power, Henry Bowen, was unwilling to use different forms of motive power, such as electric and diesel locomotives, he encouraged experimentation with steam. In 1930, the motive power group came up with an innovative locomotive with the Selkirk wheel arrangement. Number 8000 used a boiler encompassing three different pressure vessels. Steam at 250 psi operated two outer cylinders and the booster engine, as in other Selkirks. High-pressure steam at 850 psi powered a third cylinder, located between the main cylinders. And a system of pipes charged with steam at the extreme pressure of 1,600 psi transferred heat between the low- and high-pressure vessels in the boiler. Constructed as an oil burner, 8000 was assigned to run between Field and Revelstoke. It underwent exten-

The innovative and unusual looking Number 8000, the Selkirk with three cylinders and a three-part boiler, 1934. Seen at Calgary's Ogden Shops shortly after major modifications, 8000 was more efficient than the other Selkirks, but it was not liked by crews because it handled differently from other locomotives, and there was fear that the extremely high boiler pressure would result in a fatal explosion. The curved pipe directly behind the smokestack is a smoke deflector that was moved into position when the locomotive was passing through tunnels. The deflector directed smoke above the locomotive, so that visibility from the cab would not be obscured.

COLLECTION OF THE AUTHOR

It is the morning of October 28, 1933, and the British visitor, locomotive 6100 and a standard consist of the London, Midland and Scottish Railway's "Royal Scot," is being serviced at the CPR's North Bend, B.C., station. To comply with North American operating practices, the 6100 was equipped with an electric headlight and a standard brass bell, two items not used in British railways at that time. While the 6100 was a most efficient locomotive, consuming special anthracite coal, CPR officials were more impressed with the design of the passenger cars, whose curved sides and tops can be seen clearly.

PROVINCIAL ARCHIVES OF ALBERTA/A3999

sive modifications during 1933 and was returned to service in 1934. Although more efficient than the standard Selkirks, 8000, like the long-departed Malléts, was not regarded favourably by most engineers and maintenance personnel. It required special procedures to operate and maintain, was unreliable in service, and some feared that the extremely high pressures might lead to a boiler explosion. The locomotive was withdrawn from service in 1937, when a major overhaul came due, and no further examples were produced.

A more successful endeavour was the streamlining of new locomotives. In 1933, the London, Midland and Scottish Railway sent its premier passenger train, The Royal Scot, to North America as part of the Chicago World's Fair. The train made a special transcontinental excursion, going west through the United States and return-

ing in Canada by way of the CPR main line. What impressed CPR officials most about the train were the curved sides and roofs of the passenger cars, and these features were consequently incorporated into light-weight CPR passenger cars built in conjunction with new semi-streamlined locomotives. The CPR had made simple attempts at streamlining as early as the 1890s, with the rounding of locomotive cabs and other exposed parts. Beginning in 1936, new locomotives were equipped with sheet-metal cowling that enclosed the exposed parts attached to the boiler to create rounded surfaces that would diminish wind resistance. To facilitate servicing, the cowling did not completely enclose high-maintenance components such as air and water pumps—hence the designation, semi-streamlined.

Semi-streamlining was applied with good effect to a new high-speed passenger

The royal train of 1901, carrying the Duke and Duchess of York, the subsequent King George V and Queen Mary. The eastbound consist has just left Field and is about to negotiate the heavy grade of the Big Hill. Containing several extra-heavy coaches, outfitted especially for the royal entourage, two midtrain helpers and a pusher locomotive were employed to ensure that the train reached the summit of the Kicking Horse Pass without incident.

WHYTE MUSEUM OF THE CANADIAN ROCKIES/V701/LC–26

Freshly polished and almost brand-new, Jubilee 3001, sporting Chinook name plates near the front of the smokebox, is seen with its train of curved-sided rolling stock at Calgary in 1936. The semi-streamlining gave the locomotive a modern appearance for the time, and the large driving wheels enabled it to reach speeds in excess of sixty miles an hour. The skirting along the front, besides deflecting the wind, covered the front coupler and the bell. The vertical slits in the front, near the top of the smokebox, permit air to enter the shroud and pass by the smokestack, helping to lift the smoke clear of the cab.

PROVINCIAL ARCHIVES OF BRITISH COLUMBIA/F–5983

locomotive with a 4–4–4 wheel arrangement. Named Jubilee, in honour of the fiftieth anniversary of transcontinental passenger service on the CPR, these diminutive loco-motives were equipped with large, eighty-inch-diameter driving wheels with low-friction roller bearings, and a boiler that operated at 300 psi, higher than any other CPR locomotive except the 8000.[38] Intended for high-speed runs between cities, num-ber 3001 was assigned in September 1936 to a new passenger express running between Edmonton and Calgary, called the Chinook, after the warm dry winds encountered in the region. Stylized name plates were mounted on the sides of the boiler jacket near the front of the smokebox, and with the new curved-sided cars, the train cut almost an hour off the travel time of regular trains.

The CNR introduced streamlining to some of its locomotives as well. In 1936, five 4–8–4s, or Northerns, were constructed with full streamlining. The full cowling also incorporated smoke deflectors designed by the National Research Council of Canada to prevent smoke from obscuring the engineer's vision. While a later order, delivered in 1936, also included roller bearings, full streamlining was not applied to subsequent

It is June 1, 1939, and the royal train is making its way to eastern Canada along the Canadian National. Mountain type 6047 is about to depart Jasper station on its way to Edmonton. The individuals in the foreground with the armbands are personnel authorized to help with the royal train.

Erected in honour of the royal visit of 1939, a ceremonial arch greeted the King and Queen and wished them well as they left Edmonton. Prophetically, the farewell also signalled the end of peace and the end of railroading in western Canada as it had been known.

CITY OF EDMONTON ARCHIVES/ EA–160–832

locomotives, as it interfered with routine maintenance. The large streamlined Northerns were used to pull long, heavy passenger trains, and they were employed rarely in western Canada.[39] The CNR achieved more promising results with diesel-electric locomotives, which began to displace the venerable steam locomotive during the late 1930s.

By 1939, after several years of co-operation, the intense rivalry between the CNR and CPR had ebbed, and both railways accommodated the first visit to Canada by a reigning monarch. There had been a number of royal visits to Canada previously, with railroads figuring prominently in most of them. In 1901, the Duke of York, later to become King George V, travelled across Canada on the Canadian Pacific, and even rode on the pilot of a locomotive past Glacier House and the Loops. The CPR also had the honour of pulling the royal train carrying King George VI and Queen Elizabeth west to Vancouver in 1939. Two Hudson locomotives (a 4–6–4 wheel arrangement), Numbers 2850 and 2851, headed the train. The King was so impressed with how well the locomotives performed that he permitted that class to have royal

170

crowns mounted on the running boards, and they soon became known as Royal Hudsons.

The CNR took charge of the royal train at Vancouver and used a variety of locomotives, mainly Mountains (4–8–2) and Northerns, to pull the train east. Although both King George and Queen Elizabeth spent time riding in the cabs of some of the CNR locomotives, none received the honour bestowed upon the one class of CPR Hudsons. The co-operation between the two railroads in handling the royal train of 1939 signified the end of an era characterized by divisive competition. By the end of the year, Canada was at war with Germany, and unlike the situation during the First World War, Canada's railways were to become crucial to the war effort. As Sir Edward Beatty had feared in 1937, the development and proliferation of other modes of transportation, accelerated by the war, would irrevocably alter the role of railways in western Canada.

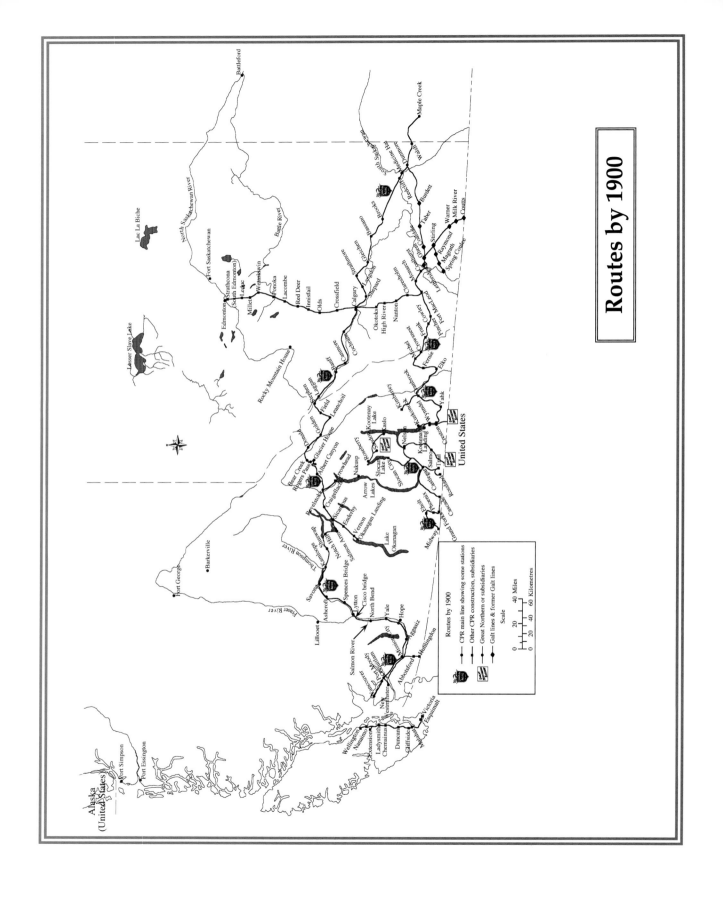

Routes by 1900

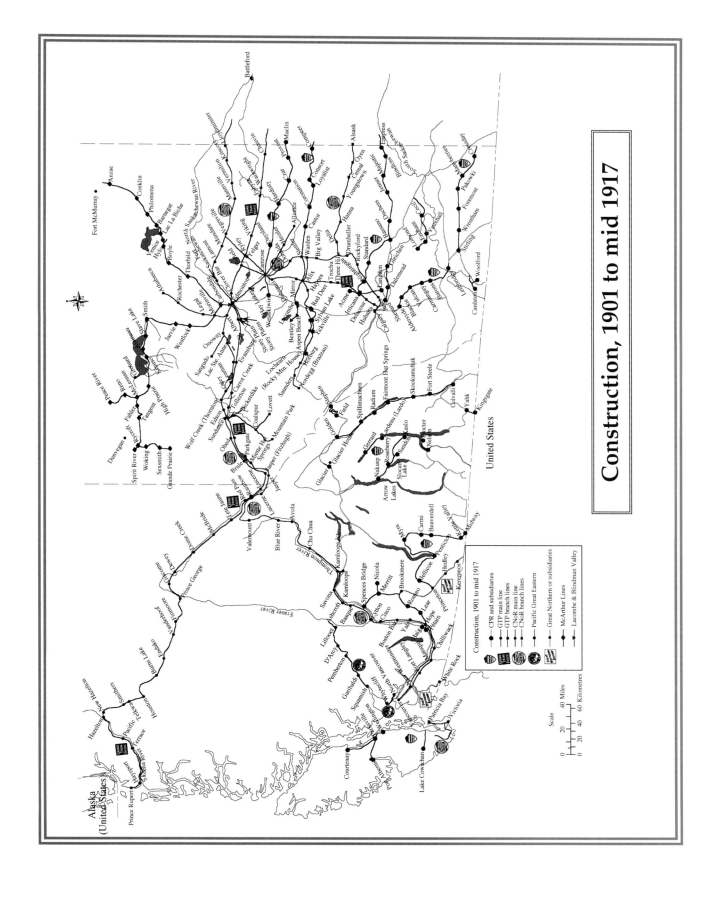

Construction, 1901 to mid 1917

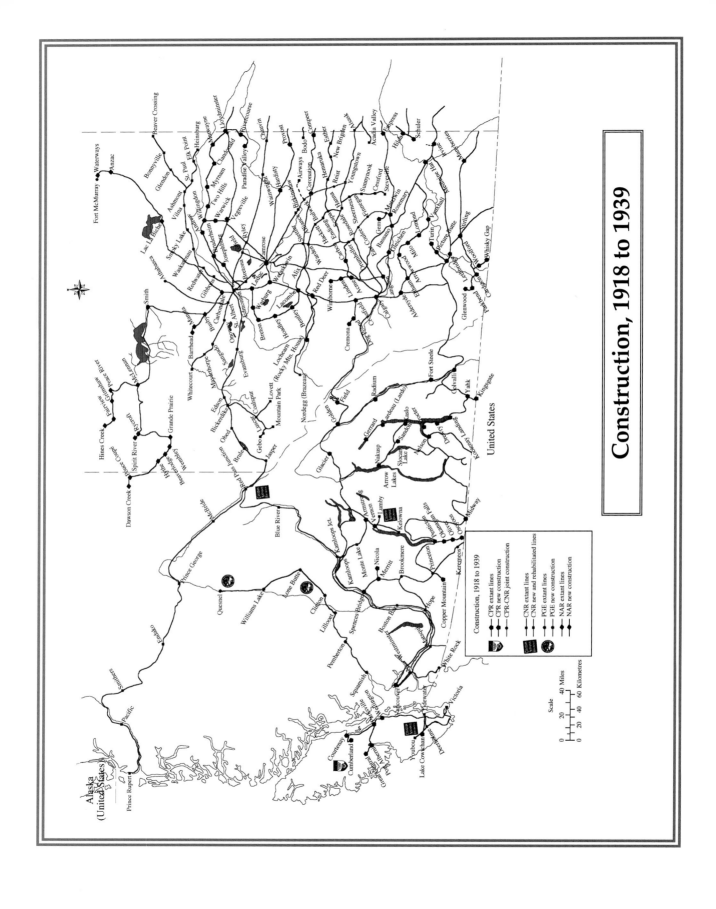

Construction, 1918 to 1939

Appendix A. Railroad Charters Granted, 1870–1939

DATE OF CHARTER	OPERATED	CHARTER ISSUED	HEAD OFFICE	FINAL NAME / FIRST NAME	FROM-TO / REMARKS	CHARTER DISSOLVED
1908	N	CA	AB	Alberta and Brazeau River Ry. Co.	Point between Olds and Innisfail, west to Rocky Mountain House via Brazeau River to the GTP	NO
1908	N	CA	BC	Alberta and British Columbia Ry. Co.	U.S. boundary Kootenay River crossing, to Elko, then east to Cowley and Calgary	NO
1909	Y	AB	AB	Alberta and Great Waterways Ry. Co.	Edmonton, Lac La Biche, Fort McMurray. Part of NAR	NO
1910	N	AB	AB	Alberta and Saskatchewan Central Ry. Lines Co.	Point NE of Sibbald to Edmonton, and another branch to the junction of the Brazeau and Saskatchewan Rivers	NO
1901	Y	CA	AB	Alberta Central Railway Co.	Point east of Red Deer to Rocky Mountain House. Also lines to: Yellowhead Pass, Saskatoon, Moose Jaw, Fort Churchill	
					Red Deer to Lochearn (Rocky Mountain House) built. Leased to CPR, 1912, for 999 years. Joint section operated with CNoR subsidiary	NO
1911	N	CA	AB	Alberta Interurban Ry. Co.	Various electric lines radiating from Calgary and Lethbridge	NO
1911	N	AB	AB	Alberta Metropolitan Ry. Co.	Calgary to points east	NO
1909	Y	AB	AB	Alberta Midland Ry. Co.	Vermilion to Bruderheim; Morinville to eastern boundary of Alberta; Edmonton to Peace River; Strathcona to Lethbridge via Calgary	
					Amalgamated with CNoR, 1909. CNoR authorized to build lines of charter, 1912	NO
1906	N	AB	AB	Alberta North Western Ry. Co.	Edmonton to western boundary of Alberta via Peace River. Also from Edmonton to Medicine Hat	NO
1906	N	AB	AB	Alberta Pacific Ry. Co	Oil Creek to Pincher on the CPR via Waterton Lakes	
				Alberta Oil, Coal and Wheat Ry. Co.	Name changed to Pincher Creek, Cardston and Montana Ry. Co., 1909. Name changed to Alberta Pacific Ry. Co., 1910. Amalgamated with Western Dominion Ry., 1914	NO
1884	Y	CA	AB	Alberta Ry. and Coal Co.	Medicine Hat to: mines; Fort McLeod; Cardston; Hope, B.C. via Crow's Nest Pass; Lethbridge to U.S. border	
					Built as three-foot narrow gauge. Leased to CPR, 1893, and gauge widened. Amalgamated into the Alberta Ry. and Irrigation Co., 1904	NO
1904	Y	CA	AB	Alberta Ry. and Irrigation Co.	Lethbridge to Coutts; Stirling to Glenwood; Raley to Whiskey Gap. All lines in Alberta	
					Amalgamated: Alberta Ry. and Coal Co.; St. Mary's River Ry. Co.; Canadian North West Irrigation Co.	NO
1894	N	CA	AB	Alberta Southern Ry. Co. #1	Calgary to U.S. boundary by Milk River	NO
1906	N	AB	AB	Alberta Southern Ry. Co. #2	Lethbridge to B.C. via Crow's Nest Pass; Calgary	NO
1910	N	AB	AB	Alberta Western Ry. Co.	South from CPR, midway between Exshaw and Morley to B.C.	NO
1910	N	CA	AB	Alberta, Peace River and Eastern Ry. Co.	Cardston to Peace River via Pincher Creek and Cochrane. Peace River to Fort Churchill via Fort McMurray. Branch to Edmonton	NO
1910	N	AB	AB	Alberta–Hudson Bay Ry. Co	East and west of High River to ends of Alberta	
				High River and Hudson Bay Ry. Co.	Name changed, 1917	NO
1907	N	CA	BC	Alsek and Yukon Ry. Co.	Pleasant Camp, B.C., north through Yukon to Alaska border	NO
1905	N	CA	AB	Anthracite Coal Ry. Co.	Lethbridge to surrounding coal mines	NO
1898	N	BC	BC	Arrowhead and Kootenay Ry. Co.	Arrowhead to north end of Kootenay Lake. Was to be leased by the CPR, 1899	YES

Date of Charter	Operated	Charter Issued	Head Office	Final Name / First Name	From-To / Remarks	Charter Dissolved
1896	N	BC	BC	Ashcroft and Cariboo Ry. Co.	Either Ashcroft or Kamloops to Port Simpson via Barkerville	YES
1889	N	CA	AB	Assiniboia, Edmonton and Unjiga Ry. Co.	Swift Current, Saskatchewan, to Edmonton and Peace River	NO
1915	N	AB	AB	Athabasca and Fort Vermilion Ry. Co.	Athabasca to Fort Vermilion	NO
1913	N	CA	AB	Athabasca and Grande Prairie Ry. Co.	Jct. of Solomon and Athabasca Rivers to Grande Prairie and Dunvegan	NO
1905	N	CA	AB	Athabasca Ry. Co.	Edmonton to Fort Smith via Lac La Biche	NO
1911	N	AB	AB	Athabasca Valley Ry. Co.	Edmonton to Fort Assiniboine	NO
1905	N	CA	AB	Athabaska Northern Ry. Co.	Edmonton to Athabaska Landing (Athabasca)	NO
1914	N	CA	BC	Atlin Ry. Co.	Atlin to Alaska boundary at Taku River	NO
1899	N	BC	BC	Atlin Short Line Ry. and Navigation Co.	Taku Arm to Atlintoo River	YES
1897	N	BC	BC	Barkerville, Ashcroft and Kamloops Ry. Co.	Ashcroft or Kamloops to Barkerville	YES
1911	N	AB	AB	Bassano and Bow Valley Ry. Co.	Bassano to points both north and south	NO
1897	Y	BC	BC	Bedlington and Nelson Ry. Co.	Bedlington to Nelson	
					Built from Port Hill to Wilkes, and owned and operated by Kootenay Ry. and Navigation Co., a subsidiary of Great Northern Ry. Abandoned and track lifted in 1916.	NO
1893	N	BC	BC	Bedlington and West Kootenay Ry. Co.	Bedlington to Kootenay Lake and vicinity	YES
1906	N	BC	BC	Bella Coola and Fraser Lake Ry. Co.	Mouth of Bella Coola River to Fort George (Prince George)	YES
1907	N	BC	BC	Bentinck Arm and Quesnel Ry. Co.	Jct. of Rau Shuswap and south fork of Fraser River to Bella Coola	YES
1899	N	BC	BC	Big Bend Transportation Co.	Several small tramways along the Columbia River in conjunction with river traffic	NO
1904	N	BC	BC	Boundary, Kamloops and Cariboo Central Ry. Co.	Midway to Kamloops via Thompson River; Hazelton and the Yukon River	NO
1886	N	CA	AB	Bow River Coal Mine Ry. and Transportation Co.	Near Medicine Hat to various mining areas	NO
1908	N	AB	AB	Bow River Collieries Ry. Co.	Bow City to: Cassils, Coutts, Taber	NO
1910	N	BC	BC	British Columbia and Alaska Ry. Co.	Lytton to: Fort George, then to Teslin Lake; Vancouver	YES
1911	N	CA	BC	British Columbia and Central Canada Ry. Co.	Mouth of Nass River to Peace River, then to Fort Churchill	NO
1911	N	CA	BC	British Columbia and Dawson Ry. Co.	Lytton to Dawson City, Ashcroft to Fraser River, and Lillooet to Vancouver	NO
1904	N	CA	BC	British Columbia and Manitoba Ry. Co.	Crawford Bay on Kootenay Lake to Hartney, Manitoba, via Fort Steele and Lethbridge	NO
1911	N	CA	BC	British Columbia and White River Ry. Co.	U.S. boundary at Bear Creek, B.C., to the White River.	NO
1906	N	BC	BC	British Columbia Central Ry. Co.	Osoyoos to Fort George	YES
1897	Y	BC	BC	British Columbia Electric Ry. Co.	Urban and Interurban lines in and around Vancouver and Victoria	NO
1906	N	BC	BC	British Columbia Northern and Alaska Ry. Co.	Vancouver to northern boundary of B.C.	YES
1903	N	BC	BC	British Columbia Northern and Mackenzie Valley Ry. Co.	Nasoga Gulf to northern boundary of B.C.	YES
1888	Y	BC	BC	British Columbia Southern Ry. Co.	Jct. of Summit and Michel Creeks to Cranbrook and lower Kootenay River. Also line to Nelson, Hope, and New Westminster.	NO
				Crow's Nest and Kootenay Lake Ry.	Lines leased to CPR, some in perpetuity	
1897	N	BC	BC	British Columbia Yukon Ry. Co.	Lynn Canal to northern boundary. Acquired by White Pass and Yukon Ry. Co.	NO
1897	N	CA	BC	British Yukon Ry. Co.	Lynn Canal via White Pass to Selkirk, Yukon	
				British Yukon Mining, Trading and Transportation Co.	Stock acquired by White Pass and Yukon Ry. Co.	NO
1913	N	AB	AB	Brule Lake Ry. Co.	GTP at Brule Lake, southeasterly towards coal areas	NO
1915	N	CA	AB	Brule, Grande Prairie and Peace River Ry. Co.	GTP at Brule Lake, to Grande Prairie, then to anticipated terminus of PGE in the Peace River block in B.C.	NO
1891	N	CA	AB	Buffalo Lake and Battleford Ry., Coal and Iron Co.	C&E railway near crossing of Blindman River, then east to Battleford, Saskatchewan	NO
1924	N	AB	AB	Burmis Carbon Ry. Co.	Burmis west to B.C. boundary, and south to the international boundary	NO

DATE OF CHARTER	OPERATED	CHARTER ISSUED	HEAD OFFICE	FINAL NAME / FIRST NAME	FROM-TO / REMARKS	CHARTER DISSOLVED
1891	N	BC	BC	Burrard Inlet and Fraser Valley Ry. Co.	Burrard Inlet southerly to the international boundary, and east towards Chilliwack	YES
1891	N	CA	BC	Burrard Inlet and Westminster Valley Ry. Co.	North shore of Burrard Inlet south to the international boundary	NO
1891	N	BC	BC	Burrard Inlet Ry. and Ferry Co.	North shore of Burrard Inlet to English Bay or Howe Sound.	
					Was to be either a railway or a tramway	YES
1907	N	CA	BC	Burrard, Westminster Boundary Ry. and Navigation Co.	Vancouver to Port Moody, and from Vancouver to Tête Jaune Cache	NO
1890	Y	CA	AB	Calgary and Edmonton Ry. Co.	Calgary to Edmonton and Peace River, and Calgary south to international boundary	
					Leased to CPR for 99 years in 1904. Majority of stock owned by CPR	NO
1906	N	CA	AB	Calgary and Fernie Ry. Co.	Calgary to Fernie via the Kananaskis Pass	NO
1913	N	CA	AB	Calgary and Fort McMurray Ry. Co.	Calgary to Fort Vermilion via Edmonton, Fort McMurray, and Fort Smith	NO
1907	N	AB	AB	Calgary and Knee Hill Ry. Co.	Calgary northeasterly to Kneehills Creek	NO
1918	N	AB	AB	Calgary and South Western Ry. Co.	Calgary to B.C. boundary, and south to Okotoks	NO
1913	N	AB	AB	Calgary Petrol Interurban Ry. Co.	Calgary to points south and southwesterly	NO
1889	N	CA	AB	Calgary, Alberta and Montana Ry. Co.	Calgary to the international boundary via High River and Fort McLeod	NO
1907	N	AB	AB	Calgary, Carbon and Red Deer Ry. Co.	Short lines north of Calgary	NO
1905	N	CA	AB	Calgary, Red Deer and Battleford Ry. Co.	Calgary east to Battleford, Saskatchewan	NO
1911	N	CA	AB	Canadian Inter-Mountain Ry. Co.	Coutts to Fernie via Milk River. Milk River to Estevan, Saskatchewan	NO
1911	Y	BC	BC	Canadian North Eastern Ry. Co.	Stewart to points east; Stewart northeasterly	
				Portland Canal Short Line Co.	Intially owned by Donald Mann. Fourteen miles operated until 1914. Charter resurrected in 1929. Sold to Consolidated Mining and Smelting, 1929	NO
1910	Y	CA	AB	Canadian Northern Alberta Ry. Co.	Edmonton westerly to coalfields near Brazeau	
					Subsidiary of Canadian Northern Ry. Became part of CNR, 1919	NO
1910	Y	BC	BC	Canadian Northern Pacific Ry. Co.	Alberta boundary southwesterly to Vancouver via Fraser River	
					Subsidiary of Canadian Northern. Became part of CNR, 1919. Canadian Northern had to adopt this name in B.C., since another railway company named Canadian Northern had already been granted a charter in B.C.	NO
1892	N	BC	BC	Canadian Northern Ry. Co.	Alberta boundary to northern terminus of the E&N railway on Vancouver Island	
					Company granted charter in B.C. before Mackenzie and Mann's enterprise	YES
1910	Y	AB	AB	Canadian Northern Western Ry. Co.	Edmonton westerly to Rocky Mountain House and coal areas. Edmonton to St. Paul des Métis	NO
					Subsidiary of Canadian Northern. Became part of CNR in 1919	
1889	N	BC	BC	Canadian Western Central Ry. Co.	Alberta boundary to northern terminus of E&N Ry. via Téte Jaune Cache, Barkerville, and Bute Inlet	YES
1909	N	AB	AB	Canadian Western Ry. Co.	CPR Crow's Nest line between Cowley and Pincher, to international boundary. Also north to Calgary and west to Michel, B.C.	NO
1898	N	BC	BC	Canadian Yukon Ry. Co.	Teslin Lake to port on B.C. coast	YES
1898	N	CA	AB	Canadian-Yukon Ry.	Edmonton to Port Simpson	
					Mackenzie and Mann were given contract to construct a portion of the line, but the project was not approved by the Senate. Mackenzie and Mann were compensated eventually	YES
1916	N	AB	AB	Canmore Ry. Co.	Canmore to various mine sites	NO
1908	N	AB	AB	Carbon Hill Ry. Co.	Burmis southwest and southeast to coalfields	NO
1903	N	CA	AB	Cardiff Ry. Co.	NE of Manyberries, west to Frank or Livingston	NO
1890	N	BC	BC	Cariboo Ry. Co.	Ashcroft to Barkerville	YES
1910	N	BC	BC	Cariboo, Barkerville and Willow River Ry. Co.	Eagle Lake to Barkerville	YES

Date of Charter	Operated	Charter Issued	Head Office	Final Name / First Name	From-To / Remarks	Charter Dissolved
1917	N	CA	AB	Cascade Scenic Ry. Co.	Incline railway up Cascade Mountain in Banff National Park	NO
1897	N	BC	BC	Cassiar Central Ry. Co.	Stickeen River to Dease Lake	YES
1913	Y	AB	AB	Central Canada Ry. Co.	ED&BC railway west of McLennan to Peace River	
					Owned by the ED&BC railway. Became part of the NAR	NO
1910	N	AB	AB	Chestermere and Calgary Suburban Ry. Co.	Calgary east to Chestermere Lake	NO
1901	N	BC	BC	Chilkat and Klehini Ry. and Navigation Co.	Confluence of Chilkat and Klehini Rivers northerly towards the Dalton Trail	YES
1891	N	BC	BC	Chilliwack Ry. Co.	CPR at Mission to Chilliwack	YES
1888	N	CA	AB	Chinook Belt and Peace River Ry. Co.	Calgary to Dunvegan via Edmonton	NO
1913	N	AB	AB	Chinook Ry. Co.	CPR at Kipp to mines	NO
1903	N	CA	BC	Coast Yukon Ry. Co.	Kitimat Inlet to Yukon River to Alaska boundary	YES
1901	N	BC	BC	Coast-Kootenay Ry. Co.	Vancouver to Chilliwack, and lines from Chilliwack to Midway and Grand Forks via the Kettle River	YES
1911	N	AB	AB	Cochrane and South Western Ry. Co.	Cochrane southwesterly to B.C. boundary	NO
1890	N	BC	BC	Columbia and Carbonate Mountain Ry. Co.	Point 17 miles up Columbia River, southwesterly to the Spillimacheen River.	YES
1889	Y	BC	BC	Columbia and Kootenay Ry. and Navigation Co.	Outlet of Kootenay Lake to jct. of Kootenay and Columbia Rivers via Selkirk Mountains	
					Leased to CPR, 1980, for 999 years	NO
1883	N	BC	BC	Columbia and Kootenay Ry. and Transportation Co.	Outlet of Kootenay Lake to jct. of Kootenay and Columbia Rivers via Selkirk Mountains	
					Charter purchased by CPR in 1889; line built by CPR	YES
1896	Y	BC	BC	Columbia and Western Ry. Co.	Castlegar to Trail	
				Trail Creek Tramway	Three-foot narrow gauge line. Leased in perpetuity to CPR in 1898 and converted to standard gauge	NO
1900	N	CA	BC	Comox and Cape Scott Ry. Co.	Wellington district, Vancouver Island, to a point in Comox district, then northerly to Cape Scott	YES
1894	Y	BC	BC	Consolidated Ry. Co.	Special	
				Consolidated Ry. and Light Co.	Incorporated to acquire several tramway companies including the Vancouver Electric Ry. Name changed, 1896. Became part of the British Columbia Electric Ry.	NO
1898	N	CA	BC	Cowichan Valley Ry. Co.	Cowichan River, Vancouver Island, to Alberni Canal	NO
1903	N	BC	BC	Cowichan, Alberni and Fort Rupert Ry. Co.	Mill or Cowichan Bay, Vancouver Island, to Fort Rupert	YES
1901	N	BC	BC	Crawford Bay Ry. Co.	Crawford Bay to Kootenay River, opposite Fort Steele	YES
1908	N	BC	BC	Crow's Nest and Northern Ry. Co.	Crow's Nest Pass, along north fork of Michel Creek	YES
1907	N	AB	AB	Crow's Nest and Prairie Electric Ry. Co.	Western end of Crow's Nest Lake easterly to Pincher Creek	NO
1917	N	AB	AB	Crow's Nest and Tent Mountain Ry. Co.	Crow's Nest southerly	NO
1900	N	BC	BC	Crow's Nest Pass Electric Light and Power Co.	Tramways in Fernie and in Kootenay district	NO
1911	N	AB	AB	Crow's Nest Pass Street Ry. Co.	Cowley to Crow's Nest Lake via Lundbreck and Burmis	NO
1901	Y	BC	BC	Crow's Nest Southern Ry. Co.	Newgate on U.S. boundary to Michel	
					Owned by Great Northern Ry. and was an extension of that railway's line from Rexford, Montana. Service discontinued in 1936 and rails removed subsequently	NO
1887	N	BC	BC	Delta Ry. Co.	Ladner's Landing to Popcum	YES
1894	N	BC	BC	Delta, New Westminster and Eastern Ry. Co.	Gulf of Georgia to New Westminster, with branch to Abbotsford	YES
1907	N	AB	AB	Diamond Ry. Co.	Mines in area of Crow's Nest Pass to CPR line	NO
1917	Y	BC	BC	Dolly Varden Ry. Co.	Mines in the vicinity of Alice Arm Abandoned in 1935 and rails removed subsequently	NO
1898	N	BC	BC	Downie Creek Ry. Co.	Albert Canyon to Revelstoke via Illecillewaet and Columbia Rivers and Downie Creek	YES
1907	N	BC	BC	East Kootenay Logging Ry. Co.	Crow's Nest to Rock Creek	NO

DATE OF CHARTER	OPERATED	CHARTER ISSUED	HEAD OFFICE	FINAL NAME / FIRST NAME	FROM–TO / REMARKS	CHARTER DISSOLVED
1897	N	BC	BC	East Kootenay Ry. Co.	Golden to Fort Steele	YES
1898	N	BC	BC	East Kootenay Valley Ry. Co.	Cranbrook to mines at Horse Thief	YES
1908	N	BC	BC	Eastern British Columbia Ry. Co.	South fork of Michel Creek easterly	NO
1906	N	AB	AB	Edmonton and Athabasca Ry. Co.	Edmonton to Fort Chipewyan via Lac La Biche	NO
1921	N	CA	AB	Edmonton and Mackenzie River Ry. Co.	Waterways to the mouth of the Hay River, Great Slave Lake	NO
1899	N	CA	AB	Edmonton and Saskatchewan Ry. Co.	Strathcona to Victoria Settlement and Cooking Lake via Fort Saskatchewan	NO
1899	Y	CA	AB	Edmonton and Slave Lake Ry. Co.	Edmonton to Peace River via Athabasca Landing and Lesser Slave Lake	
					Amalgamated with Canadian Northern Ry., 1911. Did not operate independently	NO
1916	N	CA	AB	Edmonton and Southwestern Ry. Co.	Edmonton southwesterly to Blue Rapids on the North Saskatchewan River	NO
1910	Y	AB	AB	Edmonton Interurban Ry. Co.	Edmonton to St. Albert	
					Abandoned and portions sold to the City of Edmonton in 1917, following destruction of car by fire	NO
1914	N	AB	AB	Edmonton Northwestern Radial Ry. Co.	Edmonton to Pembina River via Rivière Qui Barre	NO
1908	Y	AB	AB	Edmonton Radial Tramway (known as Edmonton Radial Railway)	Tramways within Edmonton and lines to points north, south, east, and west	
					Tramways abandoned, 1951. LRT service commenced, 1978, but within limits of the City of Edmonton	NO
1894	N	CA	AB	Edmonton Street Ry. Co.	Tramways within Edmonton	NO
1907	Y	CA	AB	Edmonton, Dunvegan and British Columbia Ry. Co.	Edmonton to Dunvegan and Peace River, then to Fort George, B.C., via Parsnip River Valley	
					Became part of NAR, 1929	NO
1913	N	AB	AB	Edmonton, Stony Plain and Wabamun Ry. Co.	Electric railway from Edmonton to shores of Lake Wabamun via Spruce Grove and Stony Plain	NO
1896	Y	CA	AB	Edmonton, Yukon and Pacific Ry. Co.	Edmonton to South Edmonton; Edmonton to Stony Plain; Edmonton to Yellowhead Pass	
				Edmonton District Ry. Co.	Owned and operated by the CNoR Amalgamated with the CNoR, 1909	NO
1913	N	AB	AB	Elbow River Suburban Ry. Co.	Elbow River from jct. of Canyon Creek easterly to Calgary	NO
1915	N	CA	AB	Entwistle and Alberta Southern Ry. Co.	Entwistle to North Saskatchewan River	NO
1875	Y	BC	BC	Esquimalt and Nanaimo Ry. Co.	Esquimalt Harbour to Nanaimo, with authority for extension to Victoria	
					Leased for 99 years to CPR, 1912	NO
1921	N	BC	BC	Fernie and Elk River Ry. Co.	Sparwood to Kananaskis Pass via Elk River Valley	YES
1903	N	BC	BC	Flathead Valley Ry. Co.	Flathead River, near U.S. boundary, to Elko	YES
1905	N	CA	BC	Fording Valley Ry. Co.	Jct. of Elk River and Michel Creek to Okotoks via the Fording River	YES
1883	N	BC	BC	Fraser River Ry. Co.	Western terminus of the CPR, west to New Westminster	YES
1915	N	CA	BC	Fraser Valley Terminal Ry. Co.	Lines in New Westminster and Richmond	NO
1894	N	CA	AB	Gleichen, Beaver Lake and Victoria Ry. Co.	Gleichen to Victoria Settlement	NO
1909	N	BC	BC	Goat River Water Power and Light Co.	Tramways within 10-mile radius of Goat River Canyon	NO
1905	N	BC	BC	Golden Light, Power and Water Co.	Tramway within 3-mile radius of Golden	NO
1909	N	BC	BC	Graham Island Ry. Co.	Lena Island, Queen Charlotte Islands, to Sheilds Island, Rennell Sound	YES
1900	N	BC	BC	Grand Forks and Kettle River Ry. Co.	Grand Forks to Carson City	NO
1914	N	AB	AB	Granger Collieries, Ltd.	Tramway from mines to CPR line	NO
1903	N	CA	AB	Great West Ry. Co.	From towns in the Crow's Nest area to the CPR Crow's Nest line	NO

DATE OF CHARTER	OPERATED	CHARTER ISSUED	HEAD OFFICE	FINAL NAME / FIRST NAME	FROM-TO / REMARKS	CHARTER DISSOLVED
1911	N	BC	BC	Greenwood-Phoenix Tramway Co.	Tramways in and around Greenwood and Phoenix	NO
1894	N	BC	BC	Hall Mines, Ltd.	Silver King Mines to Nelson	YES
1909	N	BC	BC	Hardy Bay and Quatsino Sound Ry. Co.	Hardy Bay to Coal Harbour on Quatsino Sound	YES
1888	N	BC	BC	Harrison Hot Springs Tramway Co.	Harrison Hot Springs to Agassiz and the Fraser River	YES
1928	N	CA	AB	Highwood Western Ry. Co.	West central Alberta, west to Sparwood, British Columbia	NO
1906	N	CA	BC	Hillcrest Ry. Coal and Coke Co.	Morrissey, east via Crow's Nest Pass to Cardston, Alberta	NO
1891	N	BC	BC	Hot Springs and Goat River Tramway Co.	Tramways from Hot Springs mining camp, Kootenay district, to Kootenay Lake, and from Goat River mining camp to Kootenay River	YES
1907	Y	BC	BC	Howe Sound and Northern Ry. Co.	Squamish River, Howe Sound, north to Anderson Lake via Cheakamus River	
				Howe Sound, Pemberton Valley and Northern Ry. Co.	Name changed, 1910. Charter purchased by the Pacific Great Eastern Ry.	NO
1908	N	BC	BC	Hudson Bay Pacific Ry. Co.	Port Simpson eastward via Skeena and Bulkley Rivers to eastern boundary	YES
1901	N	BC	BC	Imperial Pacific Ry. Co.	Victoria northeasterly to eastern boundary via Yellowhead Pass	YES
1910	N	BC	BC	Island Valley Ry. Co.	Skidegate Island, Graham Inlet, to mouth of Yakown River	YES
1899	N	BC	BC	Kamloops and Atlin Ry. Co.	Kamloops Lake to Atlin Lake via Hazelton	YES
1906	N	BC	BC	Kamloops and Yellowhead Pass Ry. Co.	Kamloops to Tête Jaune Cache	YES
1897	N	BC	BC	Kaslo and Lardo-Duncan Ry. Co.	Kaslo to Duncan River via Lardo and Upper Kootenay Lake	YES
1892	Y	BC	BC	Kaslo and Slocan Ry. Co.	Kaslo to mines near Carpenter and Sandon Creeks	
					Constructed as a narrow-gauge line. Leased for 99 years to CPR, 1920. Reconstructed to standard gauge	NO
1893	N	BC	BC	Kaslo and Slocan Tramway Co.	Tramway from Kaslo to Bear Lake via Kaslo Creek valley	YES
1901	Y	CA	BC	Kettle Valley Ry. Co.	U.S. boundary at Cascade City to Carson City via Kettle River valley	
					Leased to CPR for 999 years, 1913	NO
1901	Y	CA	BC	Kootenay and Arrowhead Ry. Co.	Lardo to Arrowhead via Duncan	NO
					Leased to CPR for 999 years, 1901. CPR owns all capital stock	
1886	N	CA	BC	Kootenay and Athabasca Ry. Co.	Kootenay Lake to Gold River via Columbia River	YES
1898	N	BC	BC	Kootenay and North West Ry. Co.	Golden to Fort McLeod via Cranbrook, and Golden	YES
1901	Y	BC	BC	Kootenay Central Ry. Co.	Fort Steele south, and north to Windermere and Golden	
					Leased to CPR for 999 years, 1911	NO
1903	N	BC	BC	Kootenay Development and Tramways Co.	Kootenay Lake to Duncan River, and from Kaslo to south fork of Kaslo Creek	YES
1893	N	BC	BC	Kootenay Lake Shore and Lardo Ry. Co.	U.S. boundary at Kootenay River to Kootenay Lake	YES
1892	N	BC	BC	Kootenay Power Co.	Tramways from Nelson to a radius of 25 miles	NO
1888	N	BC	BC	Kootenay Ry. and Navigation Co.	Kootenay Lake to jct. of Kootenay and Columbia Rivers via Selkirk Mountains	YES
1906	N	AB	AB	Kootenay, Alberta and Athabasca Ry. Co.	South Kootenay Pass easterly to Fishburn / Fishburn to Peace River Crossing via Edmonton	
					Charter lapsed	YES
1903	N	BC	BC	Kootenay, Cariboo and Pacific Ry. Co.	Golden to Port Simpson or Butte Inlet via Tête Jaune Cache and Giscome Portage	YES
1910	N	AB	AB	Lacombe and Brazeau Ry. Co.	Lacombe west to the Brazeau River via Bentley and Rimbey	NO
1909	Y	AB	AB	Lacombe and North Western Ry. Co.	Lacombe to Rimbey via Bentley	
				Lacombe and Blindman Valley Electric Ry. Co.	Leased for 999 years to CPR, 1929	NO
1909	N	AB	AB	Lacombe, Bullocksville and Alix Electric Ry. Co.	Lacombe to Alix via Red Deer	NO
1901	N	BC	BC	Lake Bennett Ry. Co.	Dyea River to Lake Bennett	YES
1893	N	BC	BC	Lardeau and Kootenay Ry. Co.	Lardeau City to Nelson	YES
1897	N	BC	BC	Lardeau Ry. Co.	Galena or Thumb Bay, Upper Arrow Lake, to forks of Lardeau River	YES

DATE OF CHARTER	OPERATED	CHARTER ISSUED	HEAD OFFICE	FINAL NAME / FIRST NAME	FROM-TO / REMARKS	CHARTER DISSOLVED
1907	Y	AB	AB	Lethbridge Radial Tramway	Tramways in Lethbridge to Raymond and Stafford	
					Became a city-owned enterprise, 1913	NO
1891	N	BC	BC	Liverpool and Canoe Pass Ry. Co.	Liverpool to Canoe Pass via Fraser River	YES
1921	Y	AB	AB	Luscar Collieries, Ltd.	Mines in vicinity of Leyland and Mountain Park	
					Leased for 21 years to CNR, 1927	NO
1903	N	CA	AB	Macleod, Cardston and Montana Ry. Co.	Macleod to U.S. boundary via Stand Off and Cardston	NO
1911	N	AB	AB	Magrath Ry. Co.	Magrath to coalmines north of town	NO
1911	N	AB	AB	Maharg Electric Ry. Co.	Calgary to points south and west	NO
1909	N	BC	BC	Meadow Creek Ry. Co.	Yahk to U.S. boundary via Meadow Creek	YES
1902	N	CA	AB	Medicine Hat and Northern Alberta Ry. Co.	Medicine Hat to Victoria Settlement via Strathcona	NO
1919	N	AB	AB	Medicine Hat Central Ry. Co.	Medicine Hat to Coutts via Foremost and Whitla	NO
1911	N	AB	AB	Medicine Hat Electric Ry. Co.	Medicine Hat to Dunmore and Elk Water Lake	NO
1886	N	CA	AB	Medicine Hat Ry. and Coal Co.	Medicine Hat to adjacent coalfields and south to U.S. boundary	NO
1913	N	AB	AB	Medicine Hat Southern Ry. Co.	Medicine Hat to points south	NO
1924	N	AB	AB	Medicine Lake Collieries, Ltd.	Lovett Station, CNR to adjacent coalmines	NO
1910	N	BC	BC	Menzies Bay Ry. Co.	Menzies Bay, Vancouver Island, to jct. of Salmon and Memekay Rivers	YES
1911	N	BC	BC	Mid-Provincial and Nechaco Ry. Co.	Bella Coola to Peace River Crossing via Pine River Pass	YES
1901	N	BC	BC	Midway and Vernon Ry. Co.	Midway to Vernon. Lines also to Kamloops and Penticton	YES
1903	Y	BC	BC	Morrissey, Fernie and Michel Ry. Co.	Fernie to U.S. boundary via Morrissey Creek	
					Subsidiary of Great Northern Ry.	NO
1893	N	BC	BC	Mount Tolmie Park and Cordova Bay Ry. Co.	Victoria to Cordova Bay via Mount Tolmie	YES
1911	Y	AB	AB	Mountain Park Coal Co.	Mines at Mountain Park to GTP branch line	
					Leased to CNR for 21 years, 1927	NO
1898	N	BC	BC	Mountain Tramway and Electric Co.	Mines to points on Nakusp and Slocan Ry. and to points on Columbia and Kootenay Ry.	YES
1911	N	BC	BC	Naas and Skeena Rivers Ry. Co.	Portland Inlet to Skeena River headwaters	YES
1893	Y	CA	BC	Nakusp and Slocan Ry. Co.	Nakusp to Carpenter Creek	
					Leased to CPR for 99 years, 1920.	NO
1891	N	BC	BC	Nanaimo Electric Tramway Co.	Tramways in Nanaimo and surrounding districts	YES
1897	N	BC	BC	Nanaimo-Alberni Ry. Co.	Alberni to Nanaimo	YES
1893	N	BC	BC	Nelson and Arrow Lakes Ry. Co.	Nelson to Upper Arrow Lake via New Denver	YES
1891	Y	BC	BC	Nelson and Fort Sheppard Ry. Co.	Nelson to Fort Sheppard	
					Acquired by the Great Northern Ry., 1898	NO
1882	N	BC	BC	New Westminster and Port Moody Ry. Co.	New Westminster to Port Moody	YES
1889	N	BC	BC	New Westminster and Vancouver Short Line Ry. Co.	Near Pitt River to City of Vancouver	YES
1887	Y	BC	BC	New Westminster Southern Ry. Co.	Near Semiahmoo Bay to New Westminster	YES
					Line between Brownsville and Port Kells sold to Canadian Northern Pacific Ry., 1916. Remaining lines sold to the Great-Northern-owned Vancouver, Victoria and Eastern Ry., 1924	YES
1891	N	BC	BC	Nicola Valley Ry. Co.	Spences Bridge to Nicola Lake	
					Charter acquired by CPR in 1893	NO
1891	Y	BC	BC	Nicola, Kamloops and Similkameen Coal and Ry. Co.	Spences Bridge to Nicola	
					Leased to CPR for 999 years, 1905	NO

181

DATE OF CHARTER	OPERATED	CHARTER ISSUED	HEAD OFFICE	FINAL NAME / FIRST NAME	FROM-TO / REMARKS	CHARTER DISSOLVED
1898	N	BC	BC	North Star and Arrow Lake Ry. Co.	Cranbrook to North Star Mine and to Upper Arrow Lake via Kootenay Lake	YES
1884	Y	CA	AB	North Western Coal and Navigation Co. Ltd.	Medicine Hat to Fort McLeod. Also to mines near Belly River	
					Purchased by Alberta Ry. and Coal Co., 1891	NO
1929	Y	CA	AB	Northern Alberta Railways Co.	Edmonton to Waterways, and Edmonton to Dawson Creek via Grande Prairie	
					Incorporated properties of: Alberta & Great Waterways Ry.; Central Canada Ry.; Edmonton, Dunvegan & B.C. Ry.; Pembina Valley Ry. Owned jointly by CPR and CNR. CPR interests later sold to CNR, leading to the absorption of NAR by CNR	NO
1908	N	CA	AB	Northern Empire Ry. Co.	Point near Lethbridge to Dawson City, Yukon, via Fort McMurray	NO
1915	N	CA	BC	Northern Pacific and British Columbia Ry. Co.	Special	
					Canadian subsidiary of Northern Pacific Ry. Intended to negotiate running rights on certain Great Northern lines in Canada, especially those of the Vancouver, Victoria and Eastern Ry.	NO
1910	N	BC	BC	Northern Vancouver Island Ry. Co.	Hardy Bay or Port McNeill to Coal Harbour	YES
1890	N	BC	BC	Okanagan and Kootenay Ry. Co.	Sproat's Landing to Vernon via Lower Arrow Lake	YES
1893	N	BC	BC	Osoyoos and Okanagan Ry. Co.	Foot of Okanagan Lake to U.S. boundary, and tramway from Okanagan Lake to Dog Lake	YES
1911	N	CA	BC	Pacific and Hudson Bay Ry. Co.	Kimsquit to Port Nelson via Fort Fraser, Peace River Landing, and Fort McMurray	NO
1883	N	CA	BC	Pacific and Peace River Ry. Co.	Fort Simpson to Peace River east of Fort Dunvegan	NO
1898	N	BC	BC	Pacific and Peace River Ry. Co. (2)	Kitimat Inlet to south end of Babine Lake via Copper River and Telegraph Trail	
				Kitimat Ry. Co.	Name changed, 1899	YES
1911	N	CA	BC	Pacific and Peace Ry. Co.	Bella Coola to Dunvegan via Fort Fraser	NO
1909	N	BC	BC	Pacific Coast Mines Ltd.	Tramways in districts of Cranberry and Cedar	NO
1912	Y	BC	BC	Pacific Great Eastern Ry. Co.	North Vancouver to Fort George, connecting to GTP	
					Line did not reach Prince George in this time-frame. Capital stock of company owned by B.C. provincial government	NO
1903	N	BC	BC	Pacific Northern and Eastern Ry. Co.	Hazelton to eastern boundary of B.C	YES
1900	N	BC	BC	Pacific Northern and Omineca Ry. Co.	Kitimat Inlet to Edmonton via Peace River Pass	
					Charter acquired by the GTP, but construction halted after subsidies were paid	YES
1910	N	BC	BC	Pacific Ry. Co.	Salmon River, at U.S. boundary, northerly to the headwaters of that river	YES
1914	N	CA	BC	Pacific, Peace River and Athabasca Ry. Co.	Naas River to Prince Albert, Saskatchewan, via Fort McMurray	NO
1912	N	CA	AB	Pacific, Trans-Canada and Hudson Bay Ry. Co.	Edmonton to Prince Rupert via Athabasca Landing and Fort Smith. Also line branching from Loon River to Port Nelson on Hudson Bay	NO
1911	N	BC	BC	Peace and Naas River Ry. Co.	Naas River to eastern boundary of B.C. via Pine River Pass	YES
1910	N	AB	AB	Peace River Great Western Ry. Co.	Edmonton to Dunvegan via Lesser Slave Lake and Peace River Crossing	NO
1914	N	CA	AB	Peace River Tramway and Navigation Co.	Smith's Landing to Fort Smith	
					Charter lapsed, 1918	YES
1926	Y	AB	AB	Pembina Valley Ry.	Busby to Barrhead	
					Built by the Alberta provincial government and incorporated into the NAR, 1929	NO
1910	N	BC	BC	Penticton Ry. Co.	Penticton to a point near Osoyoos Lake	YES
1909	N	AB	AB	Pincher Creek and Southern Ry. Co.	U.S. boundary northerly to Pincher on the CPR, via coalmines to the south	NO
1899	N	BC	BC	Pine Creek Flume Co.	Various tramways in vicinity	NO
1910	N	CA	AB	Pine Pass Ry. Co.	Edmonton to Fort George via Grande Prairie and Pine River Pass	NO
1910	N	BC	BC	Port Moody, Indian River and Northern Ry. Co.	Port Moody west to Indian River	YES
1898	N	BC	BC	Portland and Stickine Ry. Co.	Observatory Inlet or Portland Canal to Telegraph Creek	YES
1907	N	BC	BC	Portland Canal Ry. Co.	Portland Canal up Bear River Valley for 30 miles	
					Charter purchased by Canadian North Eastern Railway Company in 1911	YES

DATE OF CHARTER	OPERATED	CHARTER ISSUED	HEAD OFFICE	FINAL NAME / FIRST NAME	FROM–TO / REMARKS	CHARTER DISSOLVED
1909	N	BC	BC	Prince Rupert and Port Simpson Ry. Co.	Prince Rupert to Port Simpson	YES
1901	N	BC	BC	Queen Charlotte Ry. Co.	Skidegate Inlet to Massett Inlet	YES
1907	N	BC	BC	Rainy Hollow Ry. Co.	From Alaskan boundary at the Klehini River to Rainy Hollow Copper Mines	YES
1910	N	AB	AB	Raymond	Tramways in and around Raymond	NO
1909	N	AB	AB	Red Deer Ry. Co.	Tramways within Red Deer and line to Content	NO
1889	N	CA	AB	Red Deer Valley Ry. and Coal Co.	Calgary to point on Red Deer River. Also from Cheadle station, CPR, to points north	
					Charter expired	YES
1917	N	AB	AB	Red Deer Valley Ry. Co.	Princess northwesterly via Red Deer River	NO
1893	Y	BC	BC	Red Mountain Ry. Co.	Patterson to Rossland	
					Owned by the Great Northern Ry. Line abandoned, 1921	NO
1898	N	BC	BC	Revelstoke and Cassiar Ry. Co.	Revelstoke to Dease Lake or Teslin Lake via Tête Jaune Cache	YES
1900	N	BC	BC	Rock Bay and Salmon River Ry. Co.	Johnstone Strait to Upper Campbell Lake, and to north end of Bear Lake, all on Vancouver Island	YES
1891	N	CA	AB	Rocky Mountain Ry. and Coal Co.	Anthracite to Red Deer Forks Coal Mines (Red Deer River). Later chartered to build from Calgary to coalfields near Red Deer River	NO
1909	N	AB	AB	Royal Collieries Ry. Co.	Lethbridge to adjacent coalmines	NO
1886	Y	CA	BC	Shuswap and Okanagan Ry. Co.	Sicamous to Vernon	
					Leased to and constructed by CPR; lease extended to 999 years in 1915.	NO
1901	N	CA	BC	Similkameen and Keremeos Ry. Co.	Penticton to U.S. boundary via the Similkameen Valley	NO
1898	N	BC	BC	Skeena River and Eastern Ry. Co.	Skeena River to eastern boundary of B.C.	YES
1898	N	BC	BC	Skeena River Ry., Colonization and Exploration Co.	Skeena River to Yellowhead Pass	YES
1915	N	AB	AB	Smoky Valley and Peace River Ry. Co.	Jct. of Solomon Creek and Athabasca River to Dunvegan	NO
1911	N	AB	AB	South East Calgary Electric Ry. Co.	Calgary to Shepard	NO
1898	N	BC	BC	South East Kootenay Ry. Co.	South of Fort Steele to McGillivray	YES
1899	N	BC	BC	South Kootenay Ry. Co.	Fort Steele to U.S. boundary	YES
1909	N	AB	AB	Southern Alberta Ry. Co.	Medicine Hat to Suffield, then southwesterly	NO
1903	N	CA	BC	Southern Central Pacific Ry. Co.	Vancouver to a point north of Fort Churchill via Kootenay Pass and Old Man River in Alberta	NO
1906	N	BC	BC	Southern Okanagan Ry. Co.	Penticton to U.S. boundary	YES
1906	N	BC	BC	St. Mary's and Cherry Creek Ry. Co.	Near Bayard to points along Cherry Creek	NO
1900	Y	CA	AB	St. Mary's River Ry. Co.	Stirling to Spring Coulee	
					Amalgamated with Alberta Ry. and Coal Co., 1904	NO
1906	N	BC	BC	St. Mary's Valley Ry. Co.	Marysville to Crawford Bay, Kootenay Lake	YES
1897	N	BC	BC	Stickeen and Teslin Ry., Navigation and Colonization Co.	Glenora to southern end of Teslin Lake	YES
1909	N	AB	AB	Strathcona Central Ry. Co.	Ellerslie west to North Saskatchewan River, then northeast to Strathcona	NO
1904	N	AB	AB	Strathcona Radial Tramway Co.	Various tramways	NO
1910	N	AB	AB	Taber	Tramways in town	NO
1913	N	AB	AB	Taber Transit Co.	Various tramways in the vicinity of Taber	NO
1891	N	BC	BC	Toad Mountain and Nelson Tramway Co.	Silver King Mine, Toad Mountain, to Nelson	YES
1895	N	CA	BC	Trail Creek and Columbia Ry. Co.	Trail Creek Mines to mouth of Trail Creek	NO
1913	N	AB	AB	Tramways, Ltd.	Edmonton to Bon Accord and Fort Saskatchewan	NO
1907	N	BC	BC	Tsimpsean Light and Power Co.	Tramways within 75-mile radius of the mouth of the Khtada River	NO
1891	N	BC	BC	Upper Columbia Navigation and Tramway Co.	Tramway from Golden to Columbia River	YES

DATE OF CHARTER	OPERATED	CHARTER ISSUED	HEAD OFFICE	FINAL NAME / FIRST NAME	FROM-TO / REMARKS	CHARTER DISSOLVED
1887	N	CA	BC	Upper Columbia Ry. Co.	Golden to upper Columbia Lake	NO
1902	N	BC	BC	Vancouver and Coast-Kootenay Ry. Co.	Vancouver to Midway via New Westminster and Chilliwack	NO
1901	N	BC	BC	Vancouver and Grand Forks Ry. Co.	Vancouver to Keremeos via Chilliwack, Hope, and Princeton	YES
1891	N	BC	BC	Vancouver and Lulu Island Electrical Ry. and Improvement Co.	Vancouver to Lulu Island via Sea Island	YES
1891	Y	BC	BC	Vancouver and Lulu Island Ry. Co.	Vancouver to Lulu Island	
					Leased to CPR for 999 years, 1901. Operations were passed to British Columbia Electric Ry., 1908	NO
1908	N	BC	BC	Vancouver and Nicola Valley Ry. Co.	Nicola Lake to Vancouver via Coquihalla River, Hope, and New Westminster	YES
1909	N	BC	BC	Vancouver and Northern Ry. Co.	Vancouver to north arm of Burrard Inlet via Seymour Creek Valley and Loch Lomond	YES
1900	N	BC	BC	Vancouver and Westminster Ry. Co.	Vancouver to New Westminster	YES
1881	N	BC	BC	Vancouver Coal Mining and Land Co.	Along Nanaimo's esplanade	YES
1886	N	BC	BC	Vancouver Electric Ry. and Light Co.	Tramways in Vancouver Acquired by Consolidated Ry. Co.	NO
1908	N	CA	BC	Vancouver Island and Eastern Ry. Co.	Victoria to Seymour Narrows, Vancouver Island. Also from Butte or Frederick Inlet to Edmonton via Yellowhead Pass	NO
1882	N	BC	BC	Vancouver Land and Ry. Co.	Esquimalt Harbour to Seymour Narrows, Vancouver Island	YES
1906	Y	CA	BC	Vancouver, Fraser Valley and Southern Ry. Co.	Vancouver to Chilliwack via New Westminster	
					Controlled and operated by British Columbia Electric Ry.	NO
1891	N	BC	BC	Vancouver, Northern, Peace River and Alaska Ry. and Navigation Co.	Vancouver to Stickeen River via Chilcotin Pass and Fort George	YES
1897	Y	BC	BC	Vancouver, Victoria and Eastern Ry. and Navigation Co.	Vancouver to Rossland via New Westminster. Several branch lines	
					Owned by the Great Northern Ry. Running rights provided to Canadian Northern Pacific from New Westminster to Vancouver, and from Hope to Sumas Landing	NO
1901	N	CA	BC	Vancouver, Westminster and Yukon Ry. Co.	Vancouver to New Westminster. Also Vancouver to Dawson City via Lillooet, Quesnel, and Hazelton	
					Line from Vancouver to New Westminster sold to Vancouver, Victoria and Eastern Ry., 1908. No further construction ensued.	NO
1899	N	BC	BC	Vancouver, Westminster, Northern and Yukon Ry. Co.	Vancouver to northern boundary of B.C. via Lillooet, Quesnel, and Hazelton	
					Owned initially by James J. Hill. Sold to GTP, who abandoned construction after subsidies were paid	YES
1902	N	CA	BC	Velvet (Rossland) Mine Ry. Co.	Rossland to Velvet Mines, then to U.S. boundary	NO
1906	N	AB	AB	Vermilion and Cold Lake Ry. Co.	Vermilion to Cold Lake via Frog Lake	NO
1891	N	BC	BC	Vernon and Okanagan Ry. Co.	Vernon to Osoyoos Lake	YES
1909	N	BC	BC	Victoria and Barkley Sound Ry. Co.	Victoria to Barkley Sound	YES
1873	N	BC	BC	Victoria and Esquimalt Ry. Co.	Victoria to Esquimalt Harbour	NO
1891	N	BC	BC	Victoria and North American Ry. Co.	Victoria to Beecher Bay	YES
1886	N	BC	BC	Victoria and Saanich Ry. Co.	Victoria to North Saanich	YES
1902	N	BC	BC	Victoria and Seymour Narrows Ry. Co.	Victoria to Seymour Narrows via Nanaimo and Alberni	YES
1892	Y	BC	BC	Victoria and Sidney Ry. Co.	Victoria to Sidney	
					Subsidiary of Great Northern Railway. Operated until it went into receivership, 1919, then abandoned	

DATE OF CHARTER	OPERATED	CHARTER ISSUED	HEAD OFFICE	FINAL NAME / FIRST NAME	FROM-TO / REMARKS	CHARTER DISSOLVED
1889	Y	BC	BC	Victoria Electric Ry. and Lighting Co.	Tramways in Victoria and to Esquimalt	
					Sold under foreclosure to Consolidated Ry. Co., 1896	
1901	Y	BC	BC	Victoria Terminal Ry. and Ferry Co.	Connection between Victoria and Sidney Ry. and Esquimalt and Nanaimo Ry.	
					Sold to Vancouver, Victoria and Eastern Ry. and Navigation Co.	NO
1883	N	BC	BC	Victoria Transfer Co.	Tramways in Victoria and to Esquimalt	NO
1889	N	CA	BC	Victoria, Saanich and New Westminster Ry. Co.	Victoria to Swartz Bay, Vancouver Island. Also Point Roberts to New Westminster and Vancouver	NO
1894	N	BC	BC	Victoria, Vancouver and Westminster Ry. Co.	Point Garry to New Westminster	YES
1898	N	CA	AB	Western Alberta Ry. Co.	Old Man River to Rocky Mountains via Canmore and Anthracite	NO
1910	N	CA	BC	Western Canada Power Co.	Stave River to CPR between Hammond and Ruskin	NO
1912	N	CA	AB	Western Dominion Ry. Co.	U.S. boundary south of Cardston to Fort St. John via Pincher Creek, Calgary, and Edmonton	
					Charter expired 1926	YES
1890	N	BC	BC	Westminster and Vancouver Tramway Co.	Tramway between New Westminster and Vancouver	
					Acquired by Consolidated Ry.	NO
1891	N	BC	BC	Westminster Street Ry. Co.	Tramways in and around New Westminster	
					Amalgamated with Westminster and Vancouver Tramway Co., 1891, under the latter's name	NO
1913	N	CA	AB	Wetaskiwin, Yellowhead and Revelstoke Ry. Co.	Lloydminster to Revelstoke via Westaskiwin and Yellowhead Pass	NO
1901	N	BC	BC	Yale-Northern Ry. Co.	Grand Forks to mouth of Eagle Creek	YES

Notes

Notes for Preface

1 Cardwell, 1995, p. 348.

Notes (pages 4 – 7)

1 For further information about early exploration in British Columbia, see Gosnell, 1897; Wheeler, 1905.
2 Gosnell, 1897, pp. 81–89.
3 *Ibid.*, pp. 34–37. Douglas had also been an official of the Hudson's Bay Company prior to his appointment as governor of the colony.
4 This sentiment is expressed clearly in a letter of April 25, 1862, from Charles Alleyn, secretary of the Provincial Government of Canada to Alexander Dallas, governor of the Hudson's Bay Company, in *British Parliamentary Papers, 1861–63*, p. 364.
5 Gosnell, 1903, pp. 23–24; Walbran, 1909, p. 483. Although in operation as far north as the Skeena River, the line and caches of wire were abandoned in the spring of 1867. Lasting vestiges of the Overland Telegraph are place names such as Telegraph Passage on the Skeena River, named thus because it was the site where supplies were landed. Telegraph Creek was so named because the Overland Telegraph was supposed to cross the Stikine River at that point.
6 Gosnell, 1897. See correspondence regarding proposals for a road and telegraph line in the *British Parliamentary Papers, 1861–63*.
7 Wheeler, 1905; *Columbia River Exploration, 1865*.
8 Trutch later became lieutenant–governor of British Columbia and in this capacity he promoted the construction of a railroad from the East to British Columbia. See also Gibbon, 1935.
9 *British Columbia Gazette*, December 23, 1865; Wheeler, 1905. Much later, Moberly claimed that upon discovering Eagle Pass, "I blazed a small cedar tree and wrote upon it: `This is the pass for the Overland Railway'"(cited in Wheeler, 1905, p. 195). Although Berton, 1970, has made much of this episode, it was most likely apocryphal, since there is no mention of it either in Moberly's log entries of 1865, nor in his account of the discovery and naming of Eagle Pass to Sandford Fleming in 1872 (Fleming, 1872, p. 35).

10 Spry, 1963. This was not the first occasion when a transcontinental railroad linking colonies throughout British North America was proposed. Thompson and Edgar, 1933, note that several individuals, starting in the 1830s, predicted the building of such a railway for the preservation of British interests and for the further colonization of British lands.
11 Palliser, in *British Parliamentary Papers, 1861–63*, p. 454.
12 Palliser, 1860; *British Parliamentary Papers, 1861–63*, Wheeler, 1905.
13 Hector, in *British Parliamentary Papers, 1861–63*; Wheeler, 1905; Spry, 1963.
14 Blakiston, 1858, p. 11.
15 Palliser, in *British Parliamentary Papers, 1861–63*; Spry 1963, p. 276.
16 Palliser, in *British Parliamentary Papers, 1861–63*, p. 456.

Notes (pages 8 – 27)

1 Gosnell, 1897; Wheeler, 1905, p. 150.
2 Fleming, 1872; Wheeler, 1905, p. 197.
3 *Engineering News*, January 21, 1904, pp. 51–52. For more information about the Grand Trunk Railroad and its history, see Stevens, 1973; MacKay, 1986.
4 *The Railroad Gazette*, July 6, 1888, pp. 439–40; *Engineering News*, September 29, 1888.
5 A more detailed account of the Pacific Scandal may be found in Berton, 1970.
6 Fleming, 1872; 1877.
7 Fleming, 1877.
8 *Ibid.*, 1877, p. 90.
9 Two additional routes were identified that entered British Columbia via the Pine Pass, near Peace River. These routes were not explored extensively, since the areas were less inhabited than those farther south (Fleming, 1877; 1879).
10 Fleming, 1877.
11 *Ibid.*, 1877, p. 20.
12 Gosnell, 1897; Dorman, 1938.
13 Fleming, 1877, p. 78.
14 Fleming, 1877.
15 Fleming, 1879; 1880.
16 Fleming, 1880, p. 3; Gosnell, 1897.
17 Fleming, 1880. The line was also compared to the grades of the American transcontinental railroad, the Central Pacific–Union Pacific,

completed in 1870. The comparison revealed that the Canadian Pacific would have the gentlest grades and fewer summits.

18 MacLachlan, 1986.

19 Fleming, 1880. Some confusion exists about the awarding of the contracts. Berton, 1970, Lavallée, 1974, and Turner, 1987, all claim that Onderdonk and Co. were awarded contracts 60 through 63, but Fleming's report indicates that Ryan, Goodwin & Co. won contract 61, a twenty-nine-mile section between Boston Bar and Lytton. It is likely that Onderdonk took over the contract subsequently, since there is no further mention of Ryan, Goodwin & Co.

20 Fleming, 1880, p. 353.

21 Fleming, 1877, p. 63.

22 Gibbon, 1935. This work also contains additional information about the *Skuzzy*.

23 Gosnell, 1911, p. 38. The first locomotives were small, second-hand units coming either from Onderdonk's previous projects, or from the Virginia and Truckee Railroad (Turner, 1987).

24 Contract 92, from Emory's Bar at the west end of Contract 60 to Port Moody (Burrard Inlet), British Columbia, December 1, 1881. Lavallée, 1974, indicates that the contract was awarded to Onderdonk in February 1882.

25 By 1883, four thousand Chinese were at work on Onderdonk's sections (*Engineering News*, May 12, 1883).

26 Peterson, 1895.

27 Fleming, 1879.

28 Gibbon, 1935; Berton, 1970.

29 *An Act Respecting the Canadian Pacific Railway*, 44 Victoria, Chapter 1. A summary can be found in *Engineering News*, July 6, 1888, p. 439.

30 Fleming, 1880.

31 Rogers, 1905.

32 Moberly had explored the base of the Illecillewaet in 1865, but early snowfall had prevented him from reaching the headwaters. See Moberly's account in *Columbia River Exploration*, 1865.

33 Devil's Club or *panax horridus*, is a bushy plant with broad leaves resembling large maple leaves. The stalks contain many long thorns that puncture clothing and skin easily. An added torment is that the thorns break off and cause a painful and irritating rash. Devil's Club is still to be found in this area, as the author and his father can attest.

34 Rogers, 1905; Gibbon, 1935.

35 Rogers, 1905, provides a detailed account of the expedition to discover this pass by Major Rogers's nephew Albert.

36 Hanna and Hawkes, 1924; Lavallée, 1974.

37 Lavallée, 1974.

38 Van Horne was an American, and general superintendent of the Chicago, Milwaukee and St. Paul Railroad at that time. He later became a Canadian, and was knighted for his service to the country.

39 Lavallée, 1974.

40 *Engineering News*, October 27, 1888.

41 The design of such bridges was under the supervision of Charles C. Schneider of New York, who was hired by the federal government as a consulting engineer for both the government and private sections of the Canadian Pacific (*Engineering News*, November 28, 1895).

42 *Engineering News*, October 27, 1888.

43 *Ibid*.

44 Canadian Pacific Railway, *Annual Report for 1885*.

45 *Engineering News*, October 27, 1888; Lavallée, 1974.

46 Gibbon, 1935.

47 Van Horne, in *The Railroad Gazette*, October 10, 1884, p. 748.

48 Bone, 1947.

49 Lavallée, 1974; *Engineering News*, November 28, 1895, for more examples of tunnel elimination.

50 *Engineering News*, November 28, 1895.

51 Findlay, 1889.

52 *The Railroad Gazette*, October 10, 1884, p. 748; Lavallée, 1974.

53 Lavallée, 1974.

54 *The Railroad Gazette*, July 6, 1888; Canadian Pacific Railway, Pacific Division, *Timetable 1*, June 30, 1907.

55 *The Railroad Gazette*, May 8, 1887; and Lavallée, 1985.

56 Canadian Pacific Railway, Pacific Division, *Timetable 1*, June 30, 1907.

57 Bone, 1947.

58 Canadian Pacific Railway Bridge Records.

59 Lavallée, 1974.

Notes (pages 28 – 65)

1 Turner, 1973.
2 Dorman, 1938, p. 206.
3 Gosnell, 1897; MacLachlan, 1986.
4 Turner, 1973; MacLachlan, 1986.
5 Turner, 1973.
6 Turner, 1973; MacLachlan, 1986.
7 This policy was discontinued. MacLachlan, 1986.
8 Baird, 1985.
9 Turner, 1973.
10 Dorman, 1938.
11 Otter, 1982. At present, the Belly River is the name of a stream located up-river from Lethbridge.
12 Lavallée, 1972.
13 Dorman, 1938; Otter, 1982.
14 Lavallée, 1972; Otter, 1982.
15 Otter, 1982.
16 *Engineering News*, April 5, 1890; Kennedy, 1894.
17 *Engineering News*, April 26, 1890; May 8, 1890; May 31, 1890.
18 Dorman, 1938; *Engineering News*, May 17, 1890.
19 Otter, 1982.
20 Lavallée, 1972.
21 Dorman, 1938.
22 *Engineering News*, August 18, 1883.
23 Dorman, 1938; *Engineering News*, May 17, 1890.
24 *Engineering News*, May 31, 1890; Canadian Pacific Railway, *Annual Report*s for 1890, 1891.
25 Bone, 1947, pp. 159–60.
26 Thompson and Edgar, 1933.
27 Canadian Pacific Railway, *Annual Report*s for 1891, 1892.
28 Canadian Pacific Railway, *Annual Report* for 1904; Dorman, 1938.
29 Cunningham, 1887; *Engineering News*, January 21, 1888.
30 *Canadian Pacific Railway, Pacific Division Profile showing snowshed work 1886 & 1887*; see also Canadian Pacific Railway, *Annual Report*s for 1887, 1888, for summaries of costs.
31 Cunningham, 1887; *Engineering News*, January 21, 1888.
32 Vaughan, 1912.
33 Canadian Pacific Railway, *Annual Report* for 1892.
34 Peterson, 1895; Canadian Pacific Railway, Bridge Records, Western and Pacific Divisions.

35 *Engineering News*, August 2, 1894; Peterson, 1895.
36 Canadian Pacific Railway, *Annual Report* for 1894; Baedeker, 1907, p. 274; Vaux, 1900.
37 Canadian Pacific Railway, *Annual Report* for 1886, p. 14.
38 Canadian Pacific Railway, *Annual Report* for 1890, p. 18.
39 See listing of chartered railroads in appendix.
40 Turner, 1987; Turner and Wilkie, 1994.
41 Canadian Pacific Railway, *Annual Report* for 1896, p. 10.
42 *Engineering News*, March 10, 1898; Canadian Pacific Railway, *Annual Report* for 1898.
43 Cited in Gibbon, 1935, p. 304.
44 See Cars and Caracalla, 1984, for a concise illustrated history of this European concern and its celebrated trains.
45 *Engineering News*, November 28, 1888, p. 373; see additional accounts in the November 17, 1888, issue.
46 Bonar, 1950; Elson, 1976.
47 See Canadian Pacific Railway timetables, 1886, 1888.
48 Hart, 1983; Barrett and Liscombe, 1983; Canadian Pacific Railway, *Annual Report* for 1888.
49 Pole, 1991; Finch, 1991.
50 Baedeker, 1907; Barrett and Liscombe, 1983.
51 Hopkins, 1908; Reksten, 1978; Barrett and Liscombe, 1983.
52 Bohi and Kozma, 1993; Turner, 1987.

Notes (pages 66 – 89)

1 Fleming, 1879, p. 18.
2 *Statutes of Canada*, 58–59 Victoria, Chapter 68, 1895; Hopkins, 1902.
3 Wilson, 1916. Wilson's account of his professional life disagrees with many later works which tend to dismiss him as entirely ignorant of railroad matters and one who carried on the tradition in the Grand Trunk of administering from England. See, for example, Eagle, 1989; Bowman, 1980; Regehr, 1976; Stevens, 1973. Stevens, 1973; Eagle, 1989; and Fleming, 1991, misrepresent Wilson's name. His surname was Wilson and his given names were Charles and Rivers, a fact evident in his autobiography.
4 Cited in Hopkins, 1902, p. 220.
5 Wilson, 1916; Hopkins, 1902, p. 220.

6 Hopkins, 1902, p. 220.

7 Cited in Hopkins, 1903, p. 33.

8 Hopkins, 1903; 1904.

9 Cited in Hopkins, 1904, pp. 69–70.

10 Cited in Hopkins, 1902, p. 428.

11 Thompson and Edgar, 1933; Fleming, 1991; MacKay, 1986.

12 Wilson, 1916, p. 274; see also Grand Trunk Pacific, 1907.

13 *The Railway and Marine World*, April 1910.

14 Hopkins, 1908, p. 560; Leonard, 1996.

15 Hopkins, 1909, p. 601.

16 See GTP plans in the National Archives of Canada, Ottawa. The GTP primarily used a letter designation to distinguish its plans for buildings. When the GTP became part of the Canadian National Railways, a numeric designation was used, 100–152. Unfortunately, Bohi, 1977, assigned an incorrect letter designation for the design (Type E), and several authors subsequently have perpetuated this error.

17 Fitzhugh was luckless in his bid to have a town named after him. In Saskatchewan, a station on the southern outskirts of Saskatoon was named Earl, but local residents preferred South Saskatoon. A proposed town of Hopkins never materialized because of similarity with a preexisting locality.

18 Walbran, 1909; Hopkins, 1906.

19 Cited in Hopkins, 1905, p. 554.

20 Parker and Kelliher, 1909, p. 27; *The Canadian Engineer*, January 1907. Regehr, 1976, contends that the GTP moved the line to the Yellowhead Pass to cut off the Canadian Northern and compete with them directly, as that company was preparing to extend its main line west to British Columbia. Given the stated purpose of the GTP—a high-speed trunk line—and the engineering evidence presented by Kelliher, it seems that the reason for adopting the Yellowhead Pass was to obtain the gentlest grade and not primarily to block the Canadian Northern.

21 Regehr, 1976; *Annual Report of the Department of Railways and Canals*, 1907; *The Canadian Engineer*, April 5, 1907.

22 Clegg and Corley, 1969; Grand Trunk Pacific Railway Employee Timetables, 1906–1920; Canadian National Railways Western District Employee Timetables, 1921.

23 Talbot, 1912; Roe, 1982; Thompson and Edgar, 1933.

24 *The Canadian Engineer*, February 14, 1908; July 31, 1908; Thompson and Edgar, 1933; *Annual Report of the Department of Railways and Canals*, 1915.

25 Hopkins, 1907. One of the charters was for the Pacific Northern and Omineca Railway Company, which was to run about 180 miles from Kitimaat [now Kitimat] Inlet to Hazelton. The other charter, of the Vancouver, Western and Yukon Railway, was purchased from James J. Hill, and was planned to run from Vancouver, through Fort (later Prince) George, then north to Dawson City in the Yukon.

26 Hopkins, 1908. In his final inspection of construction in 1909, before resigning as chairman of the board at the end of that year, because of ill health, Sir Rivers Wilson noted that many of the workers on the Prince Rupert section were Doukhobors (Wilson, 1916).

27 Bloch, 1994.

28 *The Canadian Engineer*, July 10, 1908; July 31, 1908; September 25, 1908.

29 Hopkins, 1906.

30 *The Railway and Marine World*, November 1911; *The Canadian Engineer*, October 19, 1911, May 2, 1912; Hopper and Kearney, 1962.

31 Rattenbury, 1913; Hopkins, 1913; Barrett and Liscombe, 1983; Reksten, 1978.

32 See, for example, Stevens, 1973; MacKay, 1986; Bowman, 1980.

33 Hopkins, 1909; 1913, p. 695.

34 *Engineering News*, January 4, 1917, p. 536.

35 *Engineering News*, April 9, 1914, p. 813. Reports differ as to who drove the last spike. Most accounts credit B. B. Kelliher, while the *Canadian Railway and Marine World* (May 1914, p. 220) claims that the last spike was driven on April 8, 1914, by the vice-president of the GTP, M. Donaldson. Bowman, 1980, claims that President Edson Chamberlin drove the last spike.

36 *The Canadian Engineer*, May 23, 1912; May 9, 1914.

37 Hopper and Kearney, 1962; Clegg and Corley, 1969.

38 *Report of the Royal Commission to Inquire into Railways and Transportation in Canada*, 1917.

39 *Annual Report of the Department of Railways and Canals*, 1918. Stevens, 1973; Regehr, 1976; Taylor, 1988, and others make a big issue of the parallel lines of the GTP and Canadian Northern west of Edmonton, claiming that this was senseless

duplication. The facts contradict such a sweeping generalization. First, the Yellowhead Pass was demonstrated to provide the gentlest grades and shortest route to the Pacific, and so a railroad using a more northerly pass would have been at a disadvantage. Second, the Peace River district in Northern Alberta and British Columbia had less development than the territory west of Edmonton, and a big risk would be taken by a railroad hoping to develop the Peace River. Third, and most important, the two railroads constructed their lines for two different purposes. The GTP was a high-speed trunk line to move goods from point to point, while the Canadian Northern was not interested in speed so much as collecting business along the way, and neither company nor the dominion government could agree to terms for a common main line.

40 *Official Report of the Debates of the House of Commons,* Seventh Session, Twelfth Parliament, 7–8 George V, 1917. Most information occurs between February 1 and September 3, 1917.

41 In Hopkins, 1920, p. 305.

Notes (pages 90 – 103)

1 Hanna and Hawkes, 1924, p. 184.
2 *Statutes of Canada*, 59 Victoria, Chapter 17, 1896. The charter also permitted lines from Edmonton to Fort Assiniboine, via St. Albert, and to Fort Saskatchewan.
3 *Statutes of Canada*, 62–63 Victoria, Chapter 64, 1899; 1 Edward VII, Chapter 57, 1901.
4 Regehr, 1976.
5 Corley, 1972.
6 *Edmonton Bulletin*, May 14, 1903.
7 Hopkins, 1904, p. 495.
8 Hanna and Hawkes, 1924; *Canadian Northern Railway Abandonment, Stony Plains Subdivision,* Memorandum from Office of Chief Engineer, Winnipeg, Manitoba, January 8, 1925; *The Railway and Marine World*, April 1910, p. 285.
9 Regehr, 1976.
10 *The Railway and Marine World*, April 1910, p. 285; June 1910, p. 487.
11 Hanna and Hawkes, 1924; Regehr, 1976; Hopper and Kearney, 1962.
12 Canadian Northern Railway, 1 903. This town was, in 1905, bisected by the boundary between the new provinces of Alberta and Saskatchewan.

13 *Engineering News*, April 5, 1906.
14 Hopper and Kearney, 1962; Canadian Northern Railway, 1908.
15 *The Railway and Marine World*, July 1909.
16 Canadian National Railways Bridge Records.
17 Hopper and Kearney, 1962.
18 *The Railway and Marine World*, July 1909.
19 Nimmo, 1914.
20 Dorman, 1938; Hopper and Kearney, 1962.
21 Dorman, 1938. The charter of the B.C. Canadian Northern Railway Company was not cancelled until 1927.
22 Canadian Northern Railway, 1910. The 1912 *Annual Report* anticipated completion by the end of 1913.
23 Hopkins, 1910, p. 606.
24 *Engineering News*, December 2, 1915; Nimmo, 1914.
25 Nimmo, 1914.
26 *Engineering News*, February 26, 1914; *The Canadian Engineer*, May 23, 1912.
27 Canadian Northern Railway, 1912, p. 7.
28 Hopper and Kearney, 1962.
29 *The Canadian Engineer*, May 23, 1912; *Canadian Railway and Marine World*, February 1913.
30 Clegg and Corley, 1969; *The Canadian Engineer*, June 27, 1912.
31 Regehr, 1976.
32 Turner, 1973; Baird, 1984; Canadian National Railways, *Public Timetable*, June 23, 1929.
33 In Hopkins, 1918, p. 521.
34 *Ibid.*, p. 533.
35 Hanna and Hawkes, 1924, p. 238.

Notes (104 – 137)

1 Monsarrat, 1909. The total length of the bridge is 5,327 feet with a height of 314 feet.
2 Monsarrat, 1909; Johnston, 1977.
3 Schwitzer, 1909; *Engineering News*, November 10, 1910, pp. 512–14.
4 *The Railway and Marine World*, April 1909.
5 Turner, 1987.
6 *Engineering News*, July 4, 1912.
7 *Engineering News*, November 11, 1915; Canadian Pacific Railway, 1914.
8 Sullivan, 1916; *Canadian Railway and Marine World*, November 1913; Tracy, 1916.
9 *Engineering News*, January 1916; Beatty, 1974.
10 *Canadian Railway and Marine World*, December 1917.

11 *Engineering News-Record*, March 10, 1921.

12 Evans, 1910; Lavallée, 1985.

13 Hopkins, 1907.

14 Thompson and Edgar, 1933; Elson, 1976.

15 Pole, 1991.

16 Pole, 1991; Lavallée, 1972.

17 Maxwell, with his older brother Edward, had already designed the Château-like station and terminal office for Vancouver, opened in 1898. See Turner, 1987; Eagle, 1989.

18 Eagle, 1989.

19 Turner, 1987.

20 *The Railway and Marine World*, June 1911; *The Canadian Engineer*, April 11, 1912; Phillips, 1965.

21 Lavallée, 1985; *The Canadian Engineer*, April 11, 1912.

22 *Engineering News*, April 27, 1905; Canadian Pacific Railway, 1906.

23 Hopkins, 1914.

24 *The Canadian Engineer*, July 31, 1908; Gilpin, 1985.

25 *Canadian Railway and Marine World*, November 1913.

26 *The Canadian Engineer*, December 11, 1908; Hopkins, 1909.

27 Macgregor, 1914.

28 Hopkins, 1910; Dawe, 1972; Canadian Pacific Railway, 1913.

29 Hopkins, 1909; Dorman, 1938.

30 *Engineering News*, October 27, 1888.

31 Cited in Hopkins, 1913, p. 648; see also Hopkins, 1910, 1911; Schneider, 1989.

32 Schneider, 1989.

33 Plans and specifications in the Provincial Archives of Alberta.

34 Buck, 1982. See also advertisements for the excursion service to Lac La Biche in June 1916 issues of the *Edmonton Bulletin* and *Edmonton Journal*.

35 Schneider, 1989; Alberta Department of Railways and Telephones, 1920.

36 Schneider, 1989.

37 List of Equipment of the Edmonton, Dunvegan and British Columbia and Central Canada Railways, April 1922, in NAR corporate records, Provincial Archives of Alberta.

38 Hatcher, 1987.

39 Alberta Department of Railways and Telephones, 1919, p. 2.

40 Much information for the McArthur lines, Alberta and Great Waterways, Edmonton, Dunvegan and British Columbia, and the Central Canada was obtained from: NAR corporate records in the Provincial Archives of Alberta; *Annual Report*s of the Alberta Department of Railways and Telephones, as well as Schneider, 1989; Hatcher, 1981, 1987.

41 Alberta Department of Railways and Telephones, 1918, 1923; Dorman, 1938; see also Schneider, 1987.

42 Dorman, 1938; Correspondence between Rodney Weaver and Lawrence Unwin, November 7, 1970; McEwan, Pratt and Company (subsidiary of Baguley Cars) *Catalog*, 1915. The last two items are located in the Provincial Archives of Alberta.

43 Correspondence between Rodney Weaver and Lawrence Unwin, November 7, 1970; Corley, 1971; CPR drawing and information sheet, 1928, all in the Provincial Archives of Alberta.

44 Dorman, 1938; Ramsey, 1962.

45 Leonard, 1996.

46 Ramsey, 1962; Horton, 1985; Hungry Wolf, 1994; Hind, 1984.

47 *Statutes of the Province of British Columbia*, 1918, 8 George V, Chapter 66; Dorman, 1938; Ramsey, 1962.

48 In Hopkins, 1922, p. 837; Hungry Wolf, 1994.

49 In Hopkins, 1901, p. 382.

50 In Hopkins, 1906, p. 134; p. 146.

51 Sanford, 1990.

52 Dorman, 1938; Turner, 1987; Sanford, 1990; Canadian Pacific Railway, 1906.

53 Cited in Hopkins, 1907, p. 153.

54 Dorman, 1938; Turner, 1987; Sanford, 1990.

55 Canadian Pacific Railway, 1915.

Notes (pages 138 – 171)

1 Hanna and Hawkes, 1924, p. 273.

2 *Ibid.*, p. 312.

3 *Ibid.*, p. 302.

4 In Hopkins, 1919, p. 806.

5 In Hopkins, 1920, p. 296.

6 *Ibid.*, p. 300.

7 *Ibid.*, p. 301.

8 In Hopkins, 1922, p. 483.

9 *Ibid.*, pp. 907–08.

10 Cruise and Griffiths, 1988; Chodos, 1973.

11 Hopkins, 1923.

12 Canadian National Railways, 1926; Lavallée, 1985.

13 Canadian National Railways, 1924, p. 12; see also subsequent *Annual Reports*.

14 Smith, 1985.

15 Canadian National Railways, 1928, 1929.

16 *Ibid.*; Hopper and Kearney, 1962.

17 MacKay, 1986; Webber, 1993.

18 Cruise and Griffiths, 1988; MacKay, 1992.

19 Turner, 1987.

20 Canadian Pacific Railway, 1929; Hart, 1983.

21 *A.T.A. Magazine*, August and November 1924; Hopkins, 1925.

22 Cruise and Griffiths, 1988; MacKay, 1992.

23 Alberta Department of Railways and Telephones, 1928, p. 4.

24 *Ibid.*, 1929, p. 16.

25 In Hopkins, 1929, p. 180.

26 Ramsey, 1962.

27 Cruise and Griffiths, 1988.

28 House of Commons, 1932, p. 183.

29 In Hopkins, 1930, p. 646; Hopkins, 1931; Canadian Pacific Railway, 1931; Canadian National Railways, 1931.

30 Canadian National Railways, 1934, p. 11.

31 In Hopkins, 1933, p. 417.

32 *Ibid.*, p. 418.

33 Debates of the House of Commons, 1932, p. 2556.

34 Beatty, 1934a, pp. 10, 13.

35 House of Commons, 1933, p. 201; Beatty, 1934b; Jackman, 1939.

36 In Hopkins, 1936, p. 616.

37 Canadian Pacific Railway, 1937.

38 Canadian Pacific Railway, 1936, 1937; Lavallée, 1985.

39 Clegg and Corley, 1969.

References

Alberta Department of Railways and Telephones. 1926–1929. *Annual reports.* Edmonton, AB: Department of Railways and Telephones.

Alberta Teachers' Alliance. 1924. *The A.T.A. Magazine,* August, November.

Baedeker, Karl. 1907. *Handbook for travellers: The Dominion of Canada with Newfoundland and an excursion to Alaska.* Leipzig: Karl Baedeker.

Baird, Ian. 1984. Canadian National on Vancouver Island. *Heritage West,* spring: 14–16.

———. 1985. *A historic guide to the E&N railway.* Victoria, BC: Heritage Architectural Guides in association with the Friends of the E&N.

Barrett, Anthony A., and Rhodri W. Liscombe. 1983. *Francis Rattenbury and British Columbia: Architecture and challenge in the imperial age.* Vancouver, BC: University of British Columbia Press.

Beatty, Edward W. 1934a. *The case for railway unification.* Montréal, QC: Canadian Political Science Association.

———. 1934b. *The logical view of the railway situation.* Vancouver, BC: Board of Trade and the Service Clubs of Vancouver.

———. 1935. Prosperity in agriculture essential. *Calgary Daily Herald,* May 25: 9.

Beatty, J.A. 1974. CP Rail's Connaught Tunnel. *Canadian Rail,* 271: 227–35.

Berton, Pierre. 1970. *The national dream: The great railway, 1871–1881.* Toronto, ON: McClelland and Stewart Limited.

Blakiston, Thomas W. 1859. *Report of the exploration of two passes through the Rocky Mountains in 1858.* Woolwich, UK: The Royal Artillery Institution.

Bloch, Michael. 1994. *Ribbentrop.* London, UK: Transworld Publishers Ltd.

Bohi, Charles. 1977. *Canadian National's western depots: The country stations in Western Canada.* West Hill, ON: Railfare Enterprises Limited.

———, and Leslie S. Kozma. 1993. *Canadian Pacific's western depots: The country stations in Western Canada.* David City, NA: South Platte Press.

Bonar, James C. 1950. *Canadian Pacific Railway company and its contributions towards the early development and continued progress of Canada.* Vol. VI, *Technical contributions.* Montréal, QC: Canadian Pacific Railway.

Bone, P. Turner. 1947. *When the steel went through: Reminiscences of a railroad pioneer.* Toronto, ON: The Macmillan Company of Canada Limited.

Bowman, Phylis. 1980. *Whistling through the west.* Prince Rupert, BC: self-published.

British parliamentary papers: Correspondence and papers relating to government postal and rail communications and other affairs in Canada 1861–63. Reprint, Shannon, RI: Irish University Press, 1969.

Buck, George H. 1982. The McKeen cars mystery. *The Marker,* 8: 141–42, 153–56.

Canadian National Railways. 1922–1939. *Annual reports.* Montréal, QC: Canadian National Railways.

———. 1925. *Canadian Northern Railway Abandonment, Stony Plains Subdivision,* Memorandum from Office of Chief Engineer, Winnipeg, Manitoba, January 8.

———. 1925–39. Bridge Records.

Canadian Northern Railway. 1903–1916. *Annual reports.* Montréal, QC: Canadian Northern Railway.

Canadian Pacific Railway. 1886–1939. *Annual reports.* Montréal, QC: Canadian Pacific Railway.

———. 1887. *Pacific Division Profile shewing snowshed work 1886 & 1887.*

———. 1894. *Canadian Pacific: The new highway to the Orient across the mountains prairies and rivers of Canada.* Montréal, QC: Canadian Pacific Railway.

———. 1929. *Bungalow camps in the Canadian Rockies*. Montréal, QC: Canadian Pacific Railway.

Cardwell, Donald. 1995. *The Norton history of technology*. New York: W.W. Norton and Company.

Cars, Jean des, and Jean-Paul Caracalla. 1984. *The orient-express: A century of railway adventures*. London, UK: Bloomsbury Books.

Chodos, Robert. 1973. *The CPR: A century of corporate welfare*. Toronto, ON: James Lorimer and Company.

Clegg, Anthony, and Raymond F. Corley. 1969. *Canadian National steam power*. Montréal, QC: Railfare Enterprises Limited.

Columbia River exploration, 1865. 1865. Victoria, BC: Government Printing Office.

Corley, Raymond F. 1971. The Edmonton Interurban Railway: A researched history. (unpublished manuscript in the Provincial Archives of Alberta).

———. 1972. The Edmonton, Yukon & Pacific Railway: A researched history. (unpublished manuscript in the City of Edmonton Archives).

Cruise, David, and Alison Griffiths. 1988. *Lords of the line*. New York: Viking Penguin Inc.

Cunningham, Granville C. 1887. Snow slides in the Selkirk Mountains. *Transactions of the Canadian society of civil engineers*. Montréal, QC: John Lovell and Son.

Dawe, Michael 1972. *The Alberta Central Railway* (unpublished manuscript in the Red Deer Archives).

Dorman, Robert. 1938. *A statutory history of steam and electric railways of Canada, 1836–1937*. Ottawa, ON: King's Printer.

Eagle, John A. 1989. *The Canadian Pacific Railway and the development of western Canada, 1896–1914*. Montréal, QC, and Kingston, ON: McGill-Queen's University Press.

Elson, Harvey W. 1976. The view from the top. *Canadian Rail*, 286: 34–43.

Evans, G.I. 1910. An experimental Mallet articulated locomotive. *The Railway and Marine World*, April: 250–65.

Finch, David. 1991. *Glacier house rediscovered*. Revelstoke, BC: Friends of Mount Revelstoke and Glacier.

Findlay, C.F. 1889. Cantilever bridges. *Transactions of the Canadian society of civil engineers*. Montréal, QC: John Lovell and Son.

Fleming, R.B. 1991. *The railway king of Canada: Sir William Mackenzie, 1849–1923*. Vancouver, BC: University of British Columbia Press.

Fleming, Sandford. 1872. *Progress report on the Canadian Pacific Railway exploratory survey*. Ottawa, ON: MacLean, Roger and Co.

———. 1877. *Report on surveys and preliminary operations on the Canadian Pacific Railway up to January 1877*. Ottawa, ON: MacLean, Roger and Co.

———. 1879. *Report in reference to the Canadian Pacific Railway*. Ottawa, ON: MacLean, Roger and Co.

———. 1880. *Report and documents in reference to the Canadian Pacific Railway*. Ottawa, ON: MacLean, Roger and Co.

Fournier, Leslie T. 1935. *Railway nationalization in Canada: The problems of the Canadian National Railways*. Toronto, ON: The Macmillan Company of Canada Limited.

Gibbon, John M. 1935. *Steel of empire: The romantic history of the Canadian Pacific, the northwest passage of today*. New York: The Bobbs-Merrill Company.

Gilpin, John. 1985. The Edmonton yards of the CPR. *The Marker*, July: 104–08.

Gosnell, R.E. 1897. *The year book of British Columbia and manual of provincial information*. Victoria, BC: np.

———. 1903. *The year book of British Columbia and manual of provincial information*. Victoria, BC: np.

———. 1911. *The year book of British Columbia and manual of provincial information.* Victoria, BC: np.

Grand Trunk Pacific. 1907. *The Grand Trunk Pacific: Canada's National Transcontinental Railway.* Montréal, QC: Grand Trunk Pacific.

Grand Trunk Pacific Hotel Development in the West. 1913. *The Contract Record*, July 30: 50–51.

Hanna, David B., and A. Hawkes. 1924. *Trains of recollection.* Toronto, ON: The Macmillan Company of Canada Limited.

Hart, E.J. 1983. *The selling of Canada: The CPR and the beginning of Canadian tourism.* Banff, AB: Altitude Publishing Ltd.

Hatcher, Colin K. 1981. *The Northern Alberta Railways.* Calgary, AB: The British Railway Modellers of North America.

———. 1987. *The Northern Alberta Railways.* Vol. II. Calgary, AB: The British Railway Modellers of North America.

Hind, Patrick O. 1984. *Pacific Great Eastern steam locomotives.* Victoria, BC: The British Columbia Railway Historical Association.

Hopkins, J.C. 1901–1938. *The Canadian annual review of public affairs.* Toronto, ON: The Annual Review Publishing Company.

Hopper, A.B., and T. Kearney. 1962. *Canadian National Railways: Synoptical history of organization, capital stock, funded debt and other general information as of December 31, 1960.* Montréal, QC: Canadian National Railways.

Horton, T.J. 1985. *The Pacific Great Eastern Railway.* Vol. I. Calgary, AB: The British Railway Modellers of North America.

House of Commons. 1932. *Select standing committee on railways and shipping: Owned, operated and controlled by the government.* Ottawa, ON: King's Printer.

———. 1933. *Select standing Committee on Railways, Telegraphs and Harbors.* Ottawa, ON: King's Printer.

Hungry Wolf, Adolf. 1994. *Route of the cariboo: PGE/BC Rail.* Skookumchuck, BC: Canadian Caboose Press.

Jackman, W.T. 1939. *Critical analysis of "the Canadian railway problem."* Montréal, QC: np.

Johnston, Alex. 1977. *The CP Rail high level bridge at Lethbridge.* Occasional paper no. 7. Lethbridge, AB: Whoop-up Country Chapter, Historical Society of Alberta.

Kennedy, James H. 1894. Location and construction of the Great Northern Railway in the Rocky Mountains. *Transactions of the Canadian society of civil engineers.* Montréal, QC: John Lovell and Son.

Lavallée, Omer. 1972. *Narrow gauge railways of Canada.* Montréal, QC: Railfare Enterprises Limited.

———. 1974. *Van Horne's road: An illustrated account of the construction and first years of operation of the Canadian Pacific transcontinental railway.* Montréal, QC: Railfare Enterprises Limited.

———. 1985. *Canadian Pacific steam locomotives.* Toronto, ON: Railfare Enterprises Limited.

Leonard, Frank. 1996. *A thousand blunders: The Grand Trunk Pacific Railway and northern British Columbia.* Vancouver, BC: University of British Columbia Press.

Macgregor, J.G. 1914. The inception and location of the Alberta Central Railway. *Canadian Railway and Marine World*, September: 398–99.

MacKay, Donald. 1986. *The Asian dream: The Pacific rim and Canada's national railway.* Vancouver, BC: Douglas and McIntyre.

———. 1992. *The people's railway: A history of Canadian National.* Vancouver, BC: Douglas and McIntyre.

———, and Lorne Perry. 1994. *Train country: An illustrated history of Canadian National Railways.* Vancouver, BC: Douglas and McIntyre.

MacLachlan, Donald F. 1986. *The Esquimalt & Nanaimo Railway: The Dunsmuir years: 1884–1905.* Victoria, BC: British Columbia Railway Historical Association.

Minter, Roy. 1987. *The White Pass: Gateway to the Klondike*. Toronto, ON: McClelland and Stewart Limited.

Monsarrat, C.N. 1909. Construction of Lethbridge Viaduct, Crow's Nest Branch, Canadian Pacific Railway Company. *Transactions of the Canadian society of civil engineers*. Montréal, QC: The Witness Press.

Nimmo, J.V. 1914. The location and construction of the Canadian Northern Pacific Railway in British Columbia. *Canadian Railway and Marine World*, May: 199–204. A similar article appears in the 1916 *Transactions of the Canadian society of civil engineers*. Montréal, QC: Southam Press.

Otter, A.A. den. 1982. *Civilizing the west: The Galts and the development of western Canada*. Edmonton, AB: The University of Alberta Press.

Palliser, John. 1860. *Further papers relative to the exploration by the expedition under Captain Palliser*. London, UK: George Edward Eyre and William Spottiswoode.

Palmer, Howard. 1914. *Mountaineering and exploration in the Selkirks: A record of pioneer work among the Canadian Alps, 1908–1912*. New York: G.P. Putnam's Sons.

Parker, H.A., and B.B. Kelliher. 1909. *Report of H.A. Parker, C.E., on mountain section, and comments of B.B. Kelliher, Chief Engineer*. Montréal, QC: Grand Trunk Pacific Railway (unpublished manuscript located in the National Archives of Canada, Ottawa).

Peterson, P. Alex. 1895. President's address. *Transactions of the Canadian society of civil engineers*. Montréal, QC: John Lovell and Son.

Phillips, Lance. 1965. *Yonder comes the train*. Cranbury, NJ: A.S. Barnes and Co., Inc.

Pole, Graeme. 1991. *The Canadian Rockies: A history in photographs*. Banff, AB: Altitude Publishing Ltd.

Ramsey, Bruce. 1962. *PGE Railway to the north*. Vancouver, BC: Mitchell Press.

Rattenbury, Francis M. 1913. Grand Trunk Pacific hotel development in the west. *The Contract Record*, July 30: 50–51.

Regehr, T.D. 1976. *The Canadian Northern: Pioneer road of the northern prairies, 1895–1918*. Toronto, ON: The Macmillan Company of Canada Limited.

Reksten, Terry. 1978. *Rattenbury*. Victoria, BC: Sono Nis Press.

Riegger, Hal. 1981. *The Kettle Valley and its railways: A pictorial history of rail development in southern British Columbia and the building of the Kettle Valley Railway*. Edmonds, WA: PFM Publications.

Roe, Frank G. 1982. *Getting the know-how: Homesteading and railroading in early Alberta*. Edmonton, AB: NeWest Press.

Rogers, Albert L. 1905. Major A. B. Rogers' first expedition up the Illecillewaet valley, in 1881, accompanied by his nephew, A.L. Rogers. In A.O. Wheeler, *The Selkirk range*. Vol. I. Ottawa, ON: Government Printing Bureau.

Sanford, Barrie. 1981. *McCulloch's wonder: The story of the Kettle Valley Railway*. North Vancouver, BC: Whitecap Books.

———. 1990. *Steel rails and iron men: A pictorial history of the Kettle Valley Railway*. Vancouver, BC / Toronto, ON: Whitecap Books.

Schneider, Ena. 1987. The peanut road. *Canadian Rail*, 398: 76–85.

———. 1989. *Ribbons of steel: The story of the Northern Alberta Railways*. Calgary, AB: Detselig Enterprises Limited.

Schwitzer, J.E. 1909. Reduction of the Kicking Horse Pass grade on the C.P.R. *The Railway and Marine World*, October: 710–11.

Smith, Cyndi. 1985. *Jasper Park Lodge: In the heart of the Canadian Rockies*. Jasper, AB: self–published.

Spry, Irene M. 1963. *The Palliser expedition: An account of John Palliser's British North American exploring expedition 1857–1860*. Toronto: The Macmillan Company of Canada Limited.

Stevens, G.R. 1973. *History of the Canadian National Railway*. New York: The Macmillan Company.

Sullivan, John G. 1916. Rogers Pass tunnel method chosen for economics. *Engineering News*, February 24: 382–83.

Talbot, Frederick A. 1912. *The making of a great Canadian railway*. Toronto: The Musson Book Company.

Taylor, Geoffrey W. 1988. *The railway contractors: The story of John W. Stewart, his enterprises and associates*. Victoria, BC: Morriss Publishing.

Thompson, Norman, and J.H. Edgar. 1933. *Canadian railway development: From the earliest times*. Toronto, ON: The Macmillan Company of Canada Limited.

Tracy, H.P. 1916. Methods of enlargement work in Rogers Pass tunnel. *Engineering News*, August 31: 411–12.

Turner, Robert D. 1973. *Vancouver Island railroads*. San Marino, CA: Golden West Books.

———. 1987. *West of the Great Divide: An illustrated history of the Canadian Pacific Railway in British Columbia 1880–1986*. Victoria, BC: Sono Nis Press.

———, and David S. Wilkie. 1994. *The Skyline Limited: The Kaslo and Slocan Railway: An illustrated history of narrow gauge railroading and sternwheelers in the Kootenays*. Victoria, BC: Sono Nis Press.

Vaughan, H.H. 1912. Rotary snow plows. *Transactions of the Canadian society of civil engineers*. Montréal, QC: John Lovell and Son.

Vaux, William S., Jr. 1900. The Canadian Pacific Railway from Laggan to Revelstoke, B.C. *Proceedings of the Engineers' Club of Philadelphia*, 17(2).

Walbran, John T. 1909. *British Columbia coast names, 1592–1906*. Ottawa: Government Printing Bureau.

Webber, Bernard. 1993. *Silk trains: The romance of Canadian silk trains or "the silks."* Kelowna, BC: The World Works Publications.

Wheeler, Arthur O. 1905. *The Selkirk range*. Vol. I. Ottawa, ON: Government Printing Bureau.

Wilson, Sir Charles Rivers. 1916. *Chapters from my official life*. London, UK: Edward Arnold.

Index

NOTE: Illustrations are in **bold** type